CREATING DATA LITERATE STUDENTS

EDITED BY

Kristin Fontichiaro   Jo Angela Oehrli   Amy Lennex

This project was made possible in part by the Institute of Museum and Library Services RE-00-15-0113-15, The University of Michigan School of Information, and University Library.

Calendar created by Edward Boatman, Graph created by Xinh Studio, Star created by Alexander Smith, Rabbit created by Niké Jenny Bruinsma, Review created by Daniel Nochta, Health Insurance created by Timothy Miller, Thought Bubble created by Kid A, Stats created by Gregor Črešnar, Text created by Gregor Črešnar, Newspaper created by unlimicon, Check Box List created by unlimicon, Chat created by iconsphere, Girl Hairstyle created by LSE Designs, Statistic Graph created by Barracuda, Clock created by Alfa Design from thenounproject.com .

Published in the United States of America by
Michigan Publishing
Manufactured in the United States of America

DOI: http://dx.doi.org/10.3998/mpub.9873254

ISBN 978-1-60785-424-1 (paper)
ISBN 978-1-60785-425-8 (e-book)

An imprint of Michigan Publishing, Maize Books serves the publishing needs of the University of Michigan community by making high-quality scholarship widely available in print and online. It represents a new model for authors seeking to share their work within and beyond the academy, offering streamlined selection, production, and distribution processes. Maize Books is intended as a complement to more formal modes of publication in a wide range of disciplinary areas.

http://www.maizebooks.org

Contents

Kristin Fontichiaro, Jo Angela Oehrli, Amy Lennex

"Just skip the statistics."
"If I liked numbers, I wouldn't have gone into librarianship."
"I'm not interested in data."

These were the kinds of statements we tended to hear when the topic of data and statistics arose among the school and even some academic librarians. In listservs and at conferences, conversations about students' reading and research skills inevitably turned to how we could help them navigate *text*. We would hear passionate arguments about the need for high school students to use scholarly articles for their research. When we saw handouts or tutorials designed to help students navigate those data-heavy materials, they rarely included advice for navigating data, statistics, or visualizations.

Simultaneously, we began to see an explosion of digital tools that made it possible to create data visualizations and infographics with just a few clicks. New challenges emerged, like pie charts that added up to 193% (not 100%!). Infographics that were little more than a random collection of factoids and icons gave us concern. In the era of the *Standards for the 21st-Century Learners* (AASL 2007), wasn't learning supposed to be deeper and more meaningful than this?

At the same time, we saw that data was being used to support arguments in ways that were unanticipated. Sometimes, politicians from across the aisle could cite identical statistics to support *opposite* stances. Could a better understanding of data make it possible to create better-informed future voters?

These issues, and others, led us to begin considering data and statistical literacy as the logical expansion of librarianship's work in information literacy. Thanks to funding from the Institute of Museum and Library Services (RE-05-15-0021-15), we launched a two-year project entitled

Supporting Librarians in Adding Data Literacy Skills to Information Literacy Instruction. Our goal was to give front-line high school librarians effective and efficient strategies for raising their own – and, by extension – their students' ability to work effectively with data.

We wanted to layout a beginner's landscape for data across the two years of our project. In Year 1 (represented in this volume), we would concentrate on the nuts and bolts of modern data and usage: data and statistical comprehension; data in arguments; and data visualization. Year 2 (to come in a forthcoming volume) would concentrate on application of data principles in areas including Big Data, crowdsourced/citizen science, personal data management, and personal data use.

We also scheduled two online data literacy education conferences (http://dataliteracy.si.umich.edu) as satellites to the 4T Virtual Conference. Volume 2 will provide discussion prompts, activities, and links so that school districts can access and use the archived webinars in future professional development.

We set our core audience as high school librarians and quickly realized that there were multiple secondary audiences, including classroom teachers, community college librarians, and librarians at four-year or research universities. In fact, at our 2016 4T Data Literacy conference, we had approximately 80 different job titles register. We weren't the only ones thinking about how to bridge the gap for high schoolers.

Our project brought together two teams of experts. As experts in data and its use, Justin Joque (University of Michigan Library), Lynette Hoelter (Interuniversity Consortium for Political and Social Research – ICPSR, housed at the University of Michigan), Jacob Carlson (University of Michigan Library), and, unofficially, Justin Schell (University of Michigan Library's Shapiro Design Lab) would help inform and provide expert oversight of the publications. As experts in teaching and learning in libraries, our team of curriculum experts would contribute real-world framing, considering how these principles could be brought into existing research practices in high school in a practical and pragmatic way.

Our curriculum team features Debbie Abilock, Susan D. Ballard, Tasha Bergson-Michelson, Jennifer Colby, Jole Seroff, Susan Smith, Wendy Steadman Stephens, and Connie Williams represent a cross-section of public and private schools, industry expertise, and library education. New academic librarians Martha Stuit and Tierney Steelberg contributed their insights.

In this volume, team members contribute their perspective and expertise on how data education can integrate effectively in the already jam-packed world of high schoolers.

We open with Chapter 1, in which *Lynette Hoelter* reminds us that data and statistics in the "real world" can be a different kind of encounter than how we experienced them in math class. She identifies the most practical, high-leverage data practices that will instantly raise your quantitative game so you can do the same for your students.

Students – even those as young as first grade – intuitively sense that numbers matter. But how do the words *around* the numbers impact how we read them? That is *Tasha Bergson-Michelson*'s exploration in Chapter 2.

In Chapter 3, *Jole Seroff* shows us what data-infused moments might look like in various moments in the research process, including a memorable look into her students' exploration of migrants and refugees.

We want students to have authentic experiences with data, but we also want their first data experiences to be with good datasets, or collections of data. *Wendy Steadman Stephens,* in Chapter 4, provides an overview of reliable data sources so you can quickly connect students to good data and keep them moving in their research.

Once you've downloaded a dataset, how do you sort, eliminate duplicate data, and find patterns? Academic librarian *Martha Stuit* answers this question in Chapter 5 when she shows how to download an existing dataset and perform common sorting and filtering functions using Microsoft Excel or Google Sheets.

With Chapter 6, we transition to data visualization – the mapping, graphing, or illustration of data in visual form. *Justin Joque*, data visualization librarian at the University of Michigan, shows us how to unpack data visualizations with a variety of questions and probes. By doing so, we better prepare our students for creating visual content that is attractive *and* impactful.

In Chapter 7, academic librarian *Tierney Steelberg* walks novices through a mini-textbook on visualization types. Her work presents common visualization formats and advice about choosing and populating a visualization.

Susan Smith (Chapter 8) shows us how we can teach high school students concrete comprehension strategies for data visualizations. Her chapter includes sample infographics with discussion prompts, practical guidelines to help students select a just-right visualization type, and a series of questions with which we can interrogate a visualization.

When it comes to making infographics, the fear is that students will too-quickly cut and paste from the web into software. *Connie Williams* shares the process of "storyframing," a way of slowing students down so they move from infobits to a cohesive argument, in Chapter 9.

Public high school librarian *Jennifer Colby* (Chapter 10) knows that when it comes to integrating something "new" into the curriculum, it needs to align with standards and test-taking. She shows us how data already fits into existing standards and tests, while also demonstrating how the Reading Apprenticeship model maps to data and statistics. Her chapter closes with numerous sample lessons and test questions: where the rubber hits the road.

In Chapter 11, *Debbie Abilock* looks ahead to advanced student users of data, showing us nuanced ways in which data can inform both large and small moments in the research process.

Chapter 12 focuses on action research, in which educators identify problems to study that are relevant and important to their classroom or schools. *Susan D. Ballard* provides a template for how teachers can engage in their own research design, data collection, and analysis, all for the purpose of improving teaching and learning. The process is flexible and accessible, meaning that once educators are experienced with the technique, they can teach it to their students.

Throughout many chapters, you'll find teaching tips whether you have 15 minutes, an hour, or a full unit to get things done.

We cannot close this introduction without thanking additional colleagues. Heather Newman, head of Marketing and Communications at the University of Michigan School of Information (UMSI) helped us organize our graphics efforts. David Young from that office was our graphic designer. Tyler Hoff, Kelly Hovinga, and Martha Stuit all made critical contributions to our project deliverables at various stages. Michigan Publishing shepherded the final design through its publication channels.

We hope this book will lead you into thoughtful explorations and fruitful learning for both you and your students. We look forward to hearing about your experiences at contactdataliteracy@umich.edu .

Happy reading!

Resources

American Association of School Librarians (AASL). 2007. *Standards for the 21st-Century Learner*. Chicago, IL: American Library Association. Accessed April 18, 2017. http://ala.org/standards .

Lynette Hoelter

Let's "set the stage" for thinking about data encountered in every-day media. With just a few key statistical concepts on your tool belt, your mindset can shift from simply accepting numbers as fact to questioning the data. For anyone who is afraid that this chapter will be math heavy – be reassured, it is not!

Quantitative literacy, quantitative reasoning, statistical literacy, and *numeracy* have become buzzwords in educational circles from K-12 through undergraduate training. Used interchangeably here, they all represent a core group of skills necessary to fully partic-ipate in today's information-rich society. Some have suggested nuances leading to unique meanings of each term, but whatever the buzzword, the goal is to boost high school students' abilities and comfort level with quantitative information.

Defining statistical literacy

For the purpose of this chapter, statistical literacy refers to a mindset or set of skills that are used in everyday life. That is, while some concepts might stem from the fields of math and science, the use of those ideas is equally, if not more, important. Statistical literacy, then, is the learning and using of quantitative skills *within a particular context*. Quantitative reasoning skills include:

 » **the ability to read and interpret a chart or graph;**
 » **calculating percentages;**
 » **working within a scientific model;**

» **evaluating the data on which arguments are based and using data in making one's own decisions and arguments;**

» **knowing what kinds of data might be useful in answering particular questions.**

"Now more than ever, students need the intellectual power to recognize societal problems; ask good questions and develop robust investigations into them; consider possible solutions and consequences; separate evidence-based claims from parochial opinions; and communicate and act upon what they learn" (National Center for the Social Studies 2013, 6). The overall goal is to understand and critically evaluate the numbers encountered as part of everyday life.

The relationship between statistics and statistical literacy

There are two primary ways instructors teach statistics: with a focus on formulas and arithmetic or with a focus on key concepts and their applications. A quick scan of popular high school and college-level statistics textbooks shows a focus on formulas and arithmetic to be most common. Students often get overwhelmed by the *math* and focus only on formulas and calculations. Unfortunately, when they leave the course, they may not remember much about the analyses they did. It is difficult for instructors and students to overcome this mindset – even when students know exams are open book/open note and that their interpretations count more than their calculations, the tendency is still to grab on to the formulas because they are, in a sense, more *concrete*. Logic and application are not always straightforward. There are right and wrong answers in the number-crunching, formulas, and arithmetic, and sometimes instructors and students are most secure in that arena.

I would argue, however, that deep learning and statistical literacy can take place when students are introduced to and asked to make decisions about statistical tests and interpret the results beyond merely repeating the numbers back. It is exactly these kinds of skills that can be incorporated across the curriculum as well. That said, fundamental concepts from statistics are important in asking and answering the questions posed in quantitative reasoning. Such topics include more theoretical ideas, and the next section defines and provides examples of each. The numbers and examples are completely made up, unless otherwise noted.

Statistics review

A refresher about key topics is always helpful — whether it's been awhile since you took statistics, you have nightmares about the class, or you never took a formal statistics course. The organization of the *review* here is based on the order in which topics are typically covered in texts.

Variables

Sometimes the thing that is least on our minds when reading data and numbers is exactly what was measured, how, and by whom. In scientific language, the *what* is thought of as a *variable*. Asking how many students in a class are boys and how many are girls involves the variable *gender*. A variable is a trait that can vary from person to person (or across time or context) and about which you have or need information. If the classroom were made up entirely of boys, gender would not be a variable because it would not differentiate the students from each other.

Variables are important for two reasons.

> » **The media often present results as cause and effect.** Thinking about exactly what variables were included (and what might have been left out) leads to questioning this assumption of causality.

> » **Thinking more broadly about what was measured, how, and by whom brings forth questions** about quality of the data and potential biases depending on the source of the data or the report.

For example, a high school that says that 90% of its graduating seniors are going on to college seems impressive, until one digs further and finds that only 40% of the seniors are graduating or that *going on to college* in this case means that the student has reported an *intention* to attend college at some point in the future.

The way something is measured also affects the way that information can be used and presented later. Asking people about the highest degree they've earned, for instance, does not allow a researcher to later examine the impact on earnings of having some college but not finishing a degree, because the people who didn't go to college and the people who did but didn't earn a degree will be considered as having exactly the same level of education. A giant first step toward quantitative literacy is this understanding that the numbers we see represent variables, the data for which were measured in a specific way, by a specific person, for a specific reason.

Percentages, rates, and percent change

Without context, numbers can seem astonishingly large or shockingly small. Standardizing numbers using percentages or rates provides context around the numbers. A percentage is calculated by dividing some part by the overall whole — taking the number of correct answers on an exam and dividing by the total possible points — and then multiplying by 100 to turn it into a percentage that ranges from 0–100. For example, a student earning 40 points out of a possible 50 points on a science quiz looks like this:

 40/50 = .8 and .8 x 100 = 80%

Percentages provide a way to see how groups of very different sizes compare on a characteristic. Let's say School A has 1,010 females taking AP Calculus and School B has 76. This should not necessarily lead to the assumption that School A is better at getting females into advanced math classes. Suppose that those schools had 2,400 and 130 students in AP Calculus, respectively. Using percentages, we would see that School A's AP Calculus curriculum is 42% female while School B's is 58% female.

School A

1010/2400 = 42% of students taking AP Calculus are female.

School B

76/130 = 58% of students taking AP Calculus are female.

Taking it one step further: if math ability was present and encouraged in male and female students equally, we would expect each program to be close to 50% female. This example demonstrates that School A may not be supporting females in math as well as it could be, and School B is supporting females at least as much as males. The original 1,010 and 76 females did not provide any of the *story* that is possible by standardizing the numbers by converting them into percentages.

Similarly, rates are the number of occurrences of something divided by the number of *possibilities* for the phenomenon to occur, typically multiplied by 1,000 (or 100,000 for large populations). Violent crime rates reported for cities, then, are the number of crimes in a given time period divided by the number of people in the city at that same time, multiplied by 1,000. Like percentages, rates allow for the comparison of the chances of something happening based-don the size of the location in question.

Let's say we know for a year:

City A population = 5,000

City A violent crimes = 37

37/5,000 = .0074 x 1,000 = 7.4

This calculation tells us City A has a violent crime rate of 7.4 per 1,000 residents.

Related to percentages are *percentiles* and *percent change*. Percentiles are often used for things like children's heights and weights or standardized test scores. The number reported as the percentile is the percent of individuals above which that child's height, weight, or score falls. Someone scoring in the 90th percentile on the SAT would have a score above 90% of the people who took the test at that time. Percent change is a bit trickier because the denominator changes with each calculation. For example, a sale item marked *70% off* is cheaper than the same item marked *50% + an additional 20% off* because in the first case, the 70% is taken off the total purchase price but in the second case, the 50% is taken off first and then, using that amount as the new denominator, the 20% is taken off.

$100 x 70% = $70 off, then $100-$70 = $30

$100 x 50% = $50 off, then $50 x 20% = $10, then $50-$10 = $40

An item that began as $100 in this example would be on sale for $30 and $40, respectively.

Likewise, large denominators mean that a small percent change can still produce a large number of people affected, whereas a large percent change to a small number will remain a small number.

How is this applied to statistical literacy?

Presenting numbers without context is a common strategy for making impressions, especially when defining issues as problems. Two thousand thefts sound like a lot, and a city might use that to push for more patrol officers on the streets. If the thefts were known to have occurred in a city of 450,000, though, people might be less panicked as they realize that just over four people in every 1,000 were victims of theft (especially if they can think of four people who leave their doors unlocked!).

The same "big deal" can be made by presenting a percentage without a sense of the base. Parma, Missouri, made the headlines when the election of its first black mayor caused 80% of the police force to resign. While the headlines were technically correct (in fact, 83.3% had resigned), this percentage was based on five resignations out of the total six officers. The facts are the same, but the emotional reaction to the resignation of 80% of the officers is different than knowing that five officers resigned.

Increases in percent change of contracting a particular disease often make headlines, especially when the percent change is large. It's important to remember that if the starting number is small, even a large jump should not be enough to send everyone to his or her physician for the latest test for that disease. It might be a 100% change, but that could mean going from one person to two affected out of thousands. On the flip side, a 1% change in the prison population could mean significant overcrowding, especially if the population has grown at the same time, because the base is large. As students become more statistically literate, they'll begin to think about the context in which numbers are presented (especially when there is no context at all), whether the right number was used as the denominator, and how large or small that denominator might be to begin.

Average/central tendency

Most people know that when they hear about the *average* or *central tendencies* of something, they should think about who is represented by that statement. If Starbucks talks about the amount of coffee an average person drinks per week, it is useful to know whether they are reporting the average for their custom- ers or for a representative sample of adults in the U.S., as those two numbers could be quite different.

There are actually several types of *averages* in statistics and using one over the other can affect interpretation of results.

Mode – Sometimes it is only possible to know what trait or num- ber is the most common among a group of people or items – like knowing that July and August are the most popular birthday months in the U.S. or that blue is most commonly reported as a favorite color. The mode, or most commonly occurring value, is the only meaningful average that can be used for variables that are measured by putting people into categories (like race, gender, or religion).

Median – The median, another type of average, is the value that splits a distribution of people or things exactly in half. The medi- an should be used for variables that result in ordered responses, such as one's highest degree earned or questions answered on a scale from strongly agree to strongly disagree or by categories (e.g., age cohorts).

Mean – Lastly, the mean represents the literal arithmetic average of something, like when someone asks everyone in a room for his or her age, adds those numbers up, and divides by the number of people in the room. The value of each individual's score is used when calculating the mean, therefore one or two extremely high or low scores can shift the resulting value.

While these seem straightforward, an agenda can be supported by choosing to present results using one average rather than another.

Being statistically literate involves asking which average is being presented and whether using another might present a more accurate picture. Schools present their *average* scores on achievement tests. Those schools where one or two students have a bad day and score very low are going to want to report the median; schools where one or two students score very high will likely want to report the mean to take advantage of those high scores. One should think about whether conclusions would be different depending which measure of central tendency was used.

Best practice is for both the mean and the median to be reported. Even better is when the average is accompanied by information about how *spread out* the scores in the distribution are (e.g., standard deviation). Suppose students are given an exam scored 0–100, and both the mean and the median come out to be 75. Knowing whether the scores clustered around 75 or were spread across the 100-point continuum provides more information about student learning than knowing the mean or median alone.

Sampling

Sampling is confusing for a lot of people. Part of this confusion is because sampling is largely a theoretical concept. Part comes from the way terms are used in referring to sample designs seems contradictory to the use of those same terms in everyday language. It may be easy to convince people that results based on just a few people might not be reliable. What about a sample of 100 people? Is that enough? Sometimes the harder battle is convincing them that a sample of 100 can actually be large enough to draw conclusions — but it is harder to get them to think about the fact that the size is not the only characteristic to consider when looking at a sample. A sample's design, rather than its size, is the key characteristic in thinking about whether results can be meaningful for a larger group of people. That is, for a sample to represent some larger group, the individuals in a sample must be chosen at random.

These designs, called probability designs, range from something that could be as straightforward as putting everyone's name in a hat and selecting a certain number (a simple random sample) to complex designs that involve multiple layers of selection, some of which include an element of chance and others that do not. The chance of selection is key. In reliable data reporting, the chance of selection, or probability design, is transparent and explained clearly to the reader.

If one wants to be able to say something about high school students in the U.S., one cannot simply take a random sample of the students in one's school because that school is not likely representative of all high schools in the country. This is a very different definition of *random* than one students bring from everyday vocabulary. To some, *random* could have a negative connotation and implies no structure about who is in or out of the sample. In contrast, in sample selection, random or probability designs require the structure of having a list of possible sample units and using some rather systematic method for selecting individuals (or households or forest plots) from that list. Standing in the hallway and on the campus quad and choosing people *at random* does not qualify as a probability sample because there is no way to know the parameters of the population of interest, and selection is not usually as *random* as we think – one might be more likely to talk to those who look at the one collecting the data or the data collector might be more comfortable talking to women than to men. This type of sample is called a *convenience sample* and is one of the many non-probability designs. A *non-probability sample* is when the data collector uses his or her own judgment about who to include in the sample and who not to include. The fact that results of non-probability samples cannot be generalized does not mean that studies based on those designs should not be done. Non-probability sample designs are the most effective way to study harder-to-find populations – imagine trying to study homelessness using a national probability sample – or topics that require understanding a particular situation or phenomenon in more depth than would be possible from a survey.

Given the declining participation in surveys and other research, scientists are debating generalizability of some sampling designs. Market research, for example, is often comfortable with a large sample no matter how the individuals in the sample were (or were not) selected. Some polling firms are using large opt-in Internet panels from which they then draw random samples and generalize results. The important thing to think about is whether the people who were included in a given sample might have characteristics that make them different from those who were not included in important ways.

Random-digit dialing is a probability sample. The results from this kind of sample could be generalized, but what if the dialing hits only landline numbers? The resulting sample will be very different than if cell phones were included. In the former case, the generalizability could only extend to people with landlines, not to the general population.

How is this applied to statistical literacy?

The numbers presented in the media and other outlets should be approached with *who* questions:

- » **who was surveyed;**
- » **who participated in the survey;**
- » **who might have been systematically excluded; and**
- » **to whom, if anyone, can the results be generalized?**

A red flag should go up if no information about the sample is provided. Similarly, seeing that the sample included a large number of people is a good first step toward credibility, but information about how the sample was selected will allow for decisions about whether the reported findings might be true for anyone beyond those who were included. The *who* is also important when the target population of a study is different than the one to whom the results are being applied. Questioning every fifth person in line at a randomly selected Starbucks at a given time is not likely to yield answers about coffee preferences and consumption that are representative of all adults in that city, even though a probability design (systematic random sampling) was employed.

Margin of error/confidence

The use of a sample of people, households, or Starbucks locations to estimate the value of a characteristic for the population of those items encompasses a bit of uncertainty. Statisticians will often report their results followed by a *margin of error* or *confidence interval* because there is a chance that any one sample chosen might not accurately represent the population. This creates an interval, or range, where the researcher can be more certain that the true value falls rather than using the exact value found in the sample. Wider intervals mean more certainty that the true value is within the range. Smaller intervals have higher chances of missing the true value. The size of the interval required to reach a given level of confidence is also related to the size of the original sample. A narrower interval can be used to achieve the same level of confidence with a larger sample than would be necessary if the sample were smaller. Often the margin of error is presented as something like "54% ±2%" and it can be interpreted to mean that the estimate of the population value falls between 52% (the reported number minus two percent) and 56% (the reported number plus two percent).

How is this applied to statistical literacy?

Providing a margin of error is one way researchers and journalists can help data consumers know how much confidence to put in the numbers reported. A large margin of error means that the numbers themselves should be taken with a grain of salt, whereas smaller margins of error engender more trust. In an effort to present *news*, media outlets have a tendency to present the figures and maybe mention the margin of error but not consider whether the resulting intervals overlap. Political polling is one place in which this happens — it might be reported that support for Clinton is 52% and for Trump is 48%, ±3%, so Clinton is ahead in the polls. However, once the margin of error is taken into consideration, the candidates essentially report they are tied because the ranges overlap (49%-55% for Clinton, and 45%-51% for Trump). We now know that had voters taken the margin of error more seriously, they might have seen earlier that either candidate could have won.

Correlation

A *correlation* describes the connection between two variables. It represents the strength and direction of the relationship between them. Correlations can be either positive or negative. A *positive correlation* means that higher values on the first variable are related to higher values on the second. A positive correlation also means that lower values on the first are related to lower values on the second. For example, height and shoe size are positively correlated – in general, taller people have larger shoe sizes than shorter people. A *negative correlation* means that as one variable increases, the other variable decreases. For example, the relationship between education and racial prejudice might be a negative correlation. People who have more education tend to score lower on scales of prejudice than those with lower levels of education.

There are two very important things to keep in mind when considering correlation.

> » **A correlation or association between two variables does not mean they are causally related.** Growing taller does not cause your shoe size to be bigger. It is likely genetics, nutrition, and other factors that are causing growth in both height and size of feet. An association between two things is necessary to say that one causes the other, but it is not sufficient. Causality requires proper time ordering (does the first variable actually occur in time before the second), a logical reason for why one should cause the other, and checking that no third factor is causing the relationship between the first two, like genetics in the example of height and shoe size.

> » **A correlation only picks up a linear association between two variables.** For example, there is a relationship between the length of time that a person is married and marital satisfaction, but it is not a linear relationship. Marital satisfaction is highest at the beginning of a marriage and later in the marriage, with a drop in between, so that the pattern is U-shaped.

How is this applied to statistical literacy?

Being aware that correlation does not necessarily mean causation is the important piece here. There is a great website (www.tylervirgen.com/spurious-correlations) that demonstrates strong correlations between variables for which there is no reasonable causal relationship, such as a .993 correlation between the divorce rate in Maine and the per capita consumption of margarine for any given year. These correlations, while entertaining, are the result of a computer sifting through massive amounts of data to find things that have similar patterns. Hopefully one would know to question a report about divorce rates and margarine consumption and not infer any kind of causal relationship, but sometimes it is not that clear. A report on the *New York Times* blog, *The Upshot*, suggested that "heavier babies do better in school," based on a "study of children in Florida [that] found that those who were heavier at birth scored higher on math and reading tests in the third to eighth grades" (Leonhardt and Cox, 2014). The time ordering is there – birth weight surely comes before third and eighth grade test scores, and the two variables (weight and test scores) are associated. The authors even note that education, race, and age of the mother were taken into account (*controlled*) and the relationship held. Before mothers of small babies seek out extra tutoring for their children, it pays to consider other factors that might be causing the relationship between weight and scores. For example, better nutrition and general health likely account for both larger babies and better cognitive functioning as measured by test scores. Understanding what a correlation means and what it does not is critical in using quantitative reasoning with such stories.

Significance

Statistical significance refers to the ability to say that a reported result would only happen x% of the time by chance. Typically these percentages are set at .1%, 1%, or 5% for them to be compelling. This precise meaning allows researchers to report findings as statistically significant when they reach these thresholds. Keep in mind that the identification of something as *significant* in statistical terms doesn't necessarily mean that there is a momentous finding. Calculating statistical significance is based in part on sample size. When there is a large enough sample, it is easy to produce findings that are statistically significant even when a relationship is weak or change is small. If a large sample of students who took a standardized test showed that there is what a statistician would call a statistically significant difference between female students who achieved an 88% score and male students who achieved an 87%, one might ask oneself whether that 1% difference really mattered. The key is to think about whether that statistical significance translates into real significance or importance.

How is this applied to statistical literacy?

Journalists are always hunting for the next big story, and significant research results can grab readers' attention, but the difference between statistical and substantive or *real* significance might be lost in the process. Quantitative reasoning involves finding out what the actual difference or relationship is and considering whether the size of that effect is important in the big picture. Reported differences in mean levels of marital satisfaction for men and women might seem like a big deal, and one probably could easily think of anecdotal evidence to support a finding that says men have significantly higher levels of marital satisfaction than do women. But what if that *difference* was that men scored 90.2 and women scored 88.4 on a 100-point index of marital satisfaction? Does that less-than-two-point difference mean men and women really experience marriage differently? Wouldn't a more accurate story be one that reports both men and women are really pretty satisfied with their marriages? Questions such as these about the implications of statistically significant findings are another sign of quantitative reasoning.

Raising statistical literacy in the classroom

The mindset of statistical literacy is developed through practice. Exposing students to news articles and guiding them through questions about how the variables were measured, who was in the sample, and whether the results are worthy of such attention is one way to delve deeper. This can be used to focus students on the task at hand or to convey the content of the day. There are a number of blogs and news sources that provide quantitative information so it is relatively easy to find something related to most topics. Getting students to think quantitatively can be done without the math behind the statistics. Perhaps a science course is looking at the effects of climate change on policy (or vice versa) and having students write a paper that includes statistics about the average temperature each year or the amount of carbon monoxide emissions eliminated by a given policy offers the opportunity to remind students about credibility of sources and types of averages.

Students in many high school courses are asked to convey information as an infographic rather than writing a more traditional research paper. Each of these assignments allows students to actively engage with research and quantitative information, offering the scaffolding needed for quantitative literacy to become habit. This chapter provides a foundation for understanding fundamental concepts from statistics so that we become more statistically literate and critical evaluators of numbers, results, and claims we encounter.

Resources

Arum, Richard and Josipa Roksa. 2010. *Academically Adrift: Limited Learning on College Campuses.* Chicago: University of Chicago Press.

Leonhardt, David and Amanda Cox. 2014. "Heavier Babies Do Better in School." *New York Times: The Upshot.* http://www.nytimes.com/2014/10/12/upshot/heavier-babies-do-better-in-school.html?_r=0

National Council for the Social Studies (NCSS). 2013. The College, Career, and Civic Life (C3) Framework for Social Studies State Standards: Guidance for Enhancing the Rigor of K-12 Civics, Economics, Geography, and History. Silver Spring, MD: National Council for the Social Studies.

2 | Statistical storytelling: The language of data

Tasha Bergson-Michelson

Noting a sharp increase over recent decades, a study released Wednesday by researchers at MIT confirmed that nearly 80 percent of all statistics are now sobering.
— The Onion 2014

Recently, I sat in on an English class as they considered the character Macbeth, looking closely at the play's soliloquies. The teacher pointed to early lines in the play, in which Macbeth notes: "Two truths are told/As happy prologues to the swelling act/Of the imperial theme" (I.iii.128-130). She asked the class to consider why Shakespeare had used the adjective "swelling." This started a discussion of words relating to rot and sickness that increase as the play progresses. When we read literary fiction, we understand word choice as an author's tool used to evoke emotional and build a certain understanding of a character or a theme. We ask why one word was used instead of another. When we switch our reading over to statistics and statistical arguments, however, we rarely model this same level of close reading.

"Close reading" has a variety of definitions. Often, in classroom practice, it means finding and extracting evidence from a text. To think about close reading of statistics as simply retrieving information, however, supports the notion, uncovered by Ann Fields, that students tend to frame research as retrieving information "waiting to be found," without regard to context, and without the need for analysis (Fields 2005, 16). Rather, in "Closing in on Close Reading," Nancy Boyles expresses a preference for close reading targeted at "craft and structure ... and integration of knowledge and ideas" (Boyles 2012). As we strive to help students become data literate, it's essential to increase their awareness of the words used with the numbers. Writers can — intentionally or unintentionally — tell stories with statistics using language that influences or changes the meaning of the data itself.

Authors who include statistics in their work have interpreted the data and found it to be worthy of inclusion. As a reader, I consider the author as a narrator and storyteller. By doing so, I'm reminded to take the author's word choice, and my emotional response to it, into account.

 The goal is to separate the information from its packaging.

Until I actively recognized that the author's word choice changed how I felt about information I was reading, I could not be confident that I was thinking critically about facts and ideas I encountered.

As a librarian, I realized students were not alert to manipulative language. After a while it occurred to me: if no one is teaching them to look for how language impacts their visceral responses, then students are not solely responsible for the quality of their critical thinking.

Thus, this chapter investigates how the language we use impacts our understanding of statistics in three arenas: reading, writing, and searching for information. It is informed by my current work as a high school librarian, as well as past work as Google's Search Educator. Elsewhere in this book, my colleagues discuss choices made with the statistics themselves: poor sampling, visualizations that change the meaning of data, cherry-picking convenient evidence to make an argument, and so forth.

The purpose here is to look specifically at how language ultimately impacts our interpretation and emotional understanding of the numbers embedded within stories we read.

Authors of news articles, scholarly studies, and advocacy reports may select language to make their readers feel afraid, enraged, empowered, mollified, and more. It is our job, as educators and research skills specialists, to help our colleagues and students learn how to transfer the analytical reading we learn to do with literature and primary sources to our everyday reading, and to separate the numbers we encounter from their emotionally persuasive packaging, a packaging I like to call *statistical storytelling.*

Experts and novices

In *How People Learn* (Bransford, Brown, and Cocking 1999), the authors distinguish between experts and novices in a curriculum area. Novices are those new to a content area. It can be difficult for them to see the big picture at first, and they may over-focus on small details. On the other hand, experts are those who are more likely to overlook details and see the big picture. This comparison is useful to keep in mind when exploring statistical storytelling with teens.

Working with teens who are reading nonfiction for either research or pleasure always reinforces for me the sway of loaded language. For example, one science class in my school assigns an adult narrative nonfiction book in an astronomy unit. The teacher wants students to practice recognizing emotionally evocative language to empower them to read science for pleasure in the future. Early in the unit, students argue that passages like the one below are devoid of emotion and totally based on facts:

> Another planet? Such a suggestion would have generally been scoffed at by most astronomers in the last days of the twentieth century. ... There were certainly small asteroids to be discovered, and occasionally a bright comet that had never been seen before would come screaming in from the far depths of space, but certainly nothing major was left out

there to find. Serious discussions by serious astronomers of another planet beyond Pluto were as likely as serious discussions by serious geologists on the location of the lost continent of Atlantis (Brown 2012, 5).

The narrative laid out by author Mike Brown is factually true. Yet, when expert readers take the time to observe the dismissive tone — which Brown constructs with his use of "scoffed," "certainly," "occasionally," and "serious" — we can see that the author is simultaneously relating a stance that truly existed within the scientific community and what he thinks about the scientists who felt this way.

Alternately, I have seen tenth graders who are tasked with selecting "pro" and "con" articles on current issues reject sources because they are disheartened by the lack of confidence expressed in the writing. For example, a student pointed to this article, and passages like the one below:

> The approximately 200 studies on media violence are remarkable primarily for their inconsistency and weak conclusions. Some studies show a correlation between television and violence; others don't. Some find that violent programming can increase aggressiveness; another finds that *Mr. Rogers' Neighborhood* does. Several studies, including the most-cited ones, are deeply flawed methodologically. (American Psychological Association, 2015).

Expert readers understand that the language of uncertainty (the repeated use of the "some studies show...others don't" structure, for example) is a sign that scientists have yet to prove a cause-and-effect relationship between variables. This kind of language is standard in scholarly research, and a data literate reader recognizes such language as a mark of integrity and a strong grounding in statistics.

However, the less-experienced student interpreted the indecisive language above quite differently. She worried that language was hedging, which in turn indicated to her that the author was not an expert on his topic. Without explicit guidance, students assume an inverse relationship between precise statistical writing and what they view as "factual" or "a good source."

Examples like these demonstrate how easily novices' prior experience with reading for information can get in the way of stronger data comprehension. Let's break down some key aspects of this phenomenon.

Pure statistical storytelling

First, let's look at a few common uses of language that are related to specific statistical practices, and then we will move on to look at language more generally, and how it changes our experience of statistics.

Clarify correlation or causation

> "When you take acetaminophen, you don't feel others' pain as much: The popular painkiller reduces empathy, study finds."
>
> – Gabermeier 2016

My colleagues have already addressed the most well-known error made in writing about statistics: describing a correlation as causation (see Chapter 1). Once we know this is a common misspeak, we can, as writers, avoid various forms of the word "cause." As readers, we can also be on the alert when we see the word "cause" or its synonyms, remembering to check and see if the original research actually found a causal link. What other turns of phrase should we be on the lookout for when we read? What words are better choices when we write?

Exercise: Identify words that indicate correlation or causation

Headlines and first paragraphs of news articles and press releases, like the one above, may be designed to pack maximum impact into minimal print space or to encourage the reader to click through to the entire story (e.g., clickbait). Mainstream media examples make it easy for educators to find material for quick exercises that explore different language traps. The goal of these exercises is to sharpen students' ability to identify language that implies causation or correlation. Ideally an exercise includes at least three steps:

>> **Sort:** Determine if headlines indicate causation, or simply correlation,

>> **Identify:** Point out the words and phrases that express the nature of the relationship, and

>> **Construct:** Collaboratively building a list of terms that fall into each category, allowing for group discussion during the process. For a sample list, see page 31.

When a recent school assembly speaker made a statement that erroneously implied causation, I heard the entire tenth grade — who had studied the difference in class a few weeks prior — whispering furiously to each other to point out the error. This demonstrates that through practice, recognizing the language used with data becomes much easier. It almost becomes second nature to spot the difference between implied causation and stated correlation. It is empowering for students to know the difference.

Here are a variety of terms that may be used either to imply correlation or causation (Vita n.d.; Miller 2004, 24). See if your group can add to it.

Words that indicate correlation	Words that indicate causation
Get Have Linked More … more/ less … less Tied Connected/Related Tend Associated	Cause Increase/decrease Benefits Impacts Enhances/undermines Effect/affect Improves/Boosts If > Then type statements (implies one-direction) Consequences

Exercise: Ripped from the headlines

This exercise can work on four levels, depending on the amount of time you have and the particular group with whom you are working:

» **Sort:** Provide a selection of headlines on diverse topics and simply sort them by whether they suggest correlation or just causation. Educator Jon Mueller keeps a running list of headlines for this purpose on his "Correlation or Causation?" page (http://jfmueller.faculty.noctrl.edu/100/correlation_or_causation.htm).

» **Compare:** Offer a list of several headlines on a single topic, which have varying degrees of causation implied. Ask participants to rank them from most strongly implying correlation to most strongly implying causation. Appendix B has examples you can use, from a study that clearly states its findings are correlated, not causal.

» **Classify:** Ask participants to classify a series of several first sentences or paragraphs of news coverage as implying just correlation or also causation. Each included excerpt is also based on an original study that clearly states its findings are correlated, not proving causation. Appendix C offers some examples you can use.

» **Rewrite:** Supply a short selection of first sentences or paragraphs that all inappropriately imply causation. Ask individuals or pairs to re-draft them so that they indicate only correlation.

Contextualize base and rate

2015 saw a 100% increase in deaths due to unprovoked attacks by sharks.

> — Author summary of research done
> by University of Florida 1996

As Lynette Hoelter explained in Chapter 1, another form of purely statistical storytelling that can impact meaning is sharing statistics without maintaining their context. Readers should be able to answer the questions, "Compared to what?" or, "Is that a big number?" (Blastland and Dilnot 2009).

There are two kinds of context that are important in statistical storytelling: the first is when we see a statistic without its basis (also known as its raw number). And the second is the opposite: seeing a raw number without any data to compare it to.

Consider these two statements:

Imprecise: "The number of fatal unprovoked shark attacks rose by 100% in 2015!"

Precise: "Six of the [shark] attacks were fatal. ... Although fatalities rose from last year's low, which saw only three shark-related deaths, they remained stable when looking at the big picture, precisely matching the decade average...."

> — University of Florida 2016

Discovering examples quickly and efficiently

- In both subscription databases and search engines, include the context terms [study], [report], and [research] in your query to locate articles that are reporting on statistical findings. (Note: the search terms to enter in the search box are delineated with brackets, though you do not need to use brackets when typing in your search terms.) For example, students needing content on the Zika virus might search for [zika report] or [zika study].

- Use date range filtering — available in many search engines and databases — to narrow in on articles from a particular timeframe.

- Search in Google News (http://news.google.com) for a current story on a topic, like [nutrition]. Alternately, you can try to find new studies, currently in the news, without regard for their topic. Headlines will often proclaim something like: "New research finds pictures of octopuses cause feelings of joy" or "New study found binge TV watching causes students to skip meals." It looks a little strange until you get used to it, but you can leverage these common turns of phrase by searching for: ["new report OR study OR research" finds OR found]. This odd-looking little search will find current articles that are discussing new research. Or, combine the two: [nutrition "new report OR study OR research" finds OR found].

- Look for an article that has an Explore in depth link on the last line of the result (see Figure 1). Clicking on that link will give you all the articles Google found on that same story.

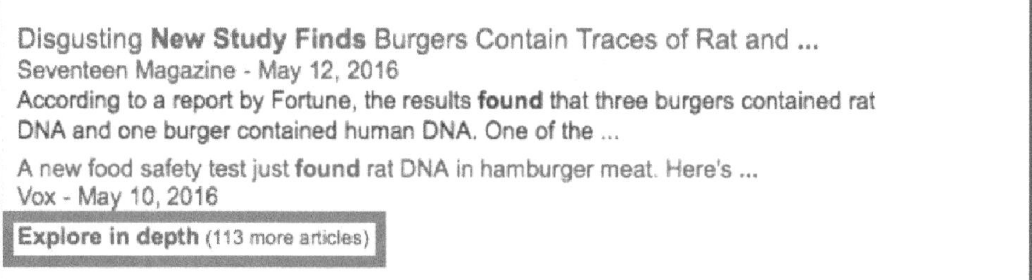

Disgusting **New Study Finds** Burgers Contain Traces of Rat and ...
Seventeen Magazine - May 12, 2016
According to a report by Fortune, the results **found** that three burgers contained rat DNA and one burger contained human DNA. One of the ...

A new food safety test just **found** rat DNA in hamburger meat. Here's ...
Vox - May 10, 2016

Explore in depth (113 more articles)

Figure 1: Accessing the "Explore in depth" feature in Google News.

The first statement shares an impressive statistic, depending on a percentage with no point of comparison. As a result, it inspires generalized fear and a sense that something is afoot in the shark population. The second statement, excerpted from a story using statistics from the Florida Museum of Natural History's International Shark Attack File at the University of Florida, explains how the 2015 number of fatalities compared to those in 2014, and also to the general trend in attacks over a larger span of years.

Authors can also make the opposite mistake, sharing a raw number without any signals to help the reader judge its size. Compare these two statements:

> *Imprecise:* "Shark attacks are common ploys in horror films, but there were only 98 unprovoked attacks worldwide in 2015!"

> *Precise:* "It's the kind of record no one wants to break: the most shark attacks in a single year. But 2015 did just that, with 98 unprovoked attacks worldwide, beating the previous record of 88 set in 2000, according to the International Shark Attack File housed at the University of Florida."
>
> – University of Florida 2016

The author of the first shares a raw number of attacks without giving the reader any independent way to determine if it is high or low. In the second, the University of Florida compares 2015 numbers against the records in the International Shark Attack File and finds that 2015 saw approximately 11% more shark attacks than the next most attack-filled year. The context given by the inclusion of this range of statistics helps the reader better understand the severity of the number of attacks.

A statistic or a dataset is not a complete argument in and of itself (The Writing Center at University of North Carolina, 2016). Jane E. Miller, the author of *The Chicago Guide to Writing about Numbers*, reminds writers to report *and* interpret (2004, 24). Data is evidence that is used in *combination with* an author's analysis to create an argument. Data, standing alone, is not sufficient.

 Data is not, in and of itself, an argument; it supports arguments.

Although we now know, from the two pieces of evidence offered above by the University of Florida, that 2015 saw a sharp increase in unprovoked shark attacks, what we do not really know is what that means in the real world. Why do shark experts think this increase is taking place? We need more information. Thus, it is appropriate that University of Florida follows the startling contention that 2015 had the highest number of shark attacks by a noticeable margin by explaining:

> Sharks plus humans equals attacks. As our population continues to rapidly grow and shark populations slowly recover, we're going to see more interactions.
>
> – University of Florida 2016

Datasets from a wide variety of disciplines could help students practice thinking about context in statistical storytelling.

Consider Figure 2, found in the Bureau of Justice Statistics' Statistical Tables report on capital punishment from 2013. It records the number of "persons executed in the United States, 1930–2013."

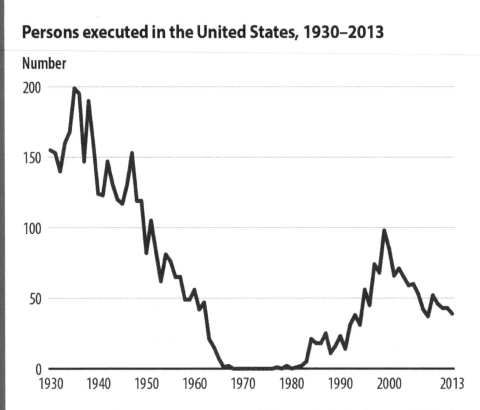

Persons executed in the United States, 1930–2013

Source: Bureau of Justice Statistics, National Prisoner Statistics Program (NPS-8), 2013.

Figure 2: Number of people executed in the United States per the Bureau of Justice Statistics 2014

As a class or in small groups, ask students what types of context are missing that could help readers understand the meaning of these trends. For example, how do these annual figures measure against the total population at the time? What meaning could we derive if we had that additional information? What was happening in various states, and on the national stage, with regard to the death penalty and the law over time?

Some helpful resources for this activity

The Death Penalty Information Center has a discussion on the history of the death penalty, as well as a timeline, that can be adapted for use in class (Death Penalty Information Center n.d.). Changes in social and judicial conditions also may play a role in the large number of executions in the early twentieth century. The Bureau of Justice Statistics' "Historical Corrections Statistics in the United States, 1850–1984" breaks down the number of executions and illegal lynchings, including statistics on race, by decade (Cahalan 1986).

Provided with additional evidence from these sources, a class could practice writing brief passages that include some basis and/or other context to data points for these execution statistics.

Which average is the best average: Mean, median, or mode?

A certain airline, when asked about the age of a specific plane that crashed, responded that the average age of its fleet is 16 years

— Tobey n.d.

Simply put, beware of the word "average." Chapter 1 defined median, mean, and mode, and described how they are different and why each one matters.

There are two major errors to avoid with averages. First, take care that the measure used (mean, median, mode, or a specific data point) matches the question being asked. In the case above, the airline was asked the specific age of a particular plane, not the "average" age fleet-wide. An "average" might have been offered to obfuscate the actual age of the specific plane in question. Secondly, as with the earlier discussion about numbers requiring context, be careful to use the average as a piece of evidence, not as a freestanding analysis. In the case of the airplane's age, the question has not been answered. One plane could be brand-new and another 32 years old to get at the mean of 16 years in age. We would refer to these two planes as likely outliers: extremes in plane age that are outside the rest of the planes' age range. Which plane would you rather be in?

Exercise: Find the correct measure

Fundamentally, a researcher must clearly define what kind of question she is asking, and match the measure to the information need. Consider the amount of exercise the students at your school are getting on a weekly basis. Imagine you have the data on every student's physical activity, in minutes of exercise a week, as shown in Figure 3.

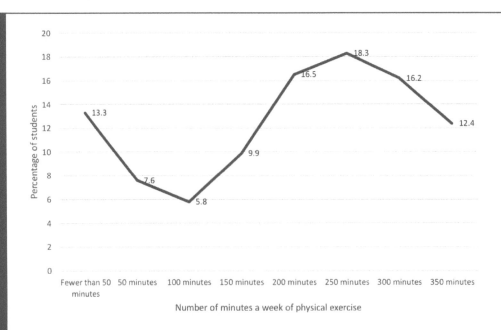

Figure 3: Number of minutes of physical exercise a week for students attending Mythical High School (Fictional data created by author).

Ask the class to calculate the mean, median, and mode for the data points on the graph. Then brainstorm stakeholders in the community who would care about the amount of exercise students are getting. Which stakeholder would benefit by knowing the mean? The median? The mode? Write statements that use the most beneficial form of average for various arguments. Responses like these make sense for this dataset:

Those who would benefit from reporting the mean
Stakeholder: Head of Food Services
Goal: Planning caloric intake for students.
Argument: "Our school lunches need to provide adequate calories for a typical student, getting n minutes of exercise a week."

Those who would benefit from reporting the median
Stakeholder: The school board member
Goal: The district wants to benchmark for physical activity on the part of the students, comparing national health guidelines to what students are currently experiencing district-wide.
Argument: "National health guidelines suggest a healthy level of activity for students is 300 minutes a week, and right now our median is n minutes a week. Fewer than half of our students are meeting these federal guidelines. We need to make this a priority for our district."

Those who would benefit from reporting the mode
Stakeholder: Physical Education District Coordinator
Goal: Requiring daily PE classes all four years of high school.
Argument: "There is a gap of almost 250 minutes of activity a week between our students who meet the Presidential standard for an active lifestyle and those who lead sedentary lives." (Presidential Active Lifestyle Award (PALA+ n.d.)).

Those who would benefit from reporting outliers
Stakeholder 1: Principal
Goal: Arguing her students are getting appropriate amounts of physical activity.

Argument: "Our students are so active, they are getting up to 240 minutes of vigorous activity every day!"

Stakeholder 2: Parent
Goal: Instituting school-wide calisthenics in zero period.
Argument: "Over thirteen percent of the class is getting no physical activity at all!"

After students complete this exercise, engage them in a discussion. Were the arguments being proposed in this exercise manipulative? Objective? Misleading? Accurate? Unfair? When we look at different ways data is communicated, is it always correct, just because it is "good" data? Is it possible for data to be both technically accurate but still misleading?

While you can use datasets in a wide variety of disciplines for this exercise, the Center for Disease Control's Youth Risk Behavior Surveillance System (YRBSS) might offer some useful ones to get you started (Center for Disease Control n.d.).

Use evidence

Once again, statistics are not some numbers sitting around, waiting to be found, imbued with some independent meaning. They really can only be understood within a context.

It is possible that many of us only ever encountered the terms mean, median, and mode in middle or high school math class. Since we are not accustomed to using them in everyday language, authors may worry that using the terms will be off putting to their audience. When an author uses the word "average," it may be an attempt to avoid intimidating readers. Perhaps writers consider "average" easier for readers to understand than "mean," "median," or "mode." Perhaps the author does not understand how the different averaging methods function well enough to write confidently using proper terminology. Since it is never a good plan to construct an argument or make a decision based on evidence one does not understand, one should only use information containing a statement of averages if one, in fact, understands it.

Given the experience we now have with writing about averages, consider what should be taken into account when reading. Always be on the lookout for whether statistics are being used as a freestanding argument or as evidence in support of an argument.

Cite your sources

"[T]he levels of driver errors we found [among dehydrated drivers] are of a similar magnitude to those found in people with a blood alcohol content of 0.08%, the current UK legal driving limit. In other words drivers who are not properly hydrated make the same number of errors as people who are over the drink drive limit."

– Professor Ron Maughan in
Loughborough University Media Centre 2015

Above and beyond the ethics of citing sources according scholarly conventions, it is helpful to readers when the text of an article makes note of the source of its data. As a reader, keep an eye out for these citations. The information in the press release above transformed into bold newspaper headlines like: "Driving While Dehydrated Just As Dangerous As Driving Drunk" (Withnall 2015).

Imagine the different perception for the reader if the story actually read:

A new study, sponsored in part by the European Hydration Institute — an industry foundation established by Coca-Cola and other organizations — suggested that driving while slightly dehydrated may lead to a similar number of errors as driving with a blood alcohol level of approximately 0.08% (Watson et al. 2015).

And how, again, would it be different if you knew that Professor Maughan, quoted at the start of this section and a contributor to the study, is also "Chair of the European Hydration Institute Science Advisory Board" (Loughborough University 2015)?

Providing the origin of the statistic provides some context for the outcome of the study, though readers cannot necessarily judge bias on funding alone. In this case, it does seems suspicious that an organization with a "pro-hydration" agenda funded a study that found dramatic consequences of not drinking enough liquids. Pairing the origin of a statistic with the number in the text helps a reader interpret the meaning and quality of the number.

In addition, students may not be aware of the different conventions for conveying an information source: I've had a student complain that an article they were reading from *The Atlantic*'s website did not footnote its sources, but her eyes had skipped right over the phrase "The OpenNet Initiative documents increasingly mature cyber attacks..." to get to the numbers that follow (Wagner 2013). Although the source was clearly named in the article, she was unfamiliar with how media sources cite articles differently than scholarly sources, so she overlooked it. For example, it can be helpful to point out to novice readers that media outlets frequently use the phrase "according to..." to signal when they are naming a source.

When writing, it is helpful to the reader to incorporate the source of a given statistic into the narrative:

> **Less helpful**: The average home price in California is 240% over the national average.

More helpful: California's Legislative Analyst's Office, the research arm of the California State Legislature, calculated that the median home price in California is 240% higher than the national average....

Most helpful: California's Legislative Analyst's Office, the research arm of the California State Legislature, calculated that, with a national median home price of $180,000, and a California median price of $440,000, the median home price in California is 240% higher than the national average.... (Taylor 2015, Gaarder 2016)[1]

The habit of incorporating the source name into the narrative does not require a teaching exercise of its own, but is rather something to remind students to do as they are writing in genres that do not use more formal citation practices. Incidentally, this habit is even more helpful (and required of all my students) when delivering presentations, where citations are not available to the audience in a meaningful manner.

As a rule of thumb, you should only use statistics you truly understand as evidence. As a reader, therefore, you should be selecting sources that provide you with sufficient amounts of information about the data you desire, communicated in a way that does not inherently change its meaning or make its meaning less clear. As a writer, you should understand the evidence you are using and speak about it in a clear and helpful manner that will not detract from the reader's ability to comprehend its true meaning.

---

[1]The use of the word "average" here is acceptable, because the sentence has already defined the central tendency being used (median). Also, check out what Joel Best has to say about the danger of "Big Round Numbers": Joel Best, *Stat-Spotting: A Field Guide to Identifying Dubious Data* (Berkeley, CA: University of California Press, 2013), 30.

Could Your Fast Food Burger or Burrito Be Making You Infertile? A New Study Concludes, Possibly...

Could your fast food be making you infertile?

Seems like there's a decent chance, or that it isn't helping, anyway, according to a new study, published in Environmental Health Perspectives, *a journal funded by the National Institutes of Health.*

Dr. Ami Zota, an assistant professor of environmental and occupational health at George Washington University, was the lead author of the study and pored over the data of 8,877 participants, collected between 2003 and 2010. They had all been asked about their diets in the past 24 hours, and they all had given a urinary sample. In those samples, Zota and her team of researchers found that the more fast food people ate, the higher the phthalates they had.

And unfortunately, phthalates isn't another name, for, say, vitamins and minerals. Believe me, I checked. I was hoping and rooting for all of us... (Williams 2016 n.p.)

Readers who pay attention to pure statistical storytelling may begin to notice that many instances of reporting actually follow the guidelines laid out previously, but still achieve a level of emotional resonance that impacts reader understanding. Let's turn now to language that is not specifically conveying numbers, but still impacts readers' understanding of those numbers. The opening lines from the above *Forbes* article about a class of chemical called phthalates, used in the packaging for fast food and linked by prior studies to infertility, follows the rules of pure statistical storytelling.

The title:

- » **uses a yes/no question,**
- » **highlights that it is reporting on a single study's findings, and**
- » **includes the word "possibly" to indicate that the author is not claiming causation.**

The text:

- » **reiterates the yes/no question in the first sentence,**
- » **refuses to provide a definitive answer to the question,**
- » **describes, quite succinctly, the sample group and methodologies used in the study.**

Technically, this statistical storytelling could have been extremely straightforward. It could have simply been a dry recounting of facts, and conveyed the study findings quite accurately.

 Author's note

I do appreciate the use of a yes/no question in a title over a title that implies causation where none exists. However, I have recently started teaching my students a highly accurate adage, "Davis's Law":

"If a headline ends in a question mark, the answer is 'no'" (Bloch 1991, 163).

(This phenomenon is often referred to as 'Betteridge's Law of Headlines,' but Davis's work predates that of Betteridge.)

Yet, I found myself chuckling as I read the article. The informal language lightens the tone. The author's voice, talking directly *to* me in that last line — rather than *at* me — makes the storytelling feel personal, like I am being taken into the author's confidence, but as much like he is making fun of himself as that he is dis cussing scientific findings. He even concludes the article with a message for readers from the lead scientist on the study, urging us not to panic.

It was surprising, then, that this slightly self-deprecating, personable and personal tone at the beginning and conclusion of the article sandwiched a very precise and incisive call to action. Williams suggests that readers bring their own plates to fast food restaurants until the chains change their packaging, and calls for "a movement" to get safer food. He also posits that his suggested changes would not constitute major economic burden for the fast food companies involved. Williams wants me to take action — he outlines suggestions for how I can fight back against fast food companies in a manner that will make their lives difficult and potentially inspire change. Yet, the lightness of his storytelling is the sugar coating on a bitter pill. He uses humor to keep me engaged through his angry retort.

Intensifiers and qualifiers

> [A] 12-year-old who took longer than 12 minutes to run a mile ... scored lower on state standardized tests than those who were more fit.
>
> > – Adams 2013

In his 2013 book *Stat-Spotting: A Field Guide to Identifying Dubious Data*, Joel Best lays out a number of ways in which language can be used to couch statistics in meanings the numbers themselves do not convey. Be on the lookout for superlatives: labeling a finding as "the best," "the worst," "the biggest," or other fantastical measures. They are often overblown.

What Best refers to as "superlatives" could fall into a category that writers call *intensifiers*. An intensifier is a word added to a sentence to amplify the feeling it conveys. The opposite of an intensifier is a "qualifier," or a word that introduces some uncertainty into a sentence. Look at these examples:

Original sentence: Students who get at least thirty minutes of activity a day perform better in their classes.

Soften with _qualifiers:_ Students who get at least thirty minutes of activity a day **may** perform **somewhat** better in their classes.

Strengthen with an _intensifier:_ Students who get at least thirty minutes of activity a day perform **much** better in their classes.

When an author makes prolific use of intensifiers, the reader senses that the author strongly supports the statement. An author who uses qualifiers gives the impression of weak support (or little/no agreement with) the topic. By watching for and identifying intensifiers and qualifiers, readers can start to read between the lines on an author's opinion.

There is an exception to this rule of thumb when reading qualifiers in scholarly articles. As with the example of the expert writing about media violence toward the start of this chapter, responsible statistical storytelling employs qualifiers to create "confident uncertainty" (The Writing Center at UNC-Chapel Hill 2016). "Uncertainty," in this case, does not refer to author's level of "grasp" of the topic, but how far developed scientific understanding of the topic is. Statisticians consider it good form to use qualifiers to underline the difficulty in proving causation.

Can students determine the difference between confident uncertainty in the spirit of responsible statistical reporting and reporting that uses qualifiers and intensifiers to convey author's opinion on the topic? In 2016, the Writing Center at University of North Carolina – Chapel Hill offered fantastic guidance for considering how and when to use qualifiers in general-subject writing. Their handout offers lists of qualifiers that help convey confident uncertainty where appropriate, but also help writers practice stating their own analytical conclusions with confidence.

Exercise: Peer review for intensifiers and qualifiers

In class, students could peer review each other's writing, identifying intensifiers and qualifiers. Where appropriate, peer reviewers can offer suggestions for places to add confident uncertainty, and suggest workable wording, in addition to identifying times that an intensifier could draw attention to an argument.

Teaching the nonfiction writer as narrator

Best points out that another way to evoke emotion in nonfiction writing is to give a situation a cute, distressing, or catchy name. For example, when a reader sees the term "The Pink Tax" used to refer to product pricing that makes items aimed at women more expensive than similar products aimed at men, be aware that someone selected that term specifically because it layered an emotional response onto their argument and, in doing so, potentially provoked a similar emotional response in the reader.

Educators have traditionally helped students identify this strategy when reading fiction in the classroom; now we can help them transfer this skill to reading nonfiction for research and "in the wild." Depending on your faculty's tastes, there are numerous ways to frame the idea of unpacking statistical writing for its emotional resonance.

My favorite frame, when working to identify emotional triggers in writing, is thinking of the writer as a narrator. When either reading or writing, we can extend this frame in a variety of ways:

» **Identify the narrator's personality:** Give participants a passage to read and ask them to describe the personality of the narrator, or describe if this person was a friend, what kind of friend would he or she be? How does the "personality" of the writing impact your response to the statistics you see?

» **Rewrite it:** Ask participants to rewrite a piece that has emotionally evocative overtones, creating a more measured tone.

» **Unpack the unreliable narrator:** Give learners a short passage of a study, news article, or advocacy piece, and ask them to highlight and discuss emotionally evocative language. You can push this exercise one step further — depending on which approach is the best fit for your faculty. Let's look at three ways to approach the question of nonfiction author as unreliable narrator:

Here are three different frameworks for discussing the notion of author as narrator, and exercises you can use for each.

Exercise: Reconstructing a popular graphic organizer

Co-contributor Wendy Stephens introduced me to a graphic organizer to use when analyzing fiction. There appear to be variations of this organizer, created by different individuals and organizations, and your students may be using it elsewhere in their schoolwork. It shows a stick figure that students labeled with:

1. **"The character says...,"**
2. **"The character thinks...,"**
3. **"The character does...."**

If we think of the nonfiction author as a story's narrator, as shown in Figure 4, it allows us to slightly tweak these questions:

1. **"The author says…,"**
2. **"The author thinks…,"**
3. **"The author wants the reader to do or to feel…."**

Consider offering these prompts on a graphic organizer or worksheet for students to practice unpacking the tone and motivation behind statistical storytelling in media, advocacy, or scholarly writing.

The author wants you to feel or do…

The author thinks…

The author says…

Figure 4: Applying story questions to nonfiction.

As with the shorter form of this lesson, asking learners to provide evidence for the answers entered on the graphic organizer is an important way for them to practice their critical reading. Learners should highlight the words and phrases in the reading which signal what the author thinks about the topic, and what s/he wants the reader to do or feel. Discuss the evidence as a group.

With the proper mindset, a lesson of this nature can be both engaging and challenging, as well as pegged for almost any age range.

There is another way to talk about these same elements, which might connect to prior learning for a different set of learners. In a sense, when I am reading nonfiction with an eye toward the author's perspective, I think of the writing as having features analogous to *connotation* and *denotation*. The *denotation*, or dictionary meaning, is like the factual information — in this case, the statistics. The *connotation* of the passage is the feeling that the author inspires (intentionally or not) in the reader; the subtext about the story. The *call to action* is what the author wants the reader to take away from the text. Novice researchers must be aware of not just text but subtext, whether reading numbers or words.

When our science students were reading their astronomy-themed narrative nonfiction, I taught a 50-minute lesson (see http://bit.ly/NonFictionAnalysis) that combined the notion of connotation and denotation with that of an unreliable narrator. Our science students successfully unpacked each of these elements from the narrative nonfiction they were reading in groups. We started to move from "the author is just clear and informative," to "the author wants us to think about him as more of an expert than the other experts" or "the author wants us to advocate for a more science-literate society!"

In this approach, these same questions might be framed like this:

>   **What was the author's topic** (what was the factual argument the author is presenting)? You could call this the "denotation" of the passage.

>   **What was the author's opinion about the topic?** You could call this the "connotation" of the passage.

» **What was the author trying to make you feel about the topic?**

» **What are some words or phrases the author used to evoke those feelings in you?**

Exercise: Aristotle's rhetorical triangle

When you have students studying formal elements of rhetoric, you may want to convey the same lesson using Aristotle's Rhetorical Triangle (shown in Figure 5), which describes how speaker, audience, and subject work together to create meaning.

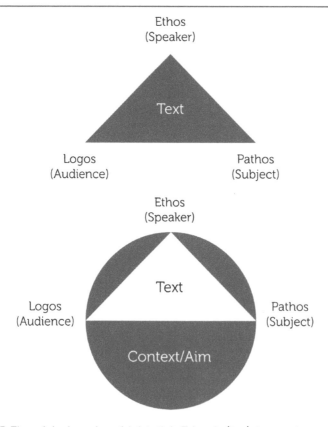

Figure 5: The original version of Aristotle's Triangle (top) demonstrates the relationship between the speaker (ethos, or expert approach), audience (logos, or logical reading), and subject (pathos, or emotional components), and how these elements work together to create the understood meaning of the text. Some scholars add an encapsulating circle to the original diagram (bottom) to communicate that the context or aim of the writing surrounds all these other elements and lends itself to how the text is understood.

The Advanced Placement Language and Composition exam focuses on rhetoric, so collaborating with classes preparing for that exam may offer opportunities to practice transfer. (Hepzibah Roskelly's 2016 article "What Do Students Need to Know About Rhetoric?" offers a succinct and clear overview of elements on which you may want to build.)

Applying the rhetorical triangle challenges us to step out of the roll of emotional reader and look at our own responses from a dispassionate distance. Consider the opening of this article on school funding from the conservative-leaning organization New Mexico WatchDog:

> For decades, it's probably the most troublesome question facing education: Why are results for U.S. public school students so mediocre, despite the billions of taxpayer dollars spent?
>
> Andrew Coulson thinks he's got the answer: Because there is no discernible correlation between spending and outcomes.
>
> "The takeaway from this study is that what we've done over the past 40 years hasn't worked," said Coulson, director of the Center For Educational Freedom at the CATO Institute. "The average performance change nationwide has declined 3 percent in mathematical and verbal skills. Moreover, there's been no relationship, effectively, between spending and academic outcomes" (Nikolewski 2014).

In this instance, the author calls on the expertise of a think tank scholar, Andrew Coulson, to provide the ethos to his argument. Drawing on evidence from such an expert provides the reader with the development of a logical argument. As is often the case when authors cite statistics, the use of data to measure change in student achievement appears to offer a logical ground truth. Of course, it is our contention throughout this work that statistics can also be a tool of pathos, as statistics can be formulated or communicated in such a way as to change the feeling they convey to the reader. Additionally, all of these elements are framed for the reader with an opening appeal to pathos, when author Rob Nikolewski employs phrases like "most troublesome question facing education" to set up the logical argument he proceeds to construct. Finally, school funding, and government spending more generally, are often at the heart of national debates which provide a broader context – and watchdog groups aim to change government behavior. This article is situated within that debate.

Select an article that makes use of statistics and identify the pathos, ethos, and logos. Consider how these elements change readers' interpretation of the statistics shared within the story.

Results required

Beyond engaging in standard close reading, it might also help students to learn about some of the pressures acting on statistical storytelling, and for them to start taking notice of resulting uses of language and structure that can impact their understanding of meaning, especially in the popular media.

One of the differences between writing done by students and the sources students consume is the expected outcome on the part of the audience. That is to say, a student who is investigating whether video games lead to violent behavior may turn in a paper that finds no difference between the two sides and receive a strong grade for good work, while a political advocate — whose funding, career, or cause may depend upon gaining publication and press attention — requires an attention-grabbing sound bite of a response. Students may not always be aware of this difference. Thus, it can be helpful to offer an example of storytelling with the same dataset at different stages in its lifecycle to see how its meaning changes as users strive to attract the public.

John Oliver's fantastic (but not appropriate for school) piece, "Scientific Studies" (2016), called out one such example:

> » **First, medical researchers,** concerned with "conflicting results regarding the role of chocolate consumption during pregnancy" wondered if there was a difference between consuming high-flavanol and low-flavanol chocolate. They "observed no significant difference" between the two, noting that "daily intake of 30g of high-flavanol chocolate did not improve placental function" compared with low-flavanol versions, noting that it "might suggest that chocolate effects are not solely and directly due to flavanol content." The original study is titled: "High-flavanol chocolate to improve placental function and to decrease the risk of preeclampsia: a double blind randomized clinical trial" (Bujold et al. 2016, S23).

> » **Next, the Society for Maternal-Fetal Medicine,** the organization hosting the conference at which the researchers were to present their study, issued a press release about the study, entitled: "The Benefits of Chocolate During Pregnancy." The release ran through the findings, reiterating the baseline statistics with regard to the methods of the study, including the fact that each subject ate 30 grams of chocolate a day for 12 weeks. However, where the original reporting concluded that "...[T]he marked improvement of the pulsatility index observed in the 2 chocolate groups might suggest that chocolate effects are not solely and directly due to flavanol content" (i.e., researchers observed a pattern of change in a notable number of subjects' placentas which was unrelated to the question they were testing, and the cause of which they could not identify), the press release argued that "This study indicates that chocolate could have a positive impact on placenta and fetal growth and development and that chocolate's effects are not solely and directly due to flavanol content" ("The Benefits of Chocolate during Pregnancy" n.d.)

> » **Finally, in the hands of the media,** the story morphed yet again, to include headlines and opening lines like:
>
> *"Pregnant women SHOULD eat chocolate as it's good for them AND baby"*
>
> *Pregnant women who crave chocolate are in for a treat – scientists say eating it could be good for them and their unborn babies.*
>
> *Having just 30g a day may boost a baby's growth, they claim* (Christensen 2016).

While students do need to understand the pressures on statistical storytellers to show impressive results to readers, educators do not want to undermine the notion that research in various disciplines can successfully help us build a greater understanding of the world around us.

Exercise: The life-cycle of reporting on research

Consider having students find storytelling about a specific study or dataset at different points in its life-cycle and identify how it changes as successive organizations make use of it.

Memory and (mis)information

There is much we still do not know about how memory works. Both academic researchers and marketing professionals experiment with emotionally evocative wording and memory,[2] accumulating growing evidence that triggering strong emotions through word choice helps shape recall. Researchers are also

[2]For example: Elizabeth A. Kensinger and Suzanne Corkin, "Memory Enhancement for Emotional Words: Are Emotional Words More Vividly Remembered than Neutral Words?," *Memory and Cognition* 31, no. 8 (2003). and Tom Channick, "The 1,072 Words That Will Change How You Write Headlines Forever," *Native Advertising*, last modified July 1, 2015, accessed May 14, 2016, http://nativeadvertising.com/contextwords/.

interested to know if headlines influence how readers understand and retain the content of the stories that follow. Lewandowsy *et al* review the scholarship on "Misinformation and Its Correction," confirming a strong research trend hypothesizing that what people first learn to be true will continue to be what they believe, even if corrected later. Only three methods seem to produce some change in what readers remember. One of these methods is offering a new narrative to replace the reader's existing one (Lewandowsky et al. 2012, 117). This finding prompted other researchers to ask whether a complete news story could counteract the impact of a misleading headline. This single study indicated that "misleading headlines affect readers' memory, their inferential reasoning and behavioral intentions" even when the article itself created a replacement narrative, if the headline is just misleading enough that the reader does not notice a glaring contradiction between it and the body of the article (Ecker et al. 2014, 323). As a result, implications of headlines may be coloring readers' understanding of statistical arguments even before the evidence is presented. Among other things, this finding would suggest even further that statistics cannot simply be evidence "waiting to be found" because the reader's understanding of their meaning may essentially be set even before they reach the statistics.

This relationship between the headline and the body of a story play out in different ways across different forms of writing. In her "How to Read and Understand a Scientific Paper: A Guide for Non-Scientists," Jennifer Raff of the University of Kansas suggested upending traditional practice and saving the abstract as the last, not first, part of a paper to read (2013). Reading the abstract first, she hypothesizes, causes the reader to believe the rest of the paper must be true and truncates the close reading process that could lead readers to find new or contradictory findings in the data or its methodology.

Similarly, the opening image of *The Atlantic*'s "Why Internet Headline Writers Hate Themselves" jokingly refers to writing a "One sentence summary that walks back the promise made in the headline" (Thompson 2015, 1). This seems counterintuitive to straightforward reporting practices, but one easily finds numerous examples of this journalistic trick:

Consider this press release from the American Psychological Association:

> **APA Review Confirms Link Between Playing Violent Video Games and Aggression**
>
> ***Finds insufficient research to link violent video game play to criminal violence***
>
> Violent video game play is linked to increased aggression in players but insufficient evidence exists about whether the link extends to criminal violence or delinquency, according to a new American Psychological Association task force report. ... (American Psychological Association 2015)

As you can see, even scholarly organizations can make this error!

Exercise: Exposing contradictions

When students are collecting sources during research, consider asking them to annotate the articles. These annotations should include contradictions they find between a headline's conclusion and the information in the opening paragraphs. Students might be surprised with how often these contradictions occur in the media. Furthermore, this practice will help them attend to the actual message of the statistics within the piece, rather than the title that initially attracted their eye.

Each of these elements of statistical storytelling help form readers' understanding of a story. Taken piece-by-piece, they may feel like too much to handle. It has been my observation, however, that practice noticing even one of these ways in which language can be used to change readers' understanding can have a great impact on the critical thinking that goes on during the overall reading and writing process.

Searching

Once students begin to get a feeling for what to watch out for in reading and writing, the same knowledge can be applied to choices made when searching for statistical stories.

"Garbage in/garbage out"

In our library, we hold the philosophy that source evaluation — the ability to assess the credibility of a resource — begins with strong search skills. All search tools provide a "garbage in/garbage out" experience. That is to say, search engines and databases "read" each page or article they contain, placing each word that appears within that source in an index. When you type a query into the search box (we're using brackets in this book to demarcate text that is typed into a search box), the search engine or database then compares the words in your query to the words indexed for each page or article, and gives you the sources that match. Google is coded to provide the flexibility to consider "related terms" — meaning it "understands" that [correlation] and [link] are often synonymous. Expert searchers know that when you use a word in your search, you should expect to see it on the page that comes back. Formal terminology tends to bring back pages with formal sources, informal language leads to informal sources. Experts consider what kind of language will be used in the *answer* they seek.

Alternatively, the novice searcher is thinking about his or her *question* (and may even have phrased the search string in the form of a question). Therefore, people who want to know *if videos games cause violence* tend to search for [video games cause violence], or even [Do video games cause violence?] but then results are more likely to skew toward articles that are confusing correlation and causation.

Of course, terms like [cause], [impact], and [average] are very tempting to include in queries. But the cleanest searches are *devoid of any words describing relationships* among factors, such as [video games violence] in a search engine, or [(video games) AND violence] in a database.

If you don't know what your answer is (for example, if you don't know that video games cause violence, for certain) then you are best to leave the verb out.

 A useful rule of thumb is: *Search for your answer, not your question.*

Familiarity with synonym searching can be crucial in this regard. Building on Best's 2013 point about naming issues to manipulate reader perceptions, the evidence researchers encounter will also skew with the search terms they chose. My students seek help when they are only finding one side of an argument when they are searching with terms that may be named differently depending on one's point of view, as shown in Figure 6.

If a searcher wants to see how various stakeholders address a single issue, it will be necessary to search separately, using each group's name for the topic, in turn. Similarly, different disciplines may use a variety of terms to refer to the same idea. For example, economists and academic librarians talk about "threshold concepts" as foundational knowledge, while others might use a term like "background knowledge."

If one searchers only for this term,	She may miss stories that use this term
[undocumented worker]	[illegal immigrant] [birthright citizenship] [anchor baby]
[obamacare]	[affordable care act]
[drone]	[unmanned aerial vehicle]
[red scare]	[anti-communism] [mccarthyism] [house un-american activities committee]

Figure 6: similar search terms with different connotations.

Exercise: Write search terms

Select a topic that is relevant to your curriculum. Try one of the following:

» **Discuss that there can be a difference between search results that feel helpful,** which is often code for "easy to find and easy to read" and those that are actually good quality. The best sources often have both of these attributes, but when one searches with a long-form question one often gets results that are "easy" to read rather than those of great quality. Brainstorm more- and less-formal ways of referring to single ideas and try searching with each term – observe the differences in results.

» **Identify synonyms that would be used by different stakeholders to describe a single idea.** Try searching with each term and observe the differences in results.

» **Practice writing searches** that do not include language that would skew toward causation unless you know that causation has actually been proven. Once again, trying searches and comparing results can be helpful.

A quick note before we move on: Web searching can work in unexpected ways. Sometimes, even poorly-constructed searches (according to expert researchers) can still prove successful. This is a chance to observe how *different* approaches produce *different* results.

Context terms

One kind of search term that is revolutionary for student search experiences is *context terms*, named by Daniel M. Russell. A context term is a source type that also functions effectively as a search term. For example, if you wanted to find a dataset show-ing which states voted Democratic or Republican in a given presidential election, you might suspect that this information would be displayed on a map. You would therefore include the term [map] in your query. Long before I started calling them context terms, I was using source types as search terms to lo-cate statistics. Building a query using terms like [study], [report], [research], [survey], and [poll] can be game-changing. Similarly, thinking about the terms that appear in the captions of datasets in scholarly works makes a huge difference. Try searching in an image collection (such as Google Images) for [*topic* figure OR table] to find the statistical images from academic papers or in-dustry reports.

You can also use terms for collections of information, like [data-base], [library], [collection], or [archive] to find the collection that holds your desired data.

Just be mindful that while the term [statistics] is increasingly being used as a title or in the metadata of pages created by trust-ed sources, is not always a helpful term in finding quality data. Experts know that quality sources do not say: "here are some statistics," or "statistics show…," they tend to say: "a recent Gallup poll found," or "see Figure 2."

Less experienced searchers often discover qualitative results, which may include a sprinkling of data, when using paid databases and open web search engines. When my students are looking for information on Turkish citizens' feelings about the country's attempts to join the European Union (EU) over the last forty years, they find articles from a variety of newspapers on online media sites, but somehow never encounter any of the results of the detailed surveys run by the EU itself. My students don't realize the EU might ask the Turkish people specific questions about their attitudes and publish the results in the form of a statistical report (European Commission Directorate-General for Communication 2013, 1-4).

One of the big issues inexperienced researchers face is *source literacy*[3]: an awareness of what kind of sources are even created and available, let alone how to find and understand them.

Exercise: Experimenting to learn context terms

I've had great luck simply posting a slide with context terms. (See Figure 7.) I then ask students to combine their basic topic search terms with one context term at a time and investigate what comes up. I never know which ones will work for which topic, and the list of potential terms changes by discipline.

I set a timer for fifteen minutes and just ask them to go for it and get through as many as possible to see what is there. While they search, I stroll around, helping build understanding for unfamiliar formats.

---

[3] A topic currently being explored by Nora Murphy. See, for example: Nora Murphy, "How to Develop Strong Source Literacy: Practice!" at http://blog.fsha.org/develop-source-literacy/ and her article "Approaching Source Illiteracy, or How a Source Is Like a Frog" in the May/June 2016 issue of *Knowledge Quest*.

Report	Conference
Survey	Case Study
Study	Book
Infographic	Forum
Figure	Thread
Table	Overview
Poll	FAQ
Survey	Database
Graph (less common)	Museum
Chart (less common)	Library
Data	Archive
Statistics	Collection
Fact sheet	Agency
Overview	Association
White paper	Institute
Presentation	Center

Figure 7: A general list of source terms that can be combined with topic-related terms to tease out less-typical results for students.

Associated search terms

There are some features that make it hard to search for specific information, yet a clever searcher can use them to great advantage. Novice searchers often forget to look beyond the anticipated headlines about their topics to the ways in which it might be discussed.

An *associated search term* is a word that is not directly related to the searcher's topic, but which has a high likelihood of appearing in the source the searcher wants to find. For example, I can find scholarly studies through paid databases and Google Scholar, but also if I know that [methods] and [discussion] are section headings of papers that may include statistical analysis, I can add them as potential search terms.

I frequently use this strategy to find projection data, for example. The notion of "projection" has many synonyms: forecast, estimate, prediction, anticipation, expectation, and sometimes the idea of a forecast is simply implied. However, reports of forecasts almost always predict some outcome "by the year *x*." An expert searcher can use this convention to find projection data. Consider the query shown in Figure 8:

Try this query	To find projections like
[childhood obesity "by the year 2020..2050" OR "by 2020..2050"]	"The researchers estimate that by 2025, China, which saw a 40 percent rise in childhood obesity between 2000 and 2013, will have the greatest..." (Lepore 2016) "The World Health Organization estimated that childhood obesity rates could rise across the globe from just over 40 million to 75 million by 2025...." (Robinson 2014) "By 2025, 268 million children aged between five and 17 years old...." (De Graaf 2016)

Figure 8: Using date ranges in searches. Putting two periods between two year dates means, "Look for results between this year and this year."

Admittedly, this technique is not for the faint of heart. I would not recommend teaching it to others until a clear need arises, but it is great to have in your toolbox for that perfect moment. Just remember, a little creativity can go a long way.

Search with precise statistical terminology

[Correlation], [link], [sample] and [predictor] can make excellent search terms. For example, to continue with the same topic, the search [predictor childhood obesity] will bring up scholarly articles outlining the predictors, and probably with data to help explain them. Just remember that [predictor childhood obesity] is open-ended and avoids confirmation bias while [exercise predictor childhood obesity] pre-supposes that the searcher already knows what causes obesity and will skew results.

Additionally, be specific when searching for averages. Have you determined that your research needs are best met by knowing a *median* statistic? Search explicitly for [median home price Atlanta] rather than [average home price Atlanta]. Consider that most search tools cannot see percentage signs (%), but can see the word [percent OR percentage] (as well as [percentile] – just don't confuse it with the others).

Searchers can use specific statistical terminology, as well, to track down studies that make use of a specific sampling method, for example: [childhood obesity multistage random sample] or [childhood obesity longitudinal]. Or, if many of the results one is finding are based on poor or unhelpful methodology, eliminate more of those results using a minus sign (-) immediately before the search term, without a space separating them. Imagine you are mostly getting results that use a method called *snowball sampling*, in which individuals recruit acquaintances to partici-pate in a study, poll, or survey. In most cases, that method does not lead to valid results. A search like [*topic* -snowball] will assure that you get no results that include the word *snowball* anywhere in the document. Similarly, if you need quantitative studies, then a qualitative method like ethnography – while valid – may not be helpful, so [iPad-ethnographic] would eliminate any iPad studies that had an ethnographic method.

Search with terms for parts of a paper

As with using context terms to find a particular type of source, you can use the formal names for parts of a scholarly paper to find your topic within a scholarly paper, as mentioned above. Are you looking for a study that will give you context for what came before it? Use the search term [literature review] in your search query. Looking for press releases, blog posts, newspaper or mag-azine articles that report a study in more accessible language, but still tell you something about how the study was carried out? Consider using search terms like [method], [discussion] or [con-clusion].

Select a topic relevant to your participants, or let them chose one for themselves. Simply try combining words describing the topic with some of the vocabulary discussed in the last two sections and ask them to observe what happens.

Conclusion

Thinking about responsible statistical language can be a bit frightening, because fewer authors than we would like speak of their work with confident uncertainty, and it can feel to students like equivocating and not appearing expert. Of course, learning to communicate with confident uncertainty where appropriate may also reincarnate the notion that it is best to use "unbiased" sources, when, in fact, such a source rarely exists. In our program, we approach bias and/or perspective as anticipated elements in our sources, and therefore aim to give students to tools to recognize it, name it, and use that understanding to place the facts they are finding in context. We believe recognizing word choices that are emotionally resonant is a powerful tool, critical for both source evaluation and synthetic thinking, and is a habit that — once formed — will become second nature for many of our students.

Acknowledgements: I owe great thanks to all my colleague-collaborators on this book, many of whom have helped me think through this idea (and many others) that make their way into the research skills curriculum at my school. I owe particular thanks here to Wendy Stephens, my partner on the statistics work in this book, who introduced me to a particular graphic organizer that crystallized my thinking, and to classroom teachers Robin von Breton and Tiffany Christ, who talked with me about my ideas, inspired me with their lesson plans, and let me into their classrooms to teach their students.

Resources

Abilock, Debbie, and Sue Smith. "No Rush: Thinking about Synthesis/Skepticism and the Brain." E-mail message to author. May 5, 2016.

Ackmann, Martha. 2003. *The Mercury 13: The Untold Story of Thirteen American Women and the Dream of Space Flight*. New York: Random House.

American Psychological Association. 2015. "APA Review Confirms Link between Playing Violent Video Games and Aggression." Press release, Aug. 13. Accessed April 15, 2017. http://www.apa.org/news/press/releases/2015/08/violent-video-games.aspx .

Bergson-Michelson, Tasha. 2016. "Introduction to Literary Analysis of Non-Fiction." Accessed April 15, 2017. https://docs.google.com/document/d/1M-NpwxF6dAsi505iq94_oP--kbrSR5HhPCOCSPi-dHU/edit?usp=sharing .

Best, Joel. 2013. *Stat-Spotting: A Field Guide to Identifying Dubious Data*. Berkeley, CA: University of California Press.

Biggs, John. 2016. "Study Finds Social Media Leads to Sleep Disturbance." *TechCrunch*, Jan. 26. Accessed April 15, 2017. https://techcrunch.com/2016/01/26/study-finds-so-cial-media-leads-to-sleep-disturbance/ .

"Blame Social Media for Your Child's Sleeplessness." 2016. *Eenadu India*, Jan. 27. Accessed April 15, 2017. http://www.eenaduindia.com/Evezonely/Parent-ing/2016/01/27134057/Blame-social-media-for-your-childs-sleeplessness.vpf .

Bloch, Arthur. 1991. *The Complete Murphy's Law: A Definitive Collection*. Rev. ed. Los Angeles, Calif.: Price Stern Sloan, 1991. Accessed April 17, 2017. https://books.google.com/books?id=tph7EdvSa0EC .

Boyles, Nancy. 2012/2013. "Closing in on Close Reading." *Educational Leadership* 70(4), Dec./Jan. Accessed April 2017. http://www.ascd.org/publications/educational-leader-ship/dec12/vol70/num04/Closing-in-on-Close-Reading.aspx .

Brown, Mike. 2012. *How I Killed Pluto and Why It Had It Coming*. New York.: Spiegel & Grau.

Bujold, Emmanuel, Asma Babar, Elise Lavoie, Mario Girard, Vicky Leblanc, Simone Lemieux, Lionel-Ange Poungui, Isabelle Marc, Belkacem Abdou, and Sylvie Dodin. 2016. "High-Flavanol Chocolate to Improve Placental Function and to Decrease the Risk of Preeclampsia: A Double Blind Randomized Clinical Trial." *American Journal of Obstetrics and Gynecology*, Jan., supplement, S23-S24.

Cahalan, Margaret Werner, and Lee Anne Parsons. 1986. *Historical Corrections Statistics in the United States*, 1850-1984. Bureau of Justice Statistics, U.S. Department of Jus-tice. Report no. NCJ - 102529. Accessed April 15, 2017. http://www.bjs.gov/content/pub/pdf/hcsus5084.pdf .

Centers for Disease Control. n.d. *1991-2013 High School Youth Risk Behavior Survey Data*. Accessed April 15, 2017. http://nccd.cdc.gov/youthonline/ .

Channick, Tom. 2015. "The 1,072 Words That Will Change How You Write Headlines Forever." Native Advertising, Jul. 1. Accessed April 15, 2017. http://nativeadvertising.com/contextwords/ .

Christensen, Aoife Ryan. 2016. "Pregnant Women SHOULD Eat Chocolate as It's Good for Them AND Baby." *Evoke*, Feb. 3. Accessed April 15, 2017. http://evoke.ie/life-style/health/mums-to-be-chocolate-ok .

Clark, Allison. 2016. "Shark Attacks Hit All-Time High in 2015." *Univeristy of Florida News*, February 8, Accessed April 15, 2017. http://news.ufl.edu/articles/2016/02/shark-attacks-hit-all-time-high-in-2015.php .

Death Penalty Information Center. 2017. "History of the Death Penalty." Death Penalty Information Center. Accessed April 15, 2017. http://www.deathpenaltyinfo.org/part-i-history-death-penalty .

De Graaf, Mia. 2016."Kids with Chronic Obesity Conditions to Sky-Rocket by 2025." *Daily Mail* (London), Oct. 8. Accessed Apr. 15, 2017. http://www.dailymail.co.uk/health/article-3827881/Kids-chronic-obesity-conditions-sky-rocket-2025-268-MIL-LION-suffering-hypertension-diabetes-liver-disease.html .

Ecker, Ullrich KH, Stephan Lewandowsky, Ee Pin Chang, and Rekha Pillai. 2014 "The Effects of Subtle Misinformation in News Headlines." *Journal of Experimental Psy-chology: Applied* 20(4): 323-35.

Equio, Amabelle. 2016. "Research Links Extreme Social Media Use With Disrupted Sleep." *American Sleep Association* (blog), Feb. 2. Accessed April 15, 2017. https://www.sleepassociation.org/2016/02/02/research-links-extreme-social-media-use-with-disrupted-sleep/ .

European Commission, Directorate-General for Communication. 2013. *Eurobarometer Standard 79 Turkey*, July. 013. Accessed Apr. 15, 2017. http://ec.europa.eu/public_opinion/archives/eb/eb79/eb79_fact_tr_en.pdf .

Gaarder, Chris. 2015. "Expensive Housing Swallows Up Middle-Class Paychecks in Over-regulated California." *National Review*, July 17. Accessed April 15, 2017. http://www.nationalreview.com/article/421293/expensive-housing-swallows-middle-class-paychecks-over-regulated-california-chris .

Gabermeier, Jeff. "When You Take Acetaminophen, You Don't Feel Others' Pain as Much." *The Ohio State University: News*. May 10. Accessed April 15, 2017. https://news.osu.edu/news/2016/05/10/empathy-reliever/ .

"How social media is wrecking your sleep." 2016. *Daily Sun* [Bangladesh], Feb. 18. Accessed April 15, 2017. http://www.daily-sun.com/arcprint/details/114811/How-Social-Media-is-Wrecking-Your-Sleep/2016-02-18 .

Kensinger, Elizabeth A., and Suzanne Corkin. 2003. "Memory Enhancement for Emotional Words: Are Emotional Words More Vividly Remembered than Neutral Words?" *Memory and Cognition* 31(8): 1169-80.

Last Week Tonight with John Oliver. 2016. "Scientific Studies." Episode 11, season 3. First aired May 14, 2016 by HBO. Performed by John Oliver.

Lepore, Sophia. 2016. "You're Welcome, World: America Is behind Climbing Childhood Obesity Rates." *Take Part*, Oct. 14. Accessed April 15, 2017. http://www.takepart.com/article/2016/10/13/2025-obesity-trend .

Levenson, Jessica C., Ariel Shensa, Jaime E. Sidani, Jason B. Colditz, Brian A. Primack. 2016. "The Association Between Social Media Use and Sleep Disturbance Among Young Adults." Preventive Medicine 85, April, 36-41.

Lewandowsky, Stephan, Ullrich KH Ecker, Colleen M. Seifert, Norbert Schwarz, and John Cook. 2012. "Misinformation and Its Correction: Continued Influence and Successful Debiasing." *Psychological Science in the Public Interest* 13(2): 106-31.

Loughborough University Media Centre. 2015. "Dehydrated Drivers Make the Same Number of Mistakes as Drink Drivers," April 20. Accessed June 4, 2017. http://www.lboro.ac.uk/media-centre/press-releases/2015/april/54-dehydrated-drivers.html .

Matteo, Anna. 2016. "Social Media Is Keeping Young Adults Awake." *Voice of America Learning English*, Mar. 14. Accessed April 15, 2017. http://learningenglish.voanews.com/a/3236261.html .

Miller, Jane E. 2004. *The Chicago Guide to Writing about Numbers*. Chicago: University of Chicago Press.

Mueller, Jon. 2017. "Correlation or Causation." North Central College, Jan. 1. Accessed April 15, 2017. http://jfmueller.faculty.noctrl.edu/100/correlation_or_causation.htm .

Myers, Maddy. 2016, "According to New Research, if You Love Social Media, You Probably Don't Sleep Well." *The Mary Sue*, April 15. Accessed April 15, 2017. http://www.themarysue.com/social-media-sleep-deprivation/ .

Nikolewski, Rob. 2014. "Study: No Connection between Spending, Student Outcomes." *Watchdog.org*, April 7. Accessed April 15, 2017. http://watchdog.org/136876/study-school-spending/ .

Office of the President's Council on Fitness, Sports & Nutrition. n.d. "Presidential Active Lifestyle Award (PALA+)." U.S. Department of Health and Human Services. Accessed April 15, 2017. https://www.fitness.gov/participate-in-programs/pala/ .

Pasolini, Antonio. 2016. "Is Social Media Keeping You Awake?" *New Atlas*, February 2. Accessed April 15, 2017. http://newatlas.com/social-media-sleep-problems/41624/ .

Radford, Benjamin. "Violent Video Games Have Not been Proven to Harm Teens." In *Teens at Risk*, ed. Christine Watkins. Opposing Viewpoints, Greenhaven Press, 2009. Accessed May 4, 2016. Opposing Viewpoints in Context (GALE|EJ3010167271).

Raff, Jennier. 2013"How to Read and Understand a Scientific Paper: A Guide for Non-Scientists." *Violent Metaphors* (blog), Aug. 25. . Accessed April 15, 2017. https://violentmetaphors.com/2013/08/25/how-to-read-and-understand-a-scientific-paper-2 .

Robinson, Erica. 2014. "WHO Warns That Childhood Obesity Could Rise to 75M by 2025." Medical Daily, July 20. Accessed April 15, 2017. http://www.medicaldaily.com/who-warns-childhood-obesity-could-rise-75m-2025-293984 .

Roskelly, Hepzibah. "What Do Students Need to Know about Rhetoric?" n.d. AP Central. Accessed April 15, 2017. http://apcentral.collegeboard.com/apc/members/repository/ap06_englang_roskelly_50098.pdf .

Snell, Tracy N. 2014. Capital Punishment 2013 -- Statistical Tables. Report no. NCJ 248448. Bureau of Justice Programs, U.S. Department of Justice. Accessed April 15, 2017. http://www.bjs.gov/content/pub/pdf/cp13st.pdf .

Society for Maternal-Fetal Medicine. 2016. "The Benefits of Chocolate during Pregnancy." News release. Accessed April 15, 2017. http://www.smfmnewsroom.org/2016/02/the-benefits-of-chocolate-during-pregnancy/ .

"Study Finds 79% Of Statistics Now Sobering." (2014). The Onion, August 20. Accessed April 15, 2017. http://www.theonion.com/article/study-finds-79-of-statistics-now-sobering-36731 .

Taylor, Mac. 2015. California's High Housing Costs - Causes and Consequences. Sacramento, CA: Legislative Analyst's Office. Accessed April 15, 2017. http://www.lao.ca.gov/reports/2015/finance/housing-costs/housing-costs.pdf .

Thompson, Derek. 2015. "Why Internet Headline Writers Hate Themselves." The Atlantic, February 6. Accessed April 15, 2017. http://www.theatlantic.com/entertainment/archive/2015/02/why-internet-headline-writers-hate-themselves/385248 .

Tobey, John. 2010. "American Air's Mishap and Statistical Misuse." Seeking Alpha (blog), Nov. 2. Accessed April 15, 2017. http://seekingalpha.com/instablog/524222-john-tobey-cfa/107308-american-air-s-mishap-and-statistical-misuse .

"Too much social media could mess up your sleep." 2016. The CW - Lubbock, January 27. Accessed April 15, 2017. http://www.lubbockcw.com/story/31071831/too-much-social-media-could-mess-up-your-sleep-study-finds .

University of Pittsburgh Schools of the Health Sciences. 2016. "Social media use in young adults linked to sleep disturbance." News release. January 26. Accessed April 15, 2017. https://www.eurekalert.org/pub_releases/2016-01/uops-smu012516.php .

Vita, Maria. n.d. "Causal or Correlational Language?" North Central College. Accessed April 15, 2017. http://jfmueller.faculty.noctrl.edu/100/vitaexercise.pdf .

Wagner, Dana. 2013 "4 Signs the Vietnamese Government Is Crushing the Country's 'Social Media Revolution." The Atlantic, March 11. Accessed April 15, 2017. http://www.theatlantic.com/international/archive/2013/03/4-signs-the-vietnamese-government-is-crushing-the-countrys-social-media-revolution/273893/ .

Watson, Phillip, Andrew Whale, Stephen A. Mears, Louise A. Reyner, and Ronald J. Maughan. 2015. "Mild Hypohydration Increases the Frequency of Driver Errors during a Prolonged, Monotonous Driving Task." Physiology and Behavior 147, Aug. 1, 313-318.

"What Is the European Hydration Institute?" n.d. European Hydration Insitute. Accessed May 10, 2016. http://www.europeanhydrationinstitute.org/what_is_the_ehi.html .

Williams, Geoff. 2016. "Could Your Fast Food Burger or Burrito Be Making You Infertile? A New Study Concludes, Possibly..." Forbes, April 30. Accessed April 15, 2017. http://www.forbes.com/sites/geoffwilliams/2016/04/30/could-your-fast-food-burger-or-burrito-be-making-you-infertile-a-new-study-concludes-possibly/ .

Withnall, Adam. 2015. "Driving While Dehydrated Can Be Just as Dangerous as Drunk Driving, Study Suggests." Independent (London, England), April 19. Accessed May 10, 2016. http://www.independent.co.uk/news/science/driving-while-dehydrated-can-be-just-as-dangerous-as-drink-driving-study-suggests-10187670.html .

The Writing Center at UNC-Chapel Hill. n.d. "Qualifiers." University of North Carolina. Accessed April 15, 2017. http://writingcenter.unc.edu/handouts/qualifiers .

―――――. n.d. "Statistics." University of North Carolina. Accessed April 15, 2017. http://writingcenter.unc.edu/handouts/statistics/ .

Appendix A: Tips for integrating lessons on unpacking language into your research process

If you have five minutes, share these rules of thumb before students begin creating their product:

- When you find a statistic or dataset you want to use, step back and think about the emotion conveyed by the source in which you found it. How do you feel after reading it? Excited? Angry? Upset? Identify the words that give you those feelings. If the words were different, would you feel the same about what you are reading?

- When you are writing, you may often try to use descriptive language. Consider the tone of your writing. How would you characterize it? Check for intensifiers and qualifiers, making sure you have used them in good measure. Add confident uncertainty where appropriate.

- When you are searching for statistics, are you keeping your searches very simple? Are you trying different terms that are used to describe your topic?

If you have 30 minutes, provide students with lists of words and phrases to use and avoid, as well as some small datasets related to the topic under discussion. Ask them to draft a paragraph using the provided statistics and being careful to craft a narrative employing careful and intentional statistical storytelling.

If you have one class period, pick a fun opening exercise to get students to think about one way in which words chosen by an author can impact their feelings about what they are reading, such as ranking news headlines on a fun topic by the level of causation implied. Introduce/review connotation and denotation. Brainstorm a list of synonyms for a common emotion, like "anger," and then consider the differences in connotation. If students are researching, have them go through a source they are using for their research and identify emotionally loaded language, name the feeling the author is trying to inspire; if they are writing, have them draft a sentence or paragraph conveying statistical information they are planning to use, trade with a partner, and check the emotional resonance of each other's writing.

If you have multiple class periods, use the first day to discuss the impact of language choice in reading and writing, drawing on some of the activities outlined in this chapter. On the second day, teach students a bit about searching for statistical information (based on this and other chapters) and have them begin to identify sources on a topic chosen by them or identified by the teacher. Remind them to keep an eye out for emotionally loaded language that might sway the reader's opinion.

Appendix B: Causation and correlation worksheet

In April 2016, researchers at the University of Pittsburgh released a study that found a correlation between sleeplessness and social media use. The study clearly stated that future work was needed to understand "directionality" and "the influence of contextual factors".

Consider these headlines reporting on that study (full citations are available in the bibliography of this chapter).

First, underline or highlight words and phrases that indicate correlation or causation.

Next, rank them in order from most suggestive of correlation to most suggestive of causation; #1 indicates strong correlation language, #9 means a clear statement of causation.

___ "Study Finds Social Media Leads to Sleep Disturbance"

___ "Is Social Media Keeping You Awake?"

___ "Social media is Keeping Young Adults Awake"

___ "Research Links Extreme Social Media Use With Disrupted Sleep"

___ "Social Media Use in Young Adults Linked to Sleep Disturbance"

___ "How Social Media is Wrecking Your Sleep"

___ "Blame Social Media for Your Child's Sleeplessness"

___ "Too Much Social Media Could Mess Up Your Sleep"

___ "According to New Research, If You Love Social Media, You Probably Don't Sleep Well"

Appendix C: Does this sound like correlation, or is there a causal hint, too?

In April 2016, researchers at the University of Pittsburgh released a study that found a correlation between sleeplessness and social media use (Levenson et al 2016). The study clearly stated that future work was needed to understand "directionality" and "the influence of contextual factors".

Read each of these first paragraphs of different news stories on the study. Decide if they are suggesting correlation or causation. Highlight or underline the words or phrases that suggest one or the other.

Examples

Just when you thought it was safe to click on that funny Facebook video of an aardvark carrying a shovel to dig a hole under a cinderblock wall while a pair of Peruvian flute-players cavort in green onesies, researchers at the University of Pittsburgh have found that social media wreaks havoc on your sleep patterns.

Obsessive social media use on Facebook, Twitter and similar platforms are linked to sleeping disturbance. According to a study conducted by the lead author, Jessica C. Levenson, Ph.D., a postdoctoral researcher at Pitt's Department of Psychiatry, published in *Preventive Medicine*, young adults who spend more time checking their social media, during the day or those who frequently check their social media accounts, are more likely to suffer from sleep disturbance.

Young adults who spend a lot of time on social media during the day or check it frequently throughout the week are more likely to suffer sleep disturbances than their peers who use social media less, according to new research from the University of Pittsburgh School of Medicine.

Young adults who spend too much time on Facebook, Twitter and Instagram may pay the price in poor sleep, new research suggests.

Social media usage correlates with sleeplessness, according to a new study, although it doesn't necessarily cause sleep troubles. According to researchers at the University of Pittsburgh School of Medicine, young adults who spend a lot of time on social media tend to also have trouble sleeping. It's not known whether sleep deprivation leads to increased social media usage, or whether all that Twitter scrolling is leading to sleep loss — but the two definitely seem to be connected.

3 | Using data in the research process

Jole Seroff

Traditional literacy, digital literacy, visual literacy, civic literacy, news literacy ... and now data literacy as well? It can take some creative thinking to figure out how all these skills fit together into a coherent curriculum for 21st century school libraries.

Many of us work with students at different junctures in their research, as they put together projects and papers or prepare debates and presentations. I've identified a few key moments in the research process that provide opportunities for interventions focused on building data literacy skills.

This chapter will outline flexible, modifiable activities you could use with your students to build background knowledge and learn to ask questions to make sense of the statistics they discover. These activities are meant to serve as starting points for incorporating more critical thinking about data in your research instruction. As you grow familiar with data literacy themes, you will likely find other connections and opportunities that are relevant for your own practice.

Building background knowledge with statistical benchmarking

The initial stages of the research process have always been particularly enjoyable for me. When students are just beginning a new project, everything is possible. They have so much to learn and don't yet know where their research might take them. Despite my own enthusiasm for this moment in the process, I've heard from colleagues and have seen in my own students that they often struggle to find a starting place for their research, to define a topic clearly, or to narrow a topic appropriately (Kuhlthau 2004).

This can be an excellent moment to infuse your lessons with data literacy skills. Students may begin with a general area of inquiry, something quite broad, or even perhaps something too narrow for the requirements of their project. Whenever they are exploring a new topic, I encourage our students to begin with background reading, which I sometimes call "stepping stone" reading. I ask them to begin with general sources, novice-level sources, and focus their attention on getting a sense of the key aspects of their topic. I want our students to understand that the first reading they do is not meant to provide their final answer, but rather to help them better understand their question.

In other words, it will build a bridge from their starting point to deeper understanding. Background reading sheds light on what they will need to know to fully answer a question, and it may help to narrow or redirect a question.

To start their thinking, I might give students an article I have selected. Alternatively, I might point them to general encyclopedias or news coverage, or even ask them to try some Google searches and examine the snippets (or brief summary) displayed on the search results page in order to begin to get a sense of the topic. In order to focus their reading and stimulate active thinking, I ask students to look for these key things: *terms of art*, *experts and organizations focused on the topic*, and *benchmark statistics*.

Terms of art and statistical benchmarks

Terms of art refers to language that has a specific meaning within a particular field or profession. For example, *hypothesis* has a specialized meaning in a science classroom, just as *formula* does in a math class. As they're getting familiar with a new topic, students can be confused by specialized terminology, so it is helpful to put them on the lookout for it through stepping stone readings. I ask them, "What are the terms used by people who know more about the topic than we do?" Once they have identified expert vocabulary related to their topic, they can use those terms in their future searches, and they're likely to get higher-quality results, including material written by or for experts in the field.

Similarly, identifying experts and major organizations associated with their topic and perhaps beginning to recognize whether these experts have a particular orientation or perspective with regard to the topic will help move them forward thoughtfully in their research. In the early stages of the research process students are building an understanding of their topic, including, perhaps, its leading thinkers, its controversial aspects, and its particular jargon. This knowledge will enable them to treat their topic with more nuance and comprehension.

How can we integrate data literacy into our practice of building background information on a topic? Gathering benchmark statistics (Best 2013), or reliable statistics against which we can weigh new data we encounter, provides an opportunity to bring data literacy practice into the process of background reading. A benchmark statistic is simply a standard or point of reference against which other things may be compared or assessed. For example, think how often you heard how many people voted for a particular candidate in a given year. If you know that there are approximately 325,000,000 people living in the United States (U.S. Census 2016), you can rapidly contextualize voter turnout. If you want to dig in further to these numbers, you might consider that not all Americans are eligible to vote, because of age and other factors. In October of 2016, *Politico* reported that the American electorate had surpassed 200 million registered voters (Goldmacher 2016). With that in mind, you have an even clearer grasp on the significance of the raw number of votes a candidate received. As our students become more data literate, they must develop the habit of looking for similar benchmarks to help them make sense of the numbers they encounter.

Brainstorming

One engaging way to use benchmark statistics with students is through brainstorming. When you're introducing a new topic, ask students to imagine: what statistical benchmarks would help me get a grasp of this topic, or be useful for comparing and evaluating new information I encounter? Encourage students to focus their questions on numbers, amounts, and percentages. Remind them that statistics are descriptive of things that are countable.

Here's an example that could be of interest to teens: according to the Centers for Disease Control and Prevention motor vehicle crashes are the leading cause of deaths for teens in the U.S. (CDC 2016). Brainstorm: what kind of benchmarks will help contextualize this statistic?

For example, students may want to know:

>> **How many teens die in traffic accidents every year?**

>> **Do they suffer traffic fatalities at a higher rate than adults do?**

>> **What are the other major causes of deaths in teens and adults?**

>> **Are teens more likely to be drivers or passengers in fatal accidents?**

>> **Considering traffic accidents in general, how often do fatalities occur?**

>> **How effective are measures such as use of seat belts and extended driver's education at preventing traffic fatalities?**

This activity can be done as a 10-minute warm up or even as a homework assignment. This kind of group discussion can fuel and contextualize the early stages of research. By generating a list of questions and tracking down relevant benchmark statistics, students engage in active thinking. This process provides insight for shaping a research topic and clarifies directions for pursuing further research.

Once your students generate a good list of data-related questions, they can employ those questions as guides for further research. As they become more fluent in their use of data, they will understand that although there aren't always statistics available on every topic, many of the questions they pose likely do have accessible answers. You could spend a 15- or 20-minute chunk of your lesson searching for benchmark statistics with a focus on selecting sources for their accuracy and currency. Information literate students will need to build their capacity to identify sources that provide reliable, relevant data.

Questioning the source

It is precisely in order to counter short-cut thinking and biased assumptions that we want to guide our students to think more critically about data when they read independently and encounter data embedded in text. It is important for students to recognize that while there may be data referenced in a source, it may have been extracted from its original dataset, context, or source. It may be so decontextualized that the argument it was intended to support may not even be explicitly expressed. Traditional information literacy skills provide valuable structure for librarians and students working with data. Consider the *source* of the data, not the location where it was found. Ask yourself:

- » **Is the source reliable?**
- » **Does the institution behind the data have an agenda that is shaping the information it presents?**
- » **When you look at multiple sources, do you find a consensus or a range of ideas?**

Students should get in the habit of asking these and other reflective questions when they encounter data just as they do when they're reading for narrative arguments.

Sample lesson

Consider a recent 50-minute class with high school seniors, in which I challenged them to develop a set of critical questions around data by working with a preselected set of resources.

In this lesson, they were responsible for reflecting on how they analyze data when it's presented as evidence in news sources. As a group we worked toward developing some rules of thumb for useful questions to ask when thinking about data.

We examined materials focused on the current migrant and refugee crisis in Africa, Europe, and the Middle East. We began by reading one source together that provided some general context for the issue: making clear distinctions between migrants and refugees and clarifying why this distinction is so important. A *refugee* is defined by the United Nations as a person fleeing her homeland due to a well-founded fear of persecution; a refugee has a right to safe asylum, and she may not be forcibly returned to her homeland. *Migrants*, however, are persons relocating out of choice, often in search of economic opportunity. Migrants are not granted a right to asylum. Through the initial group reading students learn about this distinction, and they learn that there is frequently disagreement about which individuals qualify for the refugee designation and the rights it confers. Further, they learn that a single individual may be considered a refugee when she reaches the first destination outside of her country of origin, but if she wishes to move again, she will be viewed as a migrant and may lose the rights of refugee status when she reaches her second destination. These and other complications pose real problems when it comes to calculating statistics related to this crisis.

Before breaking up into pairs to read and analyze on their own, students received a worksheet (see following pages) for taking notes, with some questions designed to focus their thinking on data they encountered. These questions directed students to examine the source of the data and to question the methods, if available, through which the data had been collected. Students were asked to look out for those discrepancies between the data presented in different sources and to hypothesize the reason for discrepancies. Further, I asked students to make note of things that surprised them and to keep a running list of new questions that came up for them as they were reading and analyzing.

I heard students engaging actively with data as I eavesdropped on the working pairs. They were wondering how displaced persons, who might want to escape official notice or who were not likely to have a fixed abode could be effectively counted. They were noticing their own surprise at the preponderance of refugees fleeing to other countries in Africa and the Middle East, and not just to Western Europe, which had been the focus of attention in Western news media. They were beginning to question whether statistics were being leveraged for political ends by leaders in countries such as Greece and Italy, that were hard-hit by the influx of refugees. They suspected that these leaders might stand to benefit from designating the new arrivals as migrants, with limited rights, rather than as refugees deserving asylum.

What questions do you have about the source of the data? (Perspective)

-

-

-

What questions do you have about how the data were collected? (Methods)

-

-

-

What surprises you? (For example, numbers that seem especially large or small, things that conflict with your assumptions, etc.)

-

-

-

What data do you find that conflicts between the sources? Where do the sources seem to disagree?

-

-

-

What new questions do you have about this topic, based on what you have read?

-

-

-

What conclusions can you draw about this topic based on what you've read? (For example, complete the sentence, *These sources show me that...*)

-

-

-

If you have extra time, look online for reliable sources and try to answer some of the questions you have!

When we reconvened as a group, we focused our discussion on taking their observations and generating some rules of thumb for thinking about data more generally. For example, when students pointed out that most of the sources were from Western countries and that the single resource from the Middle East emphasized a different perspective, we were able to conclude that it is important to look at data published from a wide range of viewpoints, which may include geographically or geopolitically diverse sources.

Students also noticed that some discrepancies in the data could be accounted for by differences in how the sources were defining migrants and refugees, or which specific geographic areas the statistics were focused on. We were able to extrapolate from that observation that it's critical to notice how terms are defined and what precisely is being counted.

When students are charged to articulate guidelines themselves, they become more engaged and empowered as learners. Nevertheless, there is a struggle inherent in designing lessons that are driven by student inquiry: the more outcomes are student-generated, the less predictable they are. It can be challenging to start a lesson without knowing where it will end up. Ultimately I remind myself that it is worth taking that risk. When I see my students engaging actively, I know they are developing powerful skills in critical thinking.

As students research: Interrogating the statistic

Now students are ready to move from group discussion to independent research. When students encounter a statistic used as evidence for an argument, I encourage them to interrogate the statistic. We interrogate statistics by exposing them to scrutiny and asking good questions about what conclusions can and cannot be drawn from them.

An excellent entry point for interrogating statistics is to help students learn to identify the original source of their data, to the best of their ability. It can be challenging to trace information back to its original source, but quality news outlets will mention the source behind the data. If that information isn't included, that's a red flag, and data literate students should learn to recognize that.

Another strategy is to have students look at conflicting statistics and evaluate their sources. This will give students an opportunity to practice interrogating the statistics: Can they determine the source of the conflict between the statistics? It could be because the information comes from different geographical locations or different time periods, or that terms are being defined differently, as in the case when it can be difficult to determine whether an individual is a migrant or a refugee. Ultimately, students can practice making a judgment when statistics conflict – which source do they feel is more credible? They should be able to make an argument to support this conclusion, perhaps citing the size of study or the relative bias of the source.

An activity of this sort can also provide an opportunity to practice both information literacy and statistical literacy skills. Students will need to evaluate the source for accuracy and bias. And they will also need to evaluate whether the numbers really mean what they seem to on their surface.

Comparing statistics

I used the article "Black Criminals, White Victims, and White Guilt" (Simpson 2015) from the Accuracy in Media website for our next example. This is a website that frames itself as a media watchdog through a conservative lens seen by some readers as biased. The basic claim of this article is that criminal justice reform in the U.S. is unnecessary because the rates of police violence against blacks have been overhyped by the media and are not actually a serious problem.

First, by applying traditional information literacy skills and looking into the organization behind this article, students will learn that this organization's stated goal is to battle what it considers a liberal bias in the media, which lends its reporting a definite perspective. When students add a data literacy lens, they will notice that the figures presented in the article are offered in raw numbers, rather than percentages or rates over time. Data literate students will pay special attention to the format in which numbers are presented. It may be the case that a particular choice was made in order to shape the reader's perception of the data. They'll keep this in mind when they compare data from multiple sources.

For contrast, I looked at an article from the *Washington Post*: "Aren't more white people than black people killed by police? Yes, but no" (Lowery 2016). A little research into the source reveals that the *Washington Post* is one of the country's leading newspapers. The article explains that while in raw numbers more white people than black people are killed by police, because black people make up a much smaller percentage of the total population they are significantly overrepresented in these kinds of deaths. According to the *Washington Post,* black Americans are 2.5 times as likely as white Americans to be shot and killed by police officers. It can be helpful for students to discuss which of these articles *seems* more compelling and why.

Practice examining arguments from opposing viewpoints builds critical thinking and information literacy skills. Students learn to read actively, considering the arguments put forth by each writer. Examining the use of data in these arguments gives students experience evaluating whether the selected data really supports the conclusion of the author.

Further along in their research, students often seek assistance crafting arguments and selecting evidence to support their claims. This is another powerful moment in the research process for building data literacy skills. From their large accumulation of research material, students must now select those statistics, information, anecdotes, and facts that best inform the argument. They begin to see that data is not merely information: it is potential evidence. When it comes to using data as evidence, what orientation do we want our students to have? What guidance can we give them?

Two interrelated concepts are useful for students to learn here: cherry-picking and confirmation bias. Finally, annotations give students an opportunity to share their thinking and analysis of sources with their instructors.

Cherry-picking

It is often said by skeptics and cynics that statistics can be used to prove anything. This notion seems validated when we see the same statistics cited to support opposing sides of an argument. Where this seems to be the case, cherry-picking, or selecting only examples that support your argument while ignoring counterexamples, may be the culprit. Cherry-picking is a critical concept for students to understand because it has become increasingly common in the world of partisan journalism, politics, social media, and blogs. Students should be on the lookout for this in sources they read and should be doubly aware of it in their own research and writing. Even when a student researcher discovers evidence that aligns with her thinking or seems ideal to support her argument, she should be sure she is not missing another side to an argument. Her research should encompass a full range of perspectives. Otherwise, she's in danger of falling prey to confirmation bias. Further, just because statistics are offered that seem to support conflicting viewpoints, that doesn't mean that both sets of statistics are equally convincing. You can set up an activity in which students examine statistics used to support conflicting arguments and then evaluate the relative strength of the two arguments.

Confirmation bias

Confirmation bias is the natural tendency to favor information which confirms our existing beliefs and preconceptions. When we encounter information that aligns with our expectations, we are less likely to think critically or question the validity of the evidence. When students are seeking information, confirmation bias can pollute their search results. Students must learn to think carefully in order to avoid doing searches where the answer is already "baked in". Because the function of a search engine is to return pages that include the terms in the search, the researcher is likely to encounter material that aligns with the ideas represented in her search. For example, a search for [black crime statistics] will produce results that show links between blacks and crime, because that is literally what the query asked the algorithm to find. Students will likely find more inclusive, nuanced, or better-balanced results if they start by searching for [U.S. crime statistics] more generally and then look closely at that data for racial breakdowns within those statistics. This approach provides more context for the information, and context is a powerful tool to combat confirmation bias. When the researcher encounters information that conflicts with her assumptions, she has the opportunity to evaluate the evidence and reconsider her position.

Cherry-picking and confirmation bias are abstract concepts that can be challenging for young scholars to master. How can we as instructors set up an environment that encourages them to engage more rigorously with sources? Annotations may be one answer. Annotations are short paragraphs that provide a student's analysis of a given source. Having students write short annotations for statistical information they include in their papers is a way to make the students' thinking transparent, and therefore easier for the teacher to assess and respond to. While not an onerous task, annotations help to build a habit of responsible use of data.

There are several online resources for discipline-specific annotation strategies, but for general purposes, most annotations include three parts, as outlined by the Purdue Online Writing Lab (n.d.): *summarization* (an overview of the key ideas), *assessment* (source evaluation and credibility), and *reflection* (student discussion of the role and relevance of this source to their overall research and project). Please see Figure 1 for details one might assign in each section of an annotation.

On a project-by-project basis, instructors could add additional criteria or questions to the annotation guidelines for a specific assignment. By doing so, they cue students to surface and confront their tacit understandings. Writing annotations can help students reflect on their assumptions, articulate their thinking, and share their understandings with educators. For more on annotations and annotated bibliographies, including a sample, see https://owl.english.purdue.edu/owl/resource/614/1/.

Annotation options for students

- **Summarization** – Students write a short overview of the main ideas and concepts of the source.
- **Assessment** – Students evaluate the source, including
  - » information quality and comprehensiveness
  - » currency of information
  - » reliability of information
  - » use of data
  - » who conducted the study and their authority, expertise, or known perspectives or political slant
  - » who funded the study and their authority, expertise, or known perspectives or political slant
- **Reflection** – Students consider how this source relates to the overall constellation of research conducted:
  - » How does this source fit into the emerging thesis of their paper or project? How does it influence their argument? What value does this source add to their thinking?

Figure 1: Three annotation strategies for students.

Conclusion

In this chapter, I have suggested a number of activities that integrate data literacy skills with traditional information literacy instruction throughout the research process. From the very first steps they take in researching a topic, active, critical thinking about data will help students gain a better understanding of a particular topic while developing powerful, transferrable skills. Incorporating data literacy in our instruction creates opportunities for practicing core information literacy skills such as source evaluation. As students get experience examining the way data is used to support arguments, they will build their capacity to incorporate statistical evidence in their own writing. The data literate student is less susceptible to misinformation and better able to weigh evidence and form her own judgments. Ultimately the goal is to develop the habit of active, critical thinking about data.

Resources

Best, Joel. 2013. *Stat-Spotting: A Field Guide to Identifying Dubious Data.* 2nd Ed. Berkeley, CA: University of California Press.

Centers for Disease Control and Prevention (CDC). 2016. "Teen Drivers" Get the Facts." Oct. 13. Retrieved December 20, 2016, from https://www.cdc.gov/motorvehiclesafety/teen_drivers/teendrivers_factsheet.html .

Goldmacher, Shane. 2016. "America Hits New Landmark: 200 Million Registered Voters." *Politico*, Oct. 19. Retrieved December 20, 2016, from http://www.politico.com/story/2016/10/how-many-registered-voters-are-in-america-2016-229993 .

Kuhlthau, Carol Collier. 2004. Seeking Meaning: A Process Approach To Library And Information Services. Westport, Conn. Libraries Unlimited.

Lowery, Wesley. 2016. "Aren't More White People Than Black People Killed By Police? Yes, But No." *Washington Post*, July 11. Retrieved December 20, 2016, from https://www.washingtonpost.com/news/post-nation/wp/2016/07/11/arent-more-white-people-than-black-people-killed-by-police-yes-but-no/ .

National Safety Council. 2016. "Motor Vehicle Deaths Increase by Largest Percent in Fifty Years." Feb. 17. Retrieved December 20, 2016, from http://www.nsc.org/Connect/NSCNewsReleases/Lists/Posts/Post.aspx?ID=103 .

Purdue Online Writing Lab. n.d. "Annotated Bibliographies." Retrieved December 20, 2016, from https://owl.english.purdue.edu/owl/resource/614/1/ .

Simpson, James. 2015. "Black Criminals, White Victims, and White Guilt." Accuracy in Media. Feb. 9. Retrieved December 20, 2016, from http://www.aim.org/special-report/black-criminals-white-victims-and-white-guilt/ .

If you have five minutes:

- **Remind students that statistics and numerical information needs to be verified, too!**

- **Help students try to track a statistic back to its source: who gathered this information?** Ask if knowing this makes the students more or less confident about the reliability of the statistic.

If you have 15 minutes:

- **Ask students to complete the worksheet from this chapter about an article you choose.**

If you have 30 minutes:

- **Practice contextualizing a statistic by generating (and answering!) a list of questions that will help you situate that statistic in relation to meaningful, familiar measures**. For example, according to the National Safety Council (2016), there were 38,000 traffic fatalities in the U.S. in 2015. Some questions students might generate include: Is there disagreement about this number? Is this higher or lower than 2014? What has the trend been in the last 5 or 10 years? What about vehicular injuries, or are we only interested in deaths? Do we know what percentage of these accidents involved alcohol and drugs? Are drivers in different age groups more or less likely to be involved in fatal accidents? etc.

If you have one class period:

- **Work with students to better understand the ways in which statistics are socially constructed.** College rankings hold inherent interest for many students. Consider the factors that go into published rankings. Do they represent the elements of a college experience that would be most meaningful to you? Try evaluating and re-ranking colleges based on your own criteria and weighting.

- **Explore the cultural construction of data by closely examining virtually any statistic.** Ask questions about how the terms of the statistic are defined, i.e., what do we mean by *disabled* or *elderly*? Inquire who constituted the pool of respondents to a survey, and what other groups might have different opinions. Consider the limitations that may have made a perfect version of a given study impossible, and the concessions or adjustments which were likely made for practical reasons. Make sure your students have an opportunity to do this independently: find their own statistic and interrogate it. Does it meet their critical standards?

If you have multiple class periods:

- **Integrate statistical literacies into a larger research process.** Examine the role of numerical information at each step of the project. Pursue background knowledge to provide context for the statistics you encounter; build a list of benchmark statistics; evaluate sources for reliability; interrogate the cultural context that informs the gathering and reporting of statistics. Soon, critical thinking about data will become second nature for your students!

4 | Real world data fluency: How to use raw data

Wendy Stephens

The implementation of the Common Core State Standards warmed the hearts of many librarians in demanding evidence as part of argumentation. Many high schoolers (as well as their teachers) sought to integrate statistical evidence – hard numbers – in their products. But too often those percentages lose context in student work, as they neglect to mention the methods of sampling or specify the populations under study.

A command of datasets will enable teachers to help students understand where data is coming from and how it is presented, enabling more sophisticated inferences about the potential value of that information. By looking specifically at datasets and examining a range of tools for reading, integrating, representing and thinking critically about data, this very transferable skill will help students as they go forward, both academically and in the workplace.

As we peer over students' shoulders to help them make sense of what they find and what they create, we recognize that we need to nurture students' ability to do just-in-time analysis with freshly-encountered data. Whether students are using a table, a graph or a chart to help make determinations and evaluations, there are some general rules of thumb:

» **To use data, you should be able to articulate how data was generated or collected.** Who generated the data? Was it self-reported? Measured in a laboratory setting?

» **Why was the dataset generated?** This includes context around who or what organization is funding a study. Some

» associations are obvious, while others demand more research, but it's important to question research agendas.

» **Look at origins of data and what those relationships are between the variables.**

» **Use the Goldilocks principle to look for the just-right dataset** — one that's not too small or not too large.

» **Did you find a provocative statistic in your research?** Follow breadcrumbs back to the source for the most thorough understanding of the data point.

» **Always look for keys, practice axis awareness, and watch the units.**

» **Watch for language shifting and unit shifting,** matching things with the bigger picture.

» **Understand external factors when considering change over time.** Society and language changes as well, populations are collapsed or differentiated, making comparisons over time difficult.

I think of real world data fluency as a facility in thinking about numbers and values — what we can learn from different amounts of things and what those relationships suggest. To foster that sort of thinking, I suggest a collection of tools and associated strategies for integrating reading, representing, and thinking critically about different data sources. Those sorts of understandings will help our students become information-literate consumers and citizens that push past headlines.

Data fluency has much in common with data literacy, but like media literacy, it seems to include more transformative elements. Students should gain experience traveling backward from headlines, soundbites, and news accounts to find data points the headlines are based upon. We want them to become comfortable understanding where data comes from and the underlying relationships between measurements. This includes how the study is diffused in the mass media and the way news accounts may or may not acknowledge the particulars of the investigation. Sometimes attribution may be simply an institutional name, but tracing back to particular research study is important.

To get started working with data in your class or library:

» **Provide students with examples of raw data with variables of interest.**

» **Discuss whether the parameters were made explicit or not.**

» **When students repurpose the data to create new products, stress attribution, citation, and responsible use of data.**

» **Practice extracting relevant data from charts, tables, and graphs. This facility is most germane in high stakes testing, too.**

» **Students might find messy data on their own, so teachers and librarians can help to structure assignments directing students to particular datasets.**

Young people who have mastered data fluency skills can make use of the myriad statistical information available today to make better informed decisions as a consumer, citizens, and social activists.

One way to start the conversation is to discuss the range of information-gathering strategies. Students should be able to identify opt-in participation like web polling or more rigorous population sampling, and discuss the way participation might affect results.

For teachers who aren't comfortable talking statistics, it is important that librarians model that teaching with data can be a cross-curricular proposition. Computational datasets and metrics exist in the humanities and across the subject areas like never before. Using datasets to explore bibliographic information or to map trends over time can be described as cultivating a computational mindset in ways that are not strictly arithmetic. There are a range of resources to help teachers in all disciplines talk about relationships in this way.

Tyler Vigen's Spurious Correlations
http://tylervigen.com

This fun, high-impact website allows for menu-based manipulation to explore sometimes humorous relationships between unrelated datasets.

The selection of the first dataset from the drop-down menu (for example, commercial space launches) produces a second menu of datasets, ranked in order of strength of correlation. Including the original numbers underpinning the relationship, the near-perfect arcs mapping honey produced by bee colonies in the U.S., and three years of visitor volume to Sea World in Florida (with a 0.9948 strength) is typical of the interesting but unrelated parallels.

With access points including morbidity and consumption of a range of dairy products, Vigen's site does drive home how two measurements can be correlated, without any representation or suggestion of a causal link between the two.

Getting hyperlocal or providing a national comparison are two potent ways to lead students to explore relationships. Social Explorer is a geographical tool including many paid datasets, but a wealth of census information is available in the free online version.

Social Explorer makes it easy to present side-by-side comparison for examining change over time or contrasting geographical distribution of different types of data. The interface seems particularly suited for historical comparisons over time – vividly illustrating population shifts brought on by Westward Expansion, industrialization, and the Great Migration.

Hovering over visualizations provides access to the original data points, and the authentic datasets are explicitly described. Intuitive to manipulate in terms of both data and mapping, Social Explorer is an excellent way for students to build fluency.

Google Ngram

https://books.google.com/ngrams

Google Ngram reflects the preoccupations of English-speaking society as they appear in print, searching the scanned volumes from Google's groundbreaking book digitization project. The default results will span 1800 – 2000, and that built-in range is important to know, especially when researching current events.

Ngram allows you to search for a single word or a series of comma-separated terms across decades of published literature. Searching [socialist, terrorist, anarchist], for example, reveals evolving trends in public consciousness as well as shifts in vocabulary usage.

Ngram is a wonderful tool for thinking in a data-centric way, without necessarily operating in a number-centric content area. It is particularly useful in the humanities to show a shift in language over time. The site attempts to index all words that have appeared in published books. The y-axis shows the percentage of times the word appears based on overall documents from a given year, rather than computing the number of mere occurrences.

Tableau Gallery
https://public.tableau.com/s/gallery

Tableau is an embeddable graphic visualization product that is increasingly being used by news organizations to develop interactive graphics for online editions. Users can hover over a visualization to view the data used in creating the visual.

Tableau Public is the free online portal to basic visualization tools; for more sophisticated usage, you may wish to download a paid version of Tableau software, which may require that you have administrative rights for your school computer. But there are interesting instructional uses for Tableau even outside construction of your own visualization. On the Gallery tab, Visualization of the Day provides an often topical, sometimes innovative, depiction to spark conversations about data relationships with geographic aspects. A favorite of reporters, the Gallery recently reflected area distributions of oil derricks in Texas, taxi ridership in New York City, or graffiti in Chicago.

For those who find relationships they want to explore in more depth, Tableau creators can offer the ability to download datasets for re-use. Under the Resources tab, these are organized under headings like Technology, Lifestyle, Government, Sports, and Entertainment. If you have a student population that tends toward ideological homogeneity you wish to challenge, the Tableau Gallery is a great place to come and look at other visualizations that a range of media outlets have built.

Five Thirty Eight's p-hacking interactive examines relationships between two bodies of information, using a graphical interactive to quickly transforming raw data into visualizations, exploding the 0.05 p-value level typically used for predictable publishable statistical significance all the while.

The interface encourages you to "Hack Your Way to Scientific Glory." The first step is choosing one of the two major political parties, and then choosing or excluding various levels of government representation through a series of checkboxes. As those changes alter the dataset under consideration, the p-value shifts. For example, by focusing on the terms of Democratic Presidents and Governors, including Employment, GDP and Stock Prices but excluding Inflation, one can produce a publishable result, as it achieves a p-value of less than 0.01, demonstrating Democrats have a positive effect on the economy. Adding in Inflation negates the significance of the finding.

The p-hacking site is designed to demonstrate that that threshold is so low that researchers can easily manipulate their findings, particularly when given a large range of data points, to claim significance where it might not exist. While researchers should establish those thresholds and variables from the outset as a part of research design, the p-hacking site allows for quick and tangible demonstrations of how multiple regression analysis can be problematic.

Google Public Data

https://www.google.com/publicdata/directory

Using data from the U.S. Census Bureau, Bureau of Economic Analysis, Bureau of Labor Statistics and other government sources, Google's public data site features quality sets with the ability to create some simple visualizations, all within an intuitive and easy-to-use interface.

Access to Census data can be found through a number of sites, but the menus Google provided through this tool allow for near-instant comparison and adjustment of graphs through easy access to the x-axis. Examining population by gender, for example, will allow you to consider the U.S. as a whole or drill down more locally. Perhaps students are interested in forecasting populations in particular countries. When accessing the Census Bureau's International Database, you can use checkboxes to include or exclude nations based on your area of interest. You can switch between cluster representations, bar graphs, and live graphs. Any attempt to measure with inadequate data will trigger a warning.

Additionally, you can upload your own datasets and use their visualization tools for plug-and-play displays. The site drives home the portability of data accessible by a variety of interfaces.

Finding existing datasets

When getting started with data, it's best to stick to the Goldilocks principle and look for a *just right* amount of data. Sometimes it's better for teachers to structure the assignments rather than let students haphazardly look for data. Student novices often run into roadblocks, not anticipating that some data simply cannot be collected and in other cases, people cannot be monitored all the time or might have reasons to not be candid. Using existing datasets helps students who might otherwise alight on a narrow data need that isn't generalizable. *Quick reads* of existing datasets also reinforce the process of drawing conclusions.

Concerned with global measures, this site makes it easy to compare one group to another by converting each statistic to being a certain percentage of 100. This makes the site a good match for younger or beginning learners.

Curious about the distribution of overall literacy globally? Students will find that 86% can read and write and 14% cannot, then find a pdf from UNESCO used to inform those percentages.

When accessing Detailed Statistics through the toolbar, scrolling to the bottom provides a link back to datasets – including the CIA World Fact Book, the World Health Organization, and World Bank – providing citations for each statistic.

100 People provides lesson plans for teachers, and using the information contained here, data becomes accessible for even the youngest students and those with learning differences. Students can make charts and graphs using data in 100-unit breakdowns, or they can take the data and work with it in analog capacities.

U.S. Census Data — People and Households

https://www.census.gov/people/

From tracing ancestry to counting the number of same-sex couples, the range of data collected by one-time and periodic supplemental surveys conducted by the U.S. Census Bureau offers a vivid portrait of evolving American life.

This menu offers access to a range of datasets, each with specified parameters, explicit terminology, and clear date of collection. There are variations between how data is conveyed. Some datasets – for example, Computer and Internet Use – offer access to tables and visualizations.

For American students, U.S. Census data is among some of the most comprehensive information available, but students should be aware the government involvement in collection presents its own issues, especially for individuals with anti-authoritarian perspectives. Any use of Census data can involve discussion about how the data is collected from the populace at regular intervals and supplemented with interview data.

Examining the distinctions between survey approaches can illuminate the way that methodologies inform outcomes. In the midst of the negotiations between the FBI and Apple over access to a locked iPhone belonging to suspected San Bernadino terrorists, the website The Verge featured two surveys about consumer privacy protections only days apart. One survey found the populace sided with the FBI in terms of mandating access, while the other survey found the majority siding with Apple on the side of privacy. The language of the surveys varied from the abstract to the concrete. Should Apple be forced, through this precedent, to unencrypt phones? Most respondents felt not. But should Apple cooperate with the terror investigation? In that case, the majority felt they should. Asking the question two different ways got two different but valid responses.

Registry of Data and Search Repositories

http://www.re3data.org/

This registry collocates a range of dataset repositories. Most subject areas focus on biological and physical sciences, but also include research on digital humanities projects, linguistics, archaeology and big data from hard science.

For example, typing [student athlete NCAA] into the home page search box retrieves the NCAA Student-Athlete Experiences Data Archive. Clicking on the archive's link (http://service.re3data.org/repository/r3d100010824) provides the url (http://www.icpsr.umich.edu/icpsrweb/NCAA/) for the datasets from a topic area with potential to interest student researchers.

The repository is in the public domain and licensed under Creative Commons CC-BY, meaning you can copy and redistribute the material in any medium or format and remix, transform, and build upon the material, as long as you give attribution.

Dryad

http://datadryad.org/

Dryad takes some 15,000 datasets and associates them with the research articles they generated. This service is provided for long-term preservation, assigning Digital Object Identifiers for proper attribution through data citation.

Dryad's curated Twitter feed demonstrates its range of data-based projects represented there and models the possibilities and technique of research using existing datasets. A recent article tackled "Disparities in influenza mortality and transmission related to sociodemographic factors within Chicago in the pandemic of 1918" (http://datadryad.org/resource/doi:10.5061/dryad.48nv3; Grantz et al., 2016).

The idea behind Dryad is allowing researchers to move beyond reading others' results to allowing readers to replicate the experimental design and confirm earlier findings. This site offers tools for the highest aims of replicability, something that should be of concern even to student researchers.

Data Portals

http://dataportals.org/search

Data Portals offers a clearinghouse for data uploaded from a range of government and nonprofit projects and agencies. Datasets are tagged and organized around subjects, allowing for searching as well as browsing their catalogued collection of links.

The attributes of each dataset – including usage rights, current activity, and the availability of application programming interfaces (APIs) – are part of the catalog's record for each set.

Want to know the geographic distribution of public toilets in Bath, U.K.? How about the books "exiled" by the Third Reich (including Dos Passos, Hemingway, and Upton Sinclair)? This treasure-trove of information offers thousands of potential jumping-off points for student researchers. It is interesting to explore the many governments and organizations that have made statistics and research available to citizenry through the open data access movement. Users can propose links to their own or other existing datasets, too.

Open Access Directory

http://oad.simmons.edu/oadwiki/Data_repositories

Another repository linking to the growing number of open data initiatives, Open Access Directory (OAD) is a crowd-sourced, wiki-based initiative to sort open data sources into disciplinary buckets as diverse as linguistics and archeology.

Of particular interest are the Interdisciplinary datasets the OAD collects, including FigShare (https://figshare.com), a site which allows access to unpublished data and studies which produced negative results, potentially revolutionizing literature reviews by allowing the inclusion of research not otherwise accessible.

Gapminder

https://www.gapminder.org/data

Gapminder is perhaps the easiest way to create visualizations based on their integrated datasets. The research tends to come from international, nongovernmental sources like the World Health Organization and the International Labor Organization.

The sets are available for download as spreadsheets or can be viewed through their web interface in both one-time versions and those which reflect change over time. Many of the data points in Gapminder will be of interest to students, for example: *how many cell phones per 100 people exist in the world?*

Tracking tends to be over time, like income per capita in different countries. Gapminder enables students to easily grasp the effects of globalization and population shifts.

Visualize Free

https://visualizefree.com/datasets.jsp

Visualize Free offers integrated datasets, as well as a mechanism for you to upload your own.

Easy-to-operate filters allow you to target particular data points on topics including Walmart locations across the country and date the store opened.

The site also offers ways to understand data gleaned from *Forbes' America's Top Colleges*, including cost, the percent of students receiving financial aid, average test scores, and faculty-to-student ratios, something particularly meaningful for high school students.

Knoema

https://knoema.com/atlas

With a definitive social science slant, Knoema offers interesting international data. One example reflects expenditures spent on food displayed as a percentage of household budgets.

The site auto-generates charts and graphs and allows for export of tables as comma delimited .csv files, so students can use spreadsheet plug-ins to customize their own visualizations. For teachers looking to exploit some of the more nuanced versions of Excel, this site could prove valuable using raw data to explore properties which inform the function of spreadsheet cells.

Representing data responsibly

One of the most exciting learning opportunities comes when students collect their own data. In Geoff Herbach's novel *Fat Boy vs. the Cheerleaders* (2014), his protagonist charts the consumption of products from the high school soda machines to support his argument that band kids, not the dance team, deserve the proceeds.

But if students collected information themselves, they'll need some help with formatting that data. The first step is usually removing duplicate or incomplete data and looking for multiple values in the same field. Students should develop some protocol for working with data and systematic methods grouping together different versions of the same reality. They will also want to consider the distribution and whether there are outliers you may want to remove. OpenRefine and Tableau Public are intuitive tools to help students clean up their own datasets.

OpenRefine
http://openrefine.org/

OpenRefine is an interactive data transformation tool, like a spreadsheet, but both easier and more powerful in specifying the attributes of a particular aspect of data. OpenRefine is dynamic in that all the data changes immediately and is reversible, taking away much of the anxiety of working with large datasets.

OpenRefine is particularly useful for consolidating different spellings or related concepts — our state library association used it for one project to bring together a population who variously described themselves as school librarians or media specialists, for example. OpenRefine is dependent upon the ability to install software on a local computer.

Tableau Public
https://public.tableau.com/s/

Tableau can use your geographically based data to create easy visualizations about the density of populations through heat mapping.

Using its ZIP code option, one of my professional organizations used it to discern where members lived to inform our targeting of certain areas in membership drives.

These are just some of the possibilities for using data with students. As a school librarian, one of the first data projects I worked on with a whole class involved a stock market contest. Each economics student chose one stock and tracked three months of closing prices before graphing the gains and losses to determine an overall profit leader. The main takeaway was that the scale of units matter in visual depictions. Excel generated a scale based on the prices in the spreadsheet, but adjusting the axes from the default let students know they had choices which would add or remove inherent drama from the graphic visualization. When students contrasted identical stock prices on 20-unit scale vs 120-unit scale, the two graphs look very different. Consciousness of units is critical in building awareness about the importance of attending to axes.

Conclusion

Teachers can encourage students to think computationally about relationships in the data with which they are working. Those are important information literacy skills. Working with data does not necessarily mean performing mathematical operations.

To master data fluency concepts within limited time frames, educators can locate existing datasets, and design assignments where students manipulating data and teasing out the relationships is the goal and then making comprehensible statements about the relationship between the data.

Presenting data in a responsible way involves students getting their point across using the language, the variables, and even the types of charts and graphs that will portray their data accurately and not necessarily overstate the data relationships. Constructing charts and graphs will make students subsequently better readers of information in these formats.

Resources

Herbach, Geoff. 2014. *Fat Boy vs. the Cheerleaders*. Naperville, IL: Sourcebooks.

5 | Manipulating data in spreadsheets

Martha Stuit

A practical side of being data literate is working with data to spot patterns, build arguments, and create visualizations. But first, you need a place to store and explore data. Knowing strategies for working with data in spreadsheets makes those tasks easier. Spreadsheets help us think about data by allowing the reader to view and interact with the individual data points that make up both summary statistics and data visualizations. By learning the features of spreadsheets outlined in this chapter, you'll find that spreadsheets more approachable for thinking about and working with data.

This chapter includes ways to identify patterns from data in spreadsheets and ideas for manipulating data. It will focus on features of Excel 2016 (with file extensions of .xlsx) and Google Sheets by walking through examples. Other versions of Excel might have slightly different steps, offer features in different menu locations, or lack features altogether. To navigate other software editions, use the Help function, search online for guidance, and/or find a manual. Data in this chapter, with the exception of a dataset in Google Sheets, are publicly available online. You can download the same data and follow along with the steps to learn the tools! In fact, trying the steps with the same data is a smart way to familiarize yourself with the strategies in this chapter. Keep in mind that there are some typical steps for using data in spreadsheets:

> » **Finding data**
> » **Downloading data to a spreadsheet**
> » **Cleaning up the data in the spreadsheet**

» **Sorting and filtering your spreadsheet to discover patterns**

» **Drawing conclusions from your spreadsheet**

Both you and your students can use the information in this chapter to manipulate your data and others' data. By the end of this chapter, you will be able to explore creating arguments and visualizations from manipulating data in spreadsheets.

Finding data

There are many places, both online and in print, to find data. While this chapter does not explore finding data in depth, there are several questions to consider when you encounter datasets that impact whether it will be easy to work with the data in a spreadsheet. You might even consider teaching these skills as part of your lesson plans with students!

» **Is the data freely available and easily accessible?** There's a lot of data online. If you have to purchase data and funding is a constraint, perhaps you could find something available for free that will also meet your needs. In any case, make sure you have an option to easily download the data.

» **What is the source of your data?** Just like any other piece of information, you should evaluate your source. Do you trust where this information is coming from?

» **Can you download the data?** Look for options to download or export your data, especially into Excel files (files with the extension .xlsx) or CSV files (files with the extension .csv). Comma separated values files (files with data divided by commas) are easily managed using common spreadsheet software.

Data.gov (https://www.data.gov/) is one of many useful places to find datasets. It catalogs datasets from the U.S. government. Data.gov offers data about a wide variety of topics, from the environment to education, and the datasets are browsable by topic. If you can't find data on what you are looking for, you might want to think about who would collect the kind of data you need and search for that organization (for example, the National Highway Traffic Safety Administration might have some information about highway fatalities). Consider what you are interested in when seeking out datasets or browse all the datasets. You can usually manipulate the search mechanisms in some data repositories to limit searches to topics, file types, and other specifications. Almost all U.S. government documents and creations are in the public domain; however, you should check a dataset's documentation for exceptions before using them. In general, datasets on crime, finances, and population might be interesting to explore in the classroom. Finding data about a topic of interest to you or your students can make it more fun to manipulate!

Downloading your data into a spreadsheet

Once you have found data online, downloading your data into a spreadsheet involves a few steps. Selecting the Excel or CSV file from a website and clicking on it to download it is often successful. The downloaded file can usually be found in your folder for downloads, unless you specify a different destination. CSV files can be opened in Excel and saved as Excel files. A possible limitation is your download settings on your computer or Internet browser. If you are unable to download a file, check those settings to make sure that they allow you to download files. Another limitation could be the amount of available storage space on your computer. If there is not enough room for the file, try clearing storage space to make room. An alternative to clearing space on your computer's hard drive is downloading the file to an external storage tool, such as a USB flash drive or external hard drive. If something goes wrong with downloading the file, try downloading it again, searching your computer files for the file, closing and reopening your browser before downloading it again, or using a different browser to download it. Check for help documentation with suggestions for troubleshooting issues on the website offering the data, too.

Let's walk through an example. We searched Data.gov for data related to farmers markets. Notice that the Data.gov landing page indicates that the data are federal and from the U.S. Department of Agriculture (USDA). The data are compiled by the Agricultural Marketing Service, an agency of the USDA.

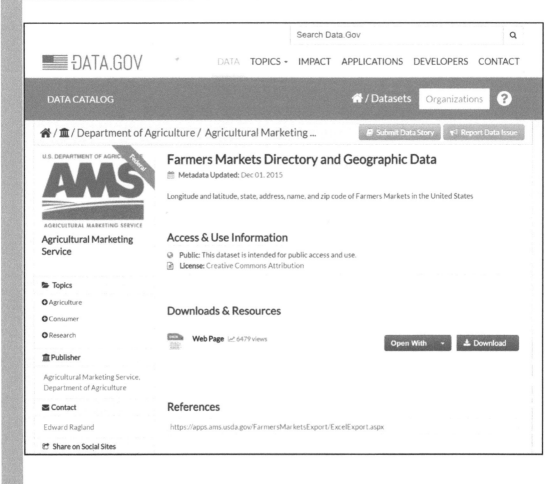

Figure 1. Landing page about farmers market data on Data.gov.
https://catalog.data.gov/dataset/farmers-markets-geographic-data

To obtain the data, click "Download." When clicking the download button, sometimes Data.gov provides a file for downloading, and other times, it redirects to another government website. In fact, you might not even get a spreadsheet, but don't despair! You might get some other kind of file. This time, "Download" takes me to the USDA website, rather than providing a file for my browser to download. When it takes you to another website, the data is often on that next web page and downloadable, or it is located somewhere on that website. Sometimes it takes a little detective work to download the data. In this case, I had to do some further digging and then found a directory of farmers markets, which is in a table on the USDA website. I clicked on "Export to Excel" to retrieve a spreadsheet that will allow me to work with the data for all the registered farmers markets in the country. Alternatively, I later observed that the URL under the word "References" on Data.gov provides a CSV file for your browser to download. Still, the table on the USDA website is updated regularly.

 Terms to look for

- Download
- Export to Excel
- References
- Get the Raw Data

By exporting the data to a spreadsheet program, the data can be manipulated, rather than just viewed in a browser. Opening the file finally gives us a spreadsheet, but it needs to be cleaned up first. For a list of spreadsheet tips, see Appendix A.

 Tips

- You can upload Excel spreadsheets to Google Sheets (To do so, upload the Excel file to Google Drive. Right click on a PC (Control click on a Mac) and then select "Open with" > "Google Sheets").
- You can also download a Google Sheet as an Excel File (in the "File" menu of Google Sheets, select "Download as" > "Microsoft Excel (.xlsx)").

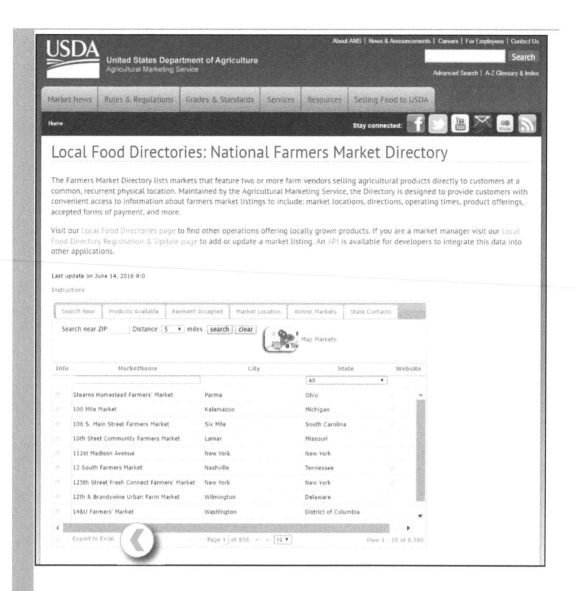

Figure 2. USDA displays the farmers market information in an online directory. Clicking "Export to Excel" in the bottom left corner of the table provides a file. https://www.ams.usda.gov/local-food-directories/farmersmarkets

Cleaning up the data in your spreadsheet

When you first download a dataset, the data may be difficult to read. For example, the rows and columns may have labels that are difficult to read. Take a look at this spreadsheet about foreclosures from the United States Department of Agriculture in Figure 3.

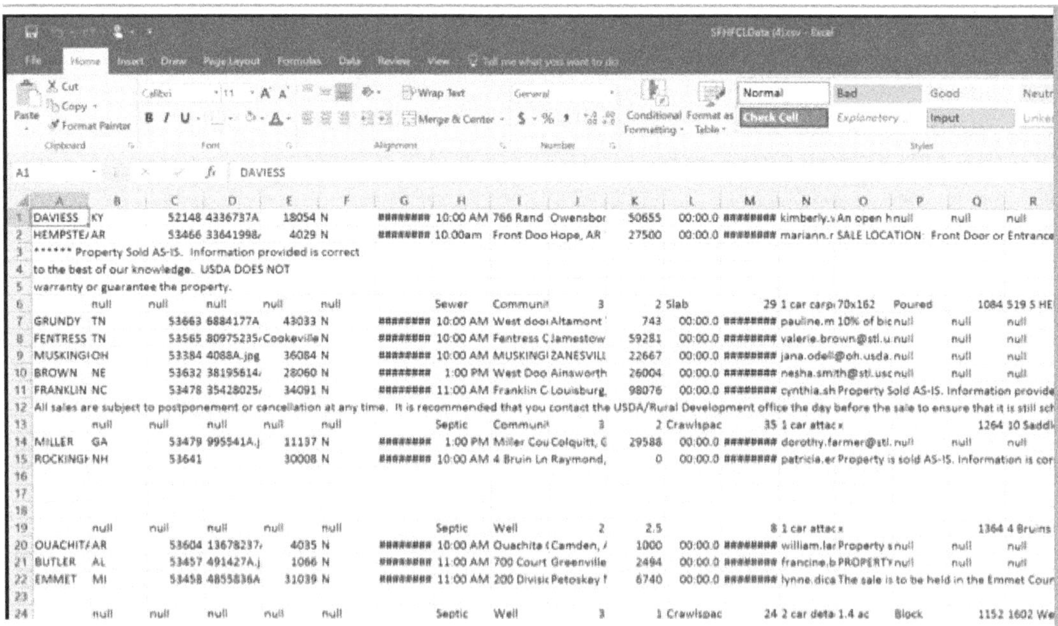

Figure 3. Spreadsheet of foreclosed properties from the United States Department of Agriculture, as found on Data.gov and downloaded from the USDA website. http://www.sc.egov.usda.gov/data/data_files.html

It is nearly impossible to tell what data are in each column because there are no explanatory headers at the top of the spreadsheet. Some data doesn't fit in the width of the column, making the information hard to read. In this case, a web page called "Rural Development Datasets" offers a Microsoft Word document, called "File Description," which contains the headers. However, it is still hard to tell with certainty what each header means because the document does not specify to which column each header belongs or definitions for the headers.

In general, it is not uncommon to encounter this kind of messy dataset. Data has not always been collected with the intention that people less familiar with the collection process might read and use it, and standard formats and practices are still being established. Luckily, there are ways to handle it. Check out these best practices, and keep them in mind when working with data:

» **Sometimes data can be "messy" or "dirty," meaning there are pieces of data that mean the same thing but**

**may be represented in different ways, have acciden-
tal errors in them, or have some other problems.** For
example, ZIP codes in the Boston area have zeroes as
the first of five digits (e.g., 02108 or 02123). Spreadsheet
software may not recognize that the zero is not superflu-
ous but essential to the number, so it may cut off the zero
from the start of the ZIP code. Another example is names
that are written or spelled differently but refer to the same
entity. For example, a column for "state" could have data
that says Michigan, Mich., and MI to represent the same
location. In order to have an accurate count of the number
of records that refer to the state of Michigan, these entries
will need to be standardized before the data can be manipulated. Otherwise, important data can be left out. Similarly,
Missus, Madame, and Mrs. need to be standardized. Male
and boy must be consolidated to a consistent gender term.
Paying attention to these details and standardizing entries
or taking them into account when you manipulate data
can save you from accidentally leaving data out of your
analysis later.

» **Look for additional documentation. As in the example
shown above, datasets are sometimes missing headers
or keys to abbreviations and codes.** This information
about the information is known as *metadata*. Metadata can
sometimes be found in separate but essential documents;
websites or files' accompanying data can offer definitions
of column headers and codes (Herzog 2016). Seeking out
and viewing this information helps with understanding
and analyzing data. This information is not always easy to
find – it often requires some digging – but it helps you be
as accurate as you can be. Guessing should be a last resort
and only if you document those guesses in your research.
Likewise, create documentation for your own data as you
generate it. If you share it or do not look at it for a while,
your metadata will clarify your data to others (and refresh
your memory).

» **When working with secondary data, save changes as a new file to indicate that the data have been modified (Herzog 2016).** In the file name, note that you have made changes to the spreadsheet (example: FarmersMarketData-Modification1.xlsx). This practice helps keep track of what you have done with the data.

One potentially intimidating part of working with spreadsheets is that they are all different, and so you might have to do some additional data organization. Column headings and other features of course vary from dataset to dataset. Going back to our farmers market data we can get our bearings by looking at column headings, as well as determining what data the rows contain.

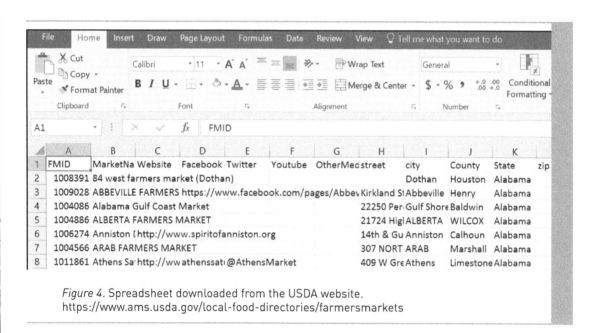

Figure 4. Spreadsheet downloaded from the USDA website.
https://www.ams.usda.gov/local-food-directories/farmersmarkets

We notice that the fields, or column headings in row 1, are human-readable with headers like "City," as well as "Credit" to indicate payment options and "Flowers" to show goods sold (visible when spreadsheet is downloaded). These are presumably the fields that the farmers market directors fill out when they register and update their information for the directory. These headings make it possible to work knowledgeably with the data. For example, it can help us navigate quickly to those farmers' markets that sell flowers or accept credit cards. Also, we can notice that each column contains one piece or category of information.

Another component to check for is duplicates in the data, because duplicate records could create errors in data interpretations. Finally, it is good practice to make sure that we have downloaded and have all of the data. According to the online table, there are 8,558 entries. Click in a cell and press Control + page down (use Command instead of Control on a Mac) to move quickly to bottom row of the data. The last row is numbered 8,559 (The number of farmers markets may be different when you download the data because numbers change over time. That's okay, though ... it won't change our discussion). Since row 1 contains column headings and thus adds a row to the total, we know that we have successfully downloaded all the data. Now that the data has been organized or cleaned up, let's work with it to sort and filter information and discover something new using its content.

Let's also save the entire file to the computer since we are making changes. Give it a name like FarmersMarketDataModification2.xlsx to indicate that it has been modified.

Sorting and filtering to discover patterns

Now that you have a spreadsheet full of data that is easier to read and understand, you'll want to organize it to make sense of it. What does all of this data mean? *Sorting* and *filtering* data can help you determine patterns. Patterns help you uncover meaning. Sorting lets you put data in various sequences, such as alphabetical order or grouping all of the rows of data related to California together. Filtering creates a smaller subset of the data, while hiding the rest of the dataset. Think of the entire spreadsheet as a grocery store where everything has been dumped on the floor. Sorting helps put all the canned vegetables in one section of the store and all the frozen items in another. Filtering would hide all of the room-temperature groceries and just show those that are refrigerated or frozen. Sorting and filtering can add value to your dataset and may be enough to draw conclusions from data, spark ideas for arguments, and make decisions about a visualization.

Now that our farmers market data is cleaned up and has clear column headings, we can sort it. In Excel, "Sort" is located under the "Data" tab, and clicking it provides a dialog box that offers options for what to sort by. To put the farmers market data in alphabetical order by state, highlight all the data by clicking in the upper left corner between column A and row 1 where the triangle is. Then click on the data tab and open the "Sort" feature, choose "Sort by" State (the column we are sorting) and "Order" by A-Z (how it will be sorted). Make sure that the checkbox next to "My data has headers" is marked.

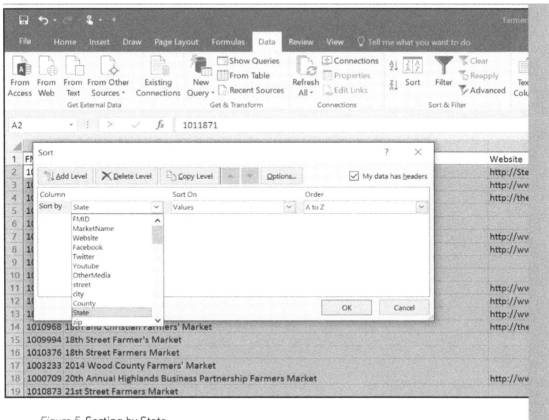

Figure 5. Sorting by State.

Since the data were not in order by state previously, sorting presents the data in a more readable way by moving farmers markets that are in the same state next to each other and ordering the states alphabetically. If the box for "My data has headers" is not checked, the "Sort by" menu will only show options for columns identified by letters, not the headers or labels for the columns. It is harder to select a column to sort by then. If you uncheck the box for "My data has headers" before sorting, the headers will disappear in the sorted data, which makes the data difficult to interpret. To remove the sorting, click "Clear" under the "Data" tab.

We can also use the "Filter" feature to zoom in on a specific section of the data and hide the rest of the data. This feature helps us view part of the dataset and makes analyzing the data more manageable by showing fewer rows. In Excel, "Filter" is located under the "Data" tab, and clicking it provides drop down menus in each column heading. Consider what category you are interested in, and identify the column that contains it. Then, use "Filter" to limit the visible data to only the data fulfilling a particular characteristic, such as location or product. For example, to view the farmers market data for only California, as shown in Figure 6,

1. **Select the "State" column.**
2. **In the dropdown menu, (accessed by clicking the triangle next to the State heading) uncheck "Select all."**
3. **Check only the box for California**
4. **Click OK, and the only rows visible will be for farmers markets in California.**

Other ideas for filters are selecting several states in a particular region or farmers markets that offer a particular product.

If you want to remove a filter for one column, click the filter icon in the column heading and click "Clear Filter From" the name of the column. If you want to remove all filters, click "Clear" in the "Sort & Filter" group of the "Data" tab.

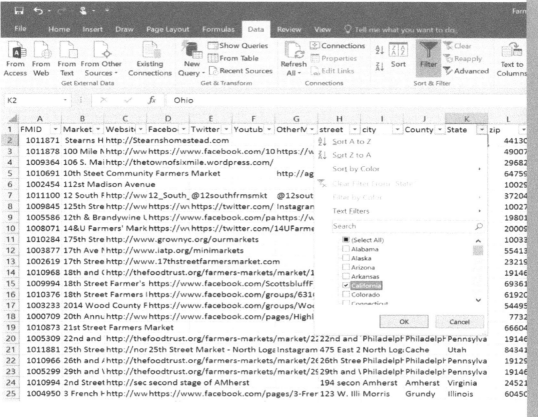

Figure 6. Filter by California.

Tips

Sorts and filters are not permanent unless you save the file with the sorts and filters activated.

- **To view all the data again, you will have to remove the filter, which makes a particular view disappear.** To return to the full dataset but save a filtered view, copy the cells and past them in a new worksheet. Make sure to give that new worksheet a name that describes the manipulated data well.

- **To spot whether data have been filtered in any spreadsheet, look for these indicators:**

  » row numbers turn blue and may skip numbers, depending on how the data are sorted and/or filtered,

  » dropdown arrows in the column headings in row 1 turns into a funnel on the columns that have been filtered, and

> » the words "Filter Mode" appear on the left end of the
>   bottom status bar.

- **"Sort" answers questions like:**
  - » Which X is the highest/greatest?
  - » Which X is the lowest/least?
  - » Which data points belong to which category?
  - » What are the categories, and how might I organize
    the data?

- **"Filter" answers questions like:**
  - » Which data belong to a category or certain categories
    in a field?
  - » Which data have a particular characteristic or char-
    acteristics of interest?
  - » Which data fulfill specific criteria?

Google Sheets also offers "Sort" and "Filter" functions under the
"Data" menu.

When you are working with data, it is helpful to automate as many
processes as possible. This allows you to play with data in many
ways in a short amount of time – the more sorting and filtering
you do,the more likely it is that you will find useful patterns.

Pivot tables

Let's turn to pivot tables, a different type of filtering which will
help us explore our data more deeply. A pivot table is a tool to
summarize data by reorganizing it in a new view. It is useful for
understanding your data because it can quickly and automatically show patterns by sorting, counting, and/or averaging data.
In searching on Data.gov, I found data for the 2010 School Improvement Grants, which were awarded by the U.S. Department
of Education to support schools with the lowest achievement.
This public dataset is not labeled with a copyright or any other
kind of license, but it is a federal dataset, so it is fair to assume
that this government data is in the public domain according to

https://www.usa.gov/government-works. Note that this dataset was summarized in 2013, a couple of years after the year being studied. Because compiling data can take a long time, it is not unusual for the most recent data available to be a few years old.

I downloaded the CSV file from Data.gov and opened it in Excel. Figure 7 shows what it looks like to start. Before making modifications to the data, save the file with a new name to avoid mixing up the raw data with any changes and findings, as we did with the other datasets. The downloaded file was automatically given the file name of userssharedsdfschoolimprovement2010grants. csv. I re-saved it as an Excel file with the file name of schoolimprovement2010grantsModified1.xlsx.

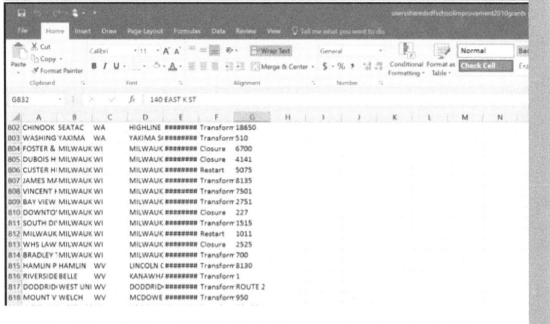

Figure 7. Unmodified spreadsheet about school improvement grants, as downloaded from Data.gov. https://catalog.data.gov/dataset/school-improvement-2010-grants

 Cite your data. While standards for data citation vary and are not well established, style manuals and data distributors often provide guidelines. Seek out guidelines to ensure you are giving proper attribution.

Because the columns are not fitted to the width of the data, it is hard to read what each cell contains. Clicking the Wrap Text icon and/or widening the columns will fix that.

Let's get to know the data. This spreadsheet has seven column headings that are are in a clear, concise format and span from A to G. By pressing Control + [End] on a PC (use Command + [Page Down] on a Mac), my cursor jumps to the last row, and I learn that there are 832 rows (831 schools listed, plus one row for the column headings), meaning that 831 schools received grants because the first row in our spreadsheet contains column headings. For an easy way to keep track of column headings in Excel, freeze the top row by selecting "Freeze Top Row" under "Freeze Panes" in the "View" tab. Then, we need to think about what we want to know from the data. I am curious which states received the most grants. To answer my question, I will create a pivot table by inserting the pivot table and putting "State" in both the "Row Labels" and "Values" fields of the pivot table.

Because each district was only eligible to receive one grant, finding two entries for the same district would show that there was some error in the data. A duplicate district (indicated in the "School Name" column) would mean that something is wrong with the data. You could check for duplicates by sorting by district name and scrolling row by row through all 831 school districts. That would be time-consuming, and if your eyes got tired, they could miss a repeated entry. Instead, let's create a pivot table.

To check for duplicates, create a pivot table by following these steps:

1. **Select the column of interest,** which for us is Column A containing the School Name, by clicking on the label for column A.

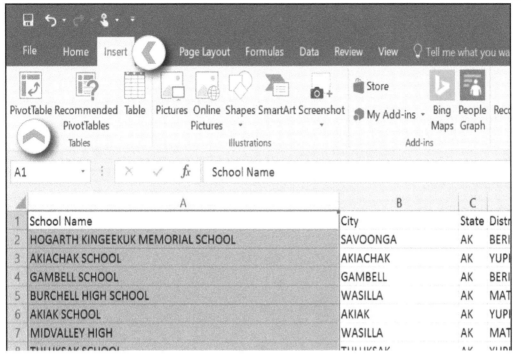

Figure 8. Select the column and click PivotTable in the "Insert" tab.

2. In the "Insert" tab, click PivotTable.

3. In the dialog box that opens, choose the options to "Select a table or range" and make sure that column A is listed.

4. Also in the dialog box, choose New Worksheet as the location to place the PivotTable. It is easier to work with pivot tables in a new tab of the spreadsheet.

5. Click "OK," and a new tab with a sidebar for PivotTable fields opens.

6. Click and drag the category of "School Name" into both the rows and values fields. Now, we will be able to see if any school names occur more than once and consequently have duplicates by looking at the new "Count of School Name" column.

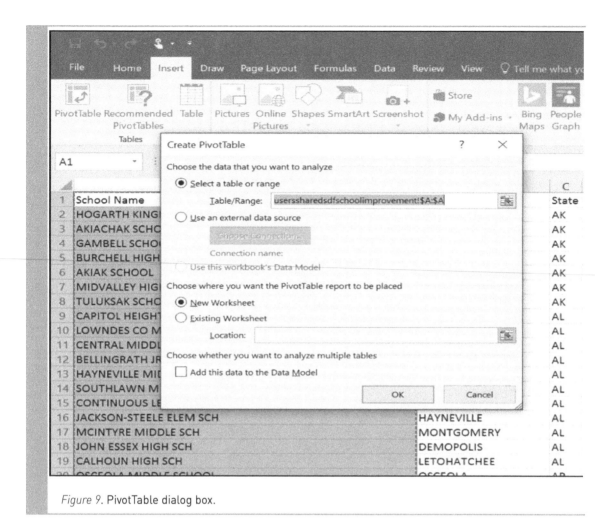

Figure 9. PivotTable dialog box.

We have completed all the steps to create our pivot table and can now learn from it. We can see that there are duplicates (as indicated by school names that have 2 next to them, instead of 1, in the "Count of School Name" column), so we need to investigate. Further investigation by returning to the original spreadsheet and searching for a duplicate name (press [Control] + f (use Command + f on a Mac) to activate the "Find" dialog box and use it to search), such as "Mount Pleasant High School" reveals that two high schools, one in Delaware and one in Tennessee, have the same name. Place names can also be abbreviated, so I also checked for "Mt Pleasant," too. Though I did not find any schools with that name in this data, it is important to consider abbreviations to avoid overlooking data. We can conclude that we do not actually have a problem with duplicates in these data.

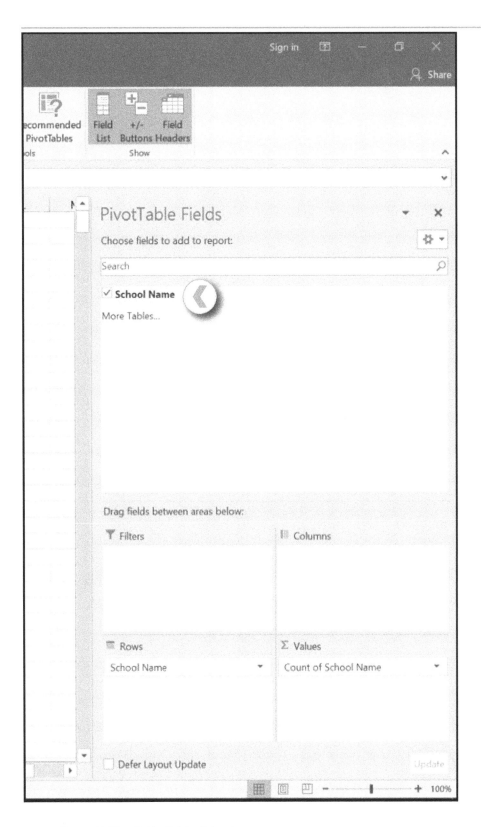

Figure 10. PivotTable fields dialog box.

509	MONTBELLO HIGH SCHOOL	1
510	MONTICELLO MIDDLE SCHOOL	1
511	MORNINGSIDE MIDDLE	1
512	MOUNT ABRAHAM UHSD #28	1
513	MOUNT HOPE HIGH SCHOOL	1
514	MOUNT PLEASANT HIGH SCHOOL	2
515	MOUNT UNION AREA SHS	1
516	MOUNT VIEW HIGH SCHOOL	1
517	MT TIPTON ELEMENTARY SCHOOL	1
518	MT. CLEMENS HIGH SCHOOL	1
519	MURTAUGH MIDDLE SCHOOL	1

Figure 11. Pivot table of schools that received school improvement grants in 2010-11.

Given that this dataset contains data for each state, another good check is to make sure that it contains 50 states. I can check the state column for unique data points to ensure that I have 50 by using a filter. Here are the steps:

1. **Highlight the State column.**

2. **Go to the "Data" tab, and click "Advanced," in the "Sort & Filter" group.**

3. **In the "Advanced Filter" dialog box, select "Copy to another location."** Then click your cursor in the "Copy to" box and select a column to the right of the data (I chose column I to separate the state data from the dataset).

4. **Be sure to click the "Unique records only" checkbox.**

Each state abbreviation will appear in the column, and the heading "State" will be at the top. We can scroll down to the end of the data in Column I to see that there are 51 rows, which seems correct for the number of states because row 1 contains the header. However, it is not quite that straightforward. What about Washington D.C. or Puerto Rico? Those would bring the count above 50. We can find documentation showing that the District of Columbia and Bureau of Indian Education have also received school improvement funding, as well as Puerto Rico (http://

www2.ed.gov/programs/sif/index.html). According to the documentation, Puerto Rico's and the Bureau of Indian Education's data appears to be separated from data for states, and North Dakota was not included in the 2010-2011 funding. Our spreadsheet contains Washington D.C. and North Dakota but Hawaii is missing. When you are working with data, think about any circumstances like these that might arise and address them from the start. Sometimes you may not know the larger facts around your data. In this case, for example, that there should be 50 entries. You need to know the context around your data. You need to find data about your data! You may even uncover other aspects to consider when you research your data – like that you need to consider information from the Bureau of Indian Affairs.

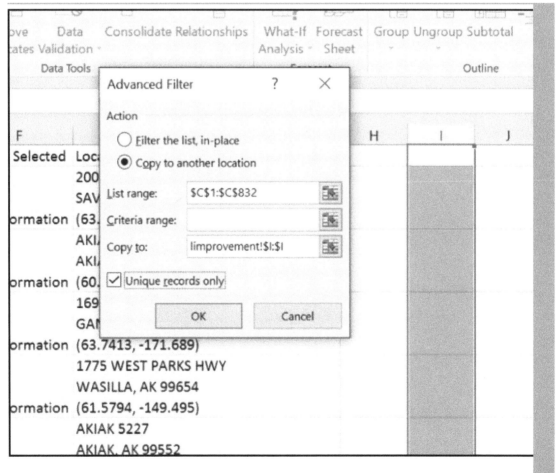

Figure 12. Using "Advanced Filter" to check the data.

Having gotten to know the data and checked over the spreadsheet, we are ready to make visualizations from this spreadsheet.

Drawing conclusions: Visualize data from a spreadsheet

Spreadsheets not only help you manipulate and learn about data but also visualize it. Simple built-in visualization tools in spreadsheet software can automatically turn your data into charts and graphs. With the school improvement data, I was curious which states had the most schools that received grants. I created a pivot table using "State" in both the "Row Labels" and "Values" fields of the pivot table to summarize number of schools that received grants per state and show only the top 10. Next, I explored visualization options to display these data.

To create a graph or chart from the school improvement data, I went through a process of inserting, modifying, and evaluating visualizations with the following steps:

1. **Select the data you want to visualize.** In this example, it's the Count of State column for the top-10 states. In the "Insert" tab, click "Recommended Charts." A dialog box will open with types of charts and graphs to choose.

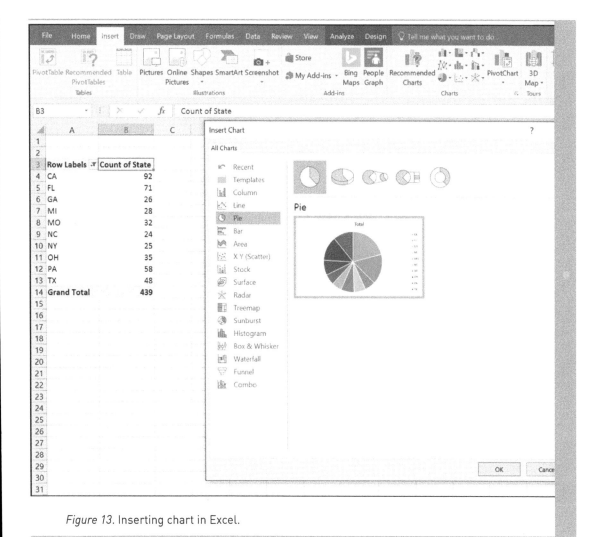

Figure 13. Inserting chart in Excel.

2. **Explore the types of charts and variations within the types by inserting and evaluating them.** Excel offers a preview in the dialog box. Select one and click OK, which will provide a chart that hovers over your spreadsheet.

3. **Manipulate your chart to add labels and change its appearance.** Click the plus sign next to the chart to add labels and the paintbrush symbol to modify its appearance.

4. **Review the chart to determine if it is the best fit for the data.** Try other charts to see which one fits best.

Consider the visualization choices. Think about which chart or graph will best showcase the data without being confusing or inaccurate. Trying out visualizations and assessing their strengths and weaknesses helps select a visualization that is a great fit for the data. For example, try out the pie chart. Given the large number of slices, it is hard to compare states and analyze how the state with the most grants, California, differs from the state that's tenth on this list, North Carolina. A different visualization could do a better job. Experiment with a line with markers. What do you think of this visualization?

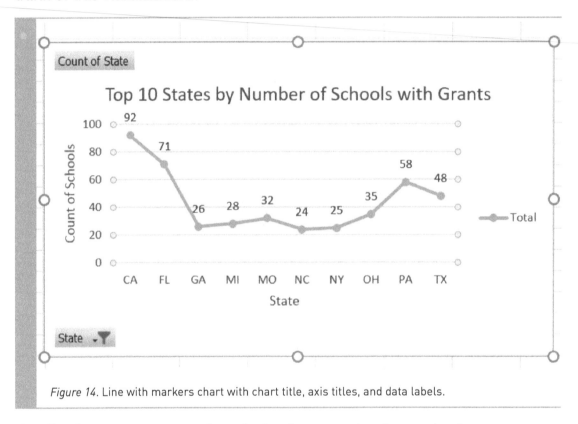

Figure 14. Line with markers chart with chart title, axis titles, and data labels.

The line is unnecessary and confusing because the data point for an individual state does not influence another state. These data are for one year, and each state has its own count. Line charts are better for data that change over time. It is clear that this is not the right visualization. Another chart or graph could illustrate these data better. A stacked bar chart is a great fit. You might consider ordering the bars from least to greatest, or greatest to least, for easier interpretation.

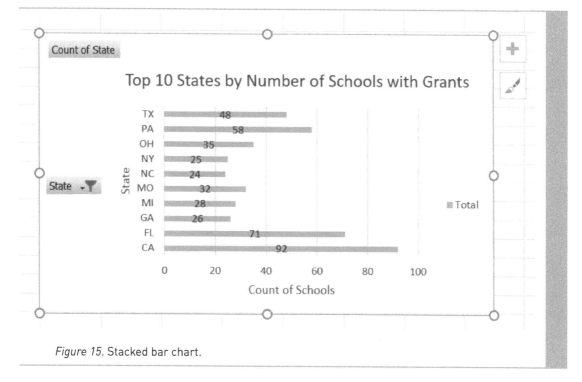

Figure 15. Stacked bar chart.

It clearly shows the range of the number of schools. It is straightforward and not confusing to look at, unlike the pie chart and line chart. Now conclusions can be drawn from the data. The chart is used to explore questions like, why might California have the most schools that received grants? Its large population might be a factor. Google Sheets also offers visualizations in the Insert menu.

Inserting your spreadsheet or graph into Word

Taking the data and visualizations from Excel or Google Sheets to Microsoft Word or Google Docs is a useful way to showcase what's earned through data manipulation in reports and other products.

Inserting (copying and pasting) an Excel spreadsheet or a piece of a spreadsheet into Word can be done in several ways. If you want a table that will never change, you can highlight, copy, and paste the spreadsheet or part of it into Word. If you want to preserve spreadsheet capabilities, you can embed the spreadsheet in Word, and Excel features will be available through Word (use "Paste Special" and paste as a "Microsoft Excel Worksheet Object"). If you want a spreadsheet in your Word document that dynamically changes whenever you change things in Excel, make sure to select the "Paste link As" option and choose "Microsoft Excel Worksheet Object." See Figure 16 to see how the different options appear. All are handy!

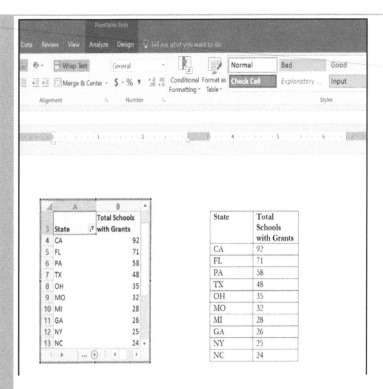

Figure 16. On this Microsoft Word page, the left spreadsheet shows how a spreadsheet pasted as an Excel object or linked to Excel appears. As data in Excel changes, so will the corresponding spreadsheet on the Word document. The right spreadsheet shows cells cut-and-pasted that are not linked to Excel. Any changes to the original Excel document will *not* be auto-transferred to the Word document.

Workarounds for Google Drive

At press time, Google Docs does not offer the feature to insert a Sheet. Copying and pasting rows and columns from Google Sheets provides a table in a Google Doc and is a good workaround. Taking a screenshot and pasting it in your Doc is another workaround. To transfer visualizations, copying and pasting from Google Sheets to Google Docs works well. Google Docs allows you to link visualizations to the spreadsheet so that they update.

Conclusion

Spreadsheets help us think about and draw conclusions from our data, allowing us to tease out patterns we might not notice otherwise. Finding data, downloading it appropriately, cleaning it up and sorting and filtering it help us understand the data and then communicate it more effectively to others. Spreadsheets can provide different views and perspectives on our data. We can even generate simple visualizations using the data within the spreadsheet software. The examples in this chapter give you a taste of ways to use spreadsheets to organize and think about your data.

Resources

Herzog, David. 2016. *Data Literacy: A User's Guide.* Los Angeles, CA: SAGE.
Office of Elementary and Secondary Education. 2015. *School Improvement 2010 Grants.* U.S. Department of Education. Distributed by Data.gov. https://catalog.data.gov/dataset/school-improvement-2010-grants.
United States Department of Agriculture. 2016, June 9. *Local Food Directories: National Farmers Market Directory.* Washington, DC: Agricultural Marketing Service, Department of Agriculture. Distributed by the Agricultural Marketing Service and Data.gov. https://www.ams.usda.gov/local-food-directories/farmersmarkets.
United States Department of Agriculture. "Rural Development Datasets." Service Center Agencies Online Services. Last modified May 5, 2016. Accessed June 12, 2016. http://www.sc.egov.usda.gov/data/data_files.html.
U.S. Department of Education. "School Improvement Grants." Data.gov. Last modified April 26, 2016. Accessed June 12, 2016. https://catalog.data.gov/dataset/school-improvement-2010-grants.
U.S. General Services Administration. "National Farmers Market Directory." Data.gov. Last modified November 18, 2015. Accessed June 9, 2016. https://catalog.data.gov/dataset/national-farmers-market-directory.
"U.S. Government Works." USA.gov. Accessed June 12, 2016. https://www.usa.gov/government-works.

If you are new to spreadsheets, need a refresher, or are not quite sure how to do something in this chapter, here are some useful features of spreadsheets in Excel. Google Sheets has some slightly different names for functions and formulas but has many similar features.

Name	What it does	Location or Formula in Excel 2016
AutoFit Column Width	Fits each column to the width of the cell with the widest data	Home tab > Cells > Format > AutoFit Column Width
Freeze Top Row	Makes the top row, which usually contains column headings, hover when scrolling down	View tab > Freeze Panes > Freeze Top Row
TRIM	Removes extra spaces before and after text	Enter the formula in a cell: =TRIM(*column* and *cell*) (example: =TRIM(A2))
Text to Columns	Splits data combined in one column into multiple columns, so that each column contains one category of data (example: first and last names)	Data tab > Text to Columns
AutoSum	Calculates the sum of a range of cells and also offers average, count, maximum, and minimum functions	Formulas tab > AutoSum
PivotTable	Summarizes the data	Insert tab > PivotTable Then, drag and drop column headings into the pivot table fields to create it

6 | Making sense of data visualization

Justin Joque

While humans have been creating maps for millennia, we only started creating statistical graphics — also referred to as data visualizations — within the last 500 years. Still, the first data visualizations, such as Edmond Halley's wind maps of the world's oceans (Figure 1), were still geographic maps, with data (in this case, wind currents) added atop the map.

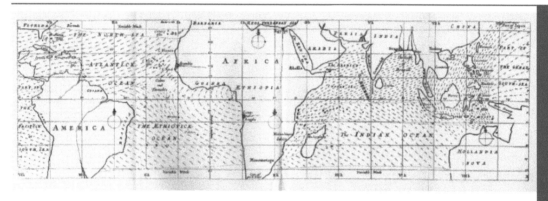

Figure 1: Edmond Halley's wind maps of the world oceans. Public domain.

From these early beginnings, data visualization has become a pervasive part of our information-intensive society. It is now used for everything from the daily weather report to advanced scientific research to managing complex business processes in real time. While data visualization can include massive datasets generated and processed by computers, we should keep in mind that the *techniques* of data visualization originate from and still include hand-drawn visuals.

There is a great diversity of technologies and techniques for making data visualizations; that being said, there are some common goals that underlie the process of visualization overall. Said simply: data visualization allows us to see something — for example, patterns, trends, or anomalies — in the data that we otherwise would not see. Lev Manovich (2010) explains that the goal of visualization "is to discover the structure of a (typically large) dataset ... a visualization is successful if it reveals this structure."

A famous dataset, known as Anscombe's Quartet (Figure 2), was designed explicitly to show how visualization can reveal the structure of data. While the statistical description of each dataset (shown first) is exactly the same, and the range of data points in each seems to be similar, we immediately see the differences when the points are graphed.

Anscombe's Quartet							
I		II		III		IV	
x	y	x	y	x	y	x	y
10.0	8.04	10.0	9.14	10.0	7.46	8.0	6.58
8.0	6.95	8.0	8.14	8.0	6.77	8.0	5.76
13.0	7.58	13.0	8.74	13.0	12.74	8.0	7.71
9.0	8.81	9.0	8.77	9.0	7.11	8.0	8.84
11.0	8.33	11.0	9.26	11.0	7.81	8.0	8.47
14.0	9.96	14.0	8.10	14.0	8.84	8.0	7.04
6.0	7.24	6.0	6.13	6.0	6.08	8.0	5.25
4.0	4.26	4.0	3.10	4.0	5.39	19.0	12.50
12.0	10.84	12.0	9.13	12.0	8.15	8.0	5.56
7.0	4.82	7.0	7.26	7.0	6.42	8.0	7.91
5.0	5.68	5.0	4.74	5.0	5.73	8.0	6.89

Property	Value	Accuracy
Mean of x	9	exact
Sample variance of x	11	exact
Mean of y	7.50	to 2 decimal places
Sample variance of y	4.125	plus/minus 0.003
Correlation between x and y	0.816	to 3 decimal places
Linear regression line	y = 3.00 + 0.500x	to 2 and 3 decimal places, respectively

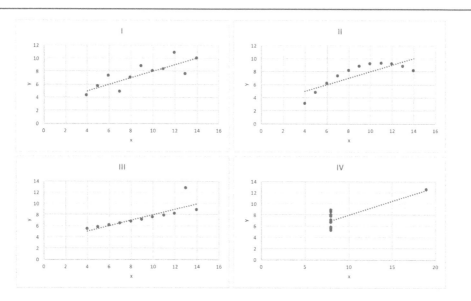

Figure 2: Anscombe's Quartet, showing how four sets of similar data can actually look quite different when visualized.

Anscombe's Quartet illustrates the fundamental principle of data visualization: to make something that is not obvious seem clearer in a compact amount of space. How does data visualization reveal data? How do these graphs show us something that is difficult to see in the raw data or even the summary statistics? Hopefully, these questions can be answered in more depth as we explore data visualization, but at this point, the history of data visualization and its relation to mapping can suggest an answer.

Data visualization allows us to map large amounts of data to a single space where it can be seen all at once. With a single graph, we can see global temperature averages over 150 years; we can see the entire history of the population of the United States, or a lifetime of stats for a favorite baseball player. Each of these examples take a series of information and maps it to a space — creates a graph — we can see with a single glance. With Anscombe's Quartet, we could read each data point one by one, but we would have a hard time keeping track of them over the time it takes to read them. But, patterns and structures emerge when seeing them all together.

> ### ❓ What does data visualization do?
>
> - It allows us to discover the structure and patterns in datasets.
> - It maps series of data to a space.

This chapter provides a framework for describing what it is that data visualization does. While there are some recommendations for best practices, our overarching purpose here is to break the task of visualization into its individual components so that you and your students can explore and understand them deeply. By doing so, we hope that students can understand the visualizations they encounter and develop language to discuss the process of making data visualizations.

Graphs

Rarely, if ever, does a visualization simply show the data as it is; if we wanted to show the data itself, we could simply list it in a table. Visualization maps the data onto a visual space, the "graph." This is important, because it means that visualizing always involves making decisions. There are not necessarily right or wrong choices, but there are better or worse choices. Making better choices about data visualization helps clearly communicate our data. Graphs are common starting points when exploring visualizations.

Working through a simple example will allow us to demonstrate the stages of moving from data to visualization. We can also see how each of these mappings requires decisions that will affect the resulting graph. Take this graph of U.S. unemployment rates going back to 1980 (Figure 3). The graph takes a time series and shows us the entire dataset (meaning all of the data points) in one visual, with the horizontal x-axis showing us the year and the vertical y-axis showing us the percentage of population that was unemployed. While this graph may seem simple, it still required making decisions and moving data into positions on the graph to create the resulting visual.

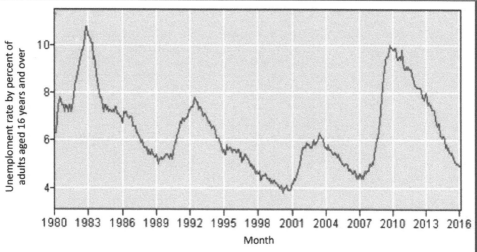

Figure 3: U.S unemployment rate, 1980-2016. Source: Bureau of Labor Statistics, https://data.bls.gov/timeseries/LNS14000000.

While this represents one way to visualize data on a graph, it's critical for us to share with students that there is often more than one way. Let's use the data points graphed above, from the Bureau of Labor Statistics, to demonstrate the kinds of decisions we might think through before graphing ... and how those decisions can lead to rather different visual outputs.

The first decision that we must make is one of scale — specifically, how should we mark the points on the x- and y-axes along with the *intervals*, or distances between points. For example,

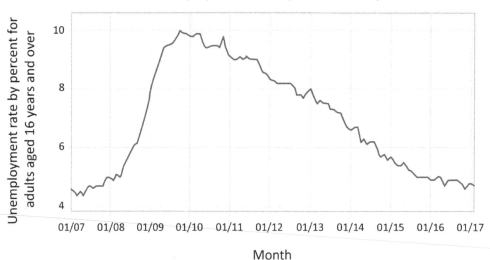

Figure 4: Graph with data points connected with a solid line. Graph shows the unemployment rate for adults, aged 16 and up, for the past decade. Data courtesy of the Bureau of Labor Statistics, http://data.bls.gov/timeseries/LNS14000000

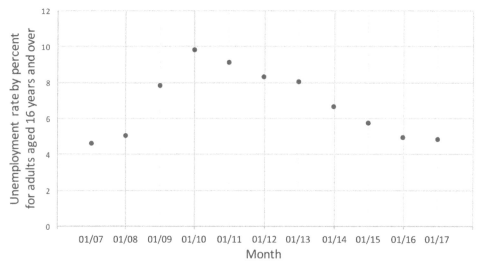

Figure 5: Scatter plot showing the unemployment rate for adults, aged 16 and up, for the past decade. Data courtesy of the Bureau of Labor Statistics, http://data.bls.gov/timeseries/LNS14000000.

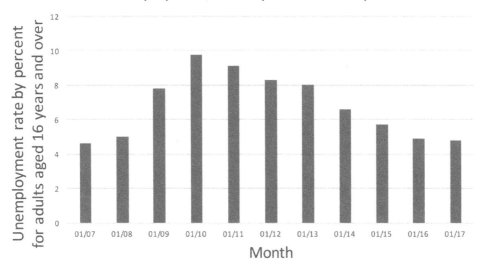

Figure 6: Bar graph showing the unemployment rate for adults, aged 16 and up, for the past decade. Data courtesy of the Bureau of Labor Statistics, http://data.bls.gov/timeseries/LNS14000000

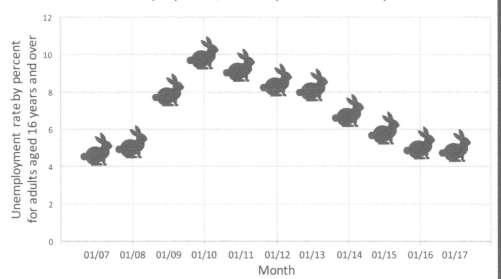

Figure 7: Unemployment rate for adults, aged 16 and up, for the past decade, with each rabbit representing the rate for each month. Data courtesy of the Bureau of Labor Statistics, http://data.bls.gov/timeseries/LNS14000000.

should the y-axis start with zero, like the graphs we are used to from math class? Or is that irrelevant as there are no points even close to zero to map? Should the y-axis go from 3 to 11? Or 4 to 15? Each of these options would be correct, but the range you pick will determine how the graph appears to the human eye. Different intervals and different starting and ending points will help determine how significant the change appears over time.

Similar decisions have to be made with the x-axis. Notice how, in Figure 4, we limit the same dataset from Figure 3 by date, showing only the data of the past 10 years. The resulting line tells a different story! Figures 5–7 contain identical data to Figure 4, but you may notice that you react differently to them. The data is the same, and the intent to display the data is honest, but each gives us a slightly different reaction. Good designers of data visualizations are aware of the impact that design choices make. Figure 6's red lines may evoke emotion, whereas the smooth line of Figure 4 feels calming. The rabbits are whimsical but perhaps make you think the data isn't conveying impactful or serious information.

Decisions like these form the bedrock of data visualization. And it's important to note here, from the very beginning, that these decisions are not part of the graphs students create in school. We need to be clear with students and ourselves that different choices may play into data visualizations "in the wild" than we are used to from math class.

While the graph with rabbits may not be the easiest to read, both the line and bar graphs provide reasonable displays of the data. The line may be slightly better at showing change over time; the bars are better for showing quantity. Since we are dealing with a change in quantity over time (the percentage of unemployment over time) both show the data well, but as we will see for different data this may not always be the case.

Pie charts

Let's move from graphs to pie charts. Figure 8 shows a pie chart of living things in my house: six total living things (two adults, two cats, one baby, and one dog).

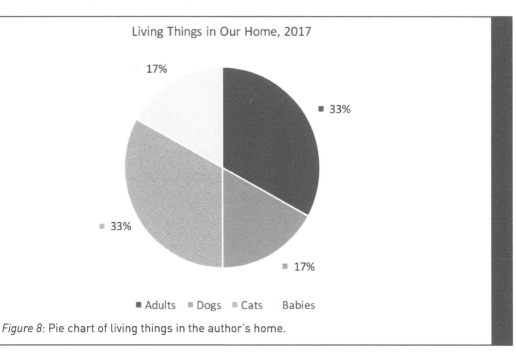

Figure 8: Pie chart of living things in the author's home.

We could easily make a bar chart or graph, with points on the x-axis for each creature type and numbers representing quantity on the y-axis. But if we did, we would be overlooking something important: how the number of any one type of creature relates to the total population. For that, a pie chart is a better visual tool.

The first thing you might notice (or already know) about pie charts is we always have a full pie and each of the slices is a part of the whole. Instead of counting numbers directly, we have to convert our data to percentages of the whole. So, instead of visualizing six things we are visualizing 100%. Before we can plot with this scale we have to transform our data from two adults, one dog, two cats, one baby to 1/3, 1/6, 1/3, 1/6 (often graphing software will do this automatically for us, but it still must be done), or directly to percentages (33%, 17%, 33%, 17%). In this case, we've rounded to the nearest whole number, so our percentage total equals 100%. In some cases, rounding may lead the total to be 99% or even 101% — that is OK, too.

With this transformation complete, we now simply define our scale as the correctly proportioned slice of pie. So instead of 2 mapping to 2 units on a graph, we map 1/3 to 1/3 of the pie (more technically, this could be thought of as 1/3 of the degrees of a circle — 120 out of 360°).

In essence, a pie chart is just a bar chart that uses proportions of a whole instead of raw counts and proportions of a circle rather than height. After we have our pieces of pie, then all we have to do is choose what color to make them and we have a relatively familiar visualization.

Many people likely know how to make a pie chart and how to read one, so what do we learn by describing it in this way? Well, there is value in discussing the process: if we understand and can describe every transformation that is done between our raw data to the final visualization, we can then imagine all sorts of different ways we could manipulate and map the data. Moreover, we can recognize when these transformations are done incorrectly and gain ways of talking about where a visualization may fail.

For instance, Figure 9 shows support backing various presidential candidates. At first glance, we see three candidates and three slices of pie. It is when we look at the percentages labeling the pie that we realize the mistake. We know that a pie chart should add up to 100% ... but here, the numbers add up to 193%! This is likely because in the survey, respondents were allowed to identify more than one candidate. (When surveys have phrases like "choose all that apply," pie charts aren't a good option.)

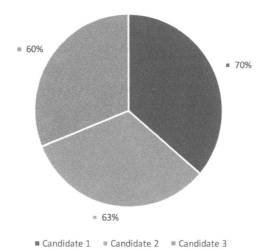

Support for Each of the Major Presidential Candidates

- 60%
- 70%
- 63%

■ Candidate 1   ■ Candidate 2   ■ Candidate 3

Figure 9: A pie chart in which the total percentage far exceeds the limit of 100%.

In this case, the numbers are accurate, but the pie chart format gives off misleading information, implying that each candidate has near-equal support when, in fact, Candidate 1 has 10% more supporters than Candidate 3!

If, instead, we simply display the data as a bar graph (Figure 10), where we are not converting the data to proportions of a whole, the information makes much more sense. The bar chart allows us to see each candidate's individual support compared against the other.

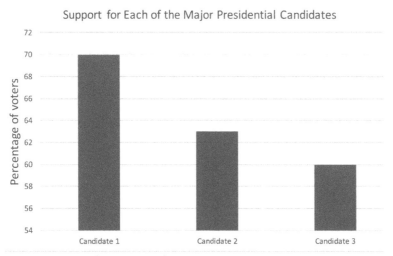

Support for Each of the Major Presidential Candidates

Figure 10: A bar chart (or bar graph) is a more effective way of representing data when people select more than one option.

Another benefit to the bar chart for the candidate data is that it is easier to judge differences in height than in area. Remember Figure 9, in which each candidate had a pie slice of near-identical size despite differences in percentages? Compare that to Figure 10. Now the differences are clear. (And remember our earlier lessons from Figures 3–7 about where to start the y-axis? If we started the y-axis for Figure 10 at zero, we might see less-pronounced differences.) While there are often good reasons to use pie charts, it is much easier to see when something is bigger than something else if you are looking at the side-by-side height rather than trying to compare the angle of a pie piece or its area.

From this example, we can see how important the notion of **proportion of a whole** is to a pie chart, and this is precisely what a pie chart excels at displaying. But, there are other aspects of datasets we may be interested in — the distribution of a dataset (i.e., how frequent certain values or outcomes are; what values make up a dataset) or how two values in a dataset relate to each other (e.g., what is the relationship between height and income — scatter plots are excellent for showing the relationship between two such values). If we are interested in distribution, a histogram is an excellent graph for understanding the values in a dataset. We can understand exactly how it works through a similar analysis.

Histograms

Imagine that we want to visualize household income in the U.S. We could make each point on the x-axis a different dollar amount — $20,000 then $21,000 then $22,000 and so on — but imagine how long the resulting graph would be! Instead, we can display information more compactly, in a smaller space, if we allow one point on the x-axis to represent a *range* of incomes. When we use one data point to represent a range, we're creating a *histogram*.

Figure 11 shows a histogram of estimated 2010 household income. Along the x-axis, we see various salary ranges. On the y-axis, we see what percentage of households fall into that income range.

How is such a histogram constructed? The first step is to "bin" data — by that, we mean to sort the data into bins, one for each salary range. In Figure 11, for example, each "bin" (except the last) holds a range of $4,999 ($5,000–$9,999; $10,000–$14,999; etc.). $4,999 is an arbitrary bin size — we could just as easily set bins that hold a range that is twice as big, or $10,000 each. Just know that the visualization will look different depending on the bin size — it will still be accurate, but different patterns may reveal themselves. It can take a few tries to figure out which bin size is most meaningful for your particular dataset. Neither of these choices is "correct" or even necessarily better than another. Each shows something slightly different about the data. Once we have made this transformation, then the histogram is really just a bar chart of these counts. The y-axis shows the count (this time, in percent) and the x-axis shows the bin that is being counted.

Tip

How do you know if you have a histogram or a bar chart? Look for number ranges on the axes, usually the x-axis.

Layered visualizations

Computers now make it easy for us to layer many kinds of data onto a single graphical image. These images can communicate a large volume of information in an efficient amount of space once one learns to read them. Figure 12 shows an example of one of these complex visualizations. This graph, from the open-source tools at Gapminder.org, the brainchild of data visualization expert

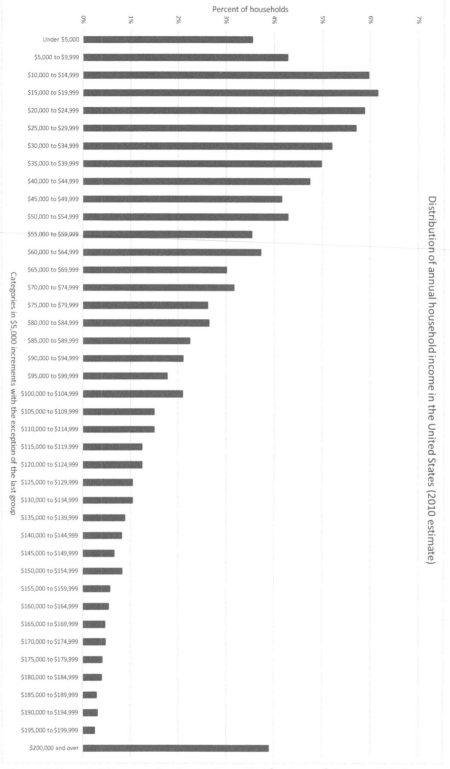

Figure 11: Household income distribution from 2010 [estimated]. Source: U.S. Census Bureau, Current Population Survey, 2011 Annual Social and Economic Supplement

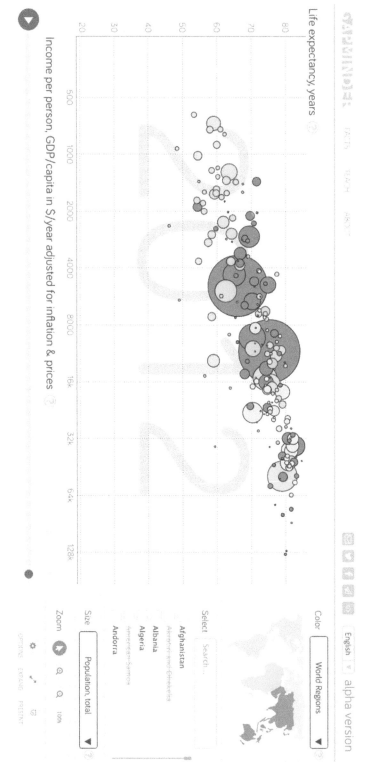

Figure 12: This chart, from the open-source tools at Gapminder.org, maps multiple variables onto a single graph.

Hans Rosling, allows us to see the relationship between a number of variables on a single graphic: life expectancy, income per person, population by country, and region of the world. Additionally, hovering over each bubble will reveal which country is represented by each bubble. We can peel back one layer at a time.

The graph puts *life expectancy* on the y-axis, with a range from 20 to 80+. Each tick mark represents a decade.

The x-axis shows *per person income*, but with one important change. Instead of equally spacing out the values on the x-axis, a logarithmic scale has been used. The first tick mark represents $500. The next tick mark doubles to $1,000 ... then doubles again at the next tick mark to $2,000 ... then $4,000 ... and so on. For students used to graphing on graph paper, with the interval between each point equal, this approach can seem illogical or confusing. However, this approach was used by Rosling and his team because this data is highly skewed (e.g., there are many countries with very low income and a few countries with very high income). If we were to plot the data linearly (like the birth rate data, with equal distance between each marked point on the axis) the vast majority of the data would be squished at the extreme ends of the x-axis.

Population is mapped in a different way: instead of using an axis to map the variable to a place, this graph represents it using the size of the bubble. Larger bubbles represent countries with larger population. This helps us establish a general sense of which nations' populations are larger and which are smaller, though one has to hover over a particular dot to reveal the nation's *name* and exact population. What this approach helps us see is that the largest countries fall somewhere in the middle of the trend.

The final variable is *region*. This is not a quantitative variable. We cannot intuitively represent it as size or position on an axis. Gapminder instead uses color — one matches the color of the bubble with the regional map provided in the upper-right corner. The graph directly converts each region into a specified color (e.g., green for North and South America). Again, being able to see where bubbles of similar color cluster adds to our understanding of human longevity and income.

Gapminder presents us with a complicated graph, but we can define each variable and how it has been mapped. By dissecting graphs in this way, we can understand exactly how they are made and what they are really showing us. For simple graphs, this level of analysis may appear unnecessary and uninformative, but as students encounter or make more complex graphs, carefully analyzing each step can reveal all sorts of insights, problems, and other ways the graph could be made.

Categories, quantities, colors, and shapes

In the prior examples, you may have noticed many of the datasets required an initial transformation before we could graph them. For example, when we made the pie chart, we converted our numbers to proportions and percents. With the histogram, we "binned" the data and graphed the count of values in each bin.

To better understand these transformations, we must distinguish between quantitative variables and qualitative variables. **Quantitative variables are numbers that measure some value**. On the other hand, **qualitative variables are categories that represent some quality**. Lingering over this distinction with students can clarify a number of issues that arise in data visualization. One important aspect of a quantitative variable is that it is the measure of some value (such as weight, height, income, or years) and not just that it is a number. For example, one occasionally sees survey data online where multiple choice answers are listed in the data as 1 or 2. If the question is about gender we can have data where a 1 represents female and a 2 represents male. Of course, these are numbers, but they are not really quantitative since they are merely stand-ins to represent categories of answers (in this case, gender). This is important to note, because a graphing program will likely not know these are categories rather than quantities, and this can easily lead to trouble with novices.

It is possible to convert values from quantitative to qualitative or vice-versa. We have already seen this in some of our examples from above. For instance, when we constructed "bins" for our histogram, we were in essence creating categories ($20,000–$24,999 is a category, even though the category represents numbers).

Taking numbers and putting them into discrete groups is a very common technique in data visualizations that allows us to create distinct bars (as in the histogram) or apply a color scale to a graph or map.

The map of median age by state in the United States (Figure 13) uses five colors to represent these values and each color corresponds to a range of values. We are visualizing numbers, but we first must convert them to groups (under 32; 32–35; 36–38; 39–41; above 41) and then color (lighter shades representing younger median ages, and darker shades representing older groups).

The decision as to what these groupings should be can dramatically impact the visualization. If, instead, we sort median ages into three categories (under 20; 20-30; and over 30), as shown in Figure 14, the map becomes nearly useless; it only tells us a little bit about Utah. All we know is that Utah has a younger median age as a state than any other state does ... but we lose the power of comparison among the other contiguous states.

Again, there is no exact formula for calculating which "bin" size is "best" — even expert designers experiment until they find an approach that delivers maximum meaning.

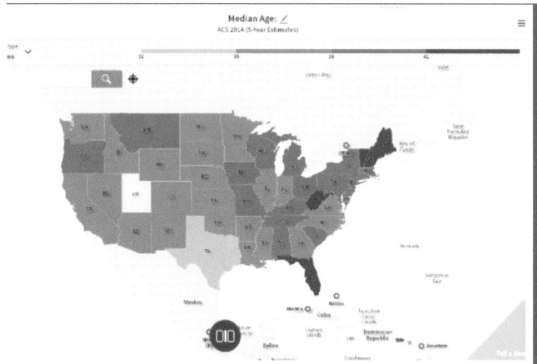

Figure 13: Map of median age in the U.S. made with SocialExplorer.com and visualized into five age groups: under 32, 32-35, 36-38, 39-41, and above 41 years of age.

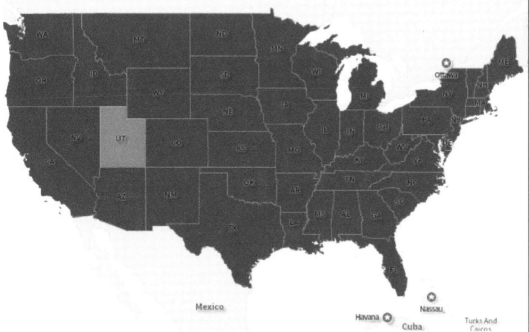

Figure 14: Map of median age in the U.S. made with SocialExplorer.com and visualized into three age groups: under 20, 20-30, and over 30 years of age.

Likewise, we can convert categories into quantities, although this is often less straightforward than the other way around. Imagine we have a survey with possible responses: strongly disagree, disagree, neutral, agree, strongly agree. It might make sense to treat these responses as 1, 2, 3, 4, 5 respectively (this is often called a Likert scale). But there are also other numerical conversions we can make based on the data.

One option is to *rank* the data and then use the ranking as a numerical value and organize the data based on that value. For example, Figure 15 is a bar chart showing state population ranked by population, with the y- or vertical axis sorted from the largest to the smallest. In a sense, then, the y-axis is displaying both qualitative data (the state name) and quantitative information (population). The data would look different if we arranged the state names alphabetically or by some other numeric variable such as the year each was granted statehood. Each rearrangement is purposeful and communicates very different information about the states.

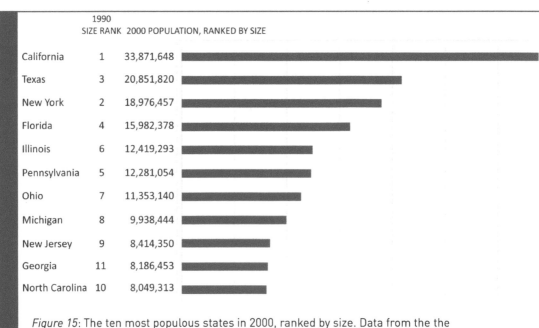

	1990 SIZE RANK	2000 POPULATION, RANKED BY SIZE
California	1	33,871,648
Texas	3	20,851,820
New York	2	18,976,457
Florida	4	15,982,378
Illinois	6	12,419,293
Pennsylvania	5	12,281,054
Ohio	7	11,353,140
Michigan	8	9,938,444
New Jersey	9	8,414,350
Georgia	11	8,186,453
North Carolina	10	8,049,313

Figure 15: The ten most populous states in 2000, ranked by size. Data from the the 2000 and 1990 decennial census.

Representing quantitative and qualitative data

Now that we have discussed how to transform between quantitative and qualitative data, we can explore ways to represent them in graphs. **Position** and **size** are the two main methods available for displaying quantitative data. In the complex Gapminder graph of life expectancy and income (Figure 12), both position and size of the dot were used to display quantitative information. Likewise, the pie chart of animate beings in Figure 8 used the size of pie pieces to represent quantities. The bar chart of state population (Figure 15) used vertical positioning as well as bar length to display the population.

Color and **symbol** are especially adept at showing qualitative data. The population maps use quantities (median age) converted into categories and then used color to differentiate each of these categories. Furthermore, for printing in black and white, shades of gray and different fill patterns (such as cross hatching) can also be used to represent qualitative data. Symbols can also be used to differentiate between categories of data — think back to childhood atlases that placed icons of cattle, factories, or sheaves of wheat inside states to represent common industries.

Color can also be used to display quantitative data directly, by creating a continuous color scale. In the topographical map of Figure 16, the continuous color scale is mapped directly to meters of depth and height, such that each value corresponds directly with a color rather than with a category. The key shows lower depths as blue hues and the highest heights as red. The continuous scale strategy tends to work well for directly mapping physical properties that have smooth transitions between values, like elevation or temperature. Keep in mind that data that tends to cluster together or be highly skewed, like income or population counts by state, can often be seen much more clearly by categorizing the values first and coloring by category.

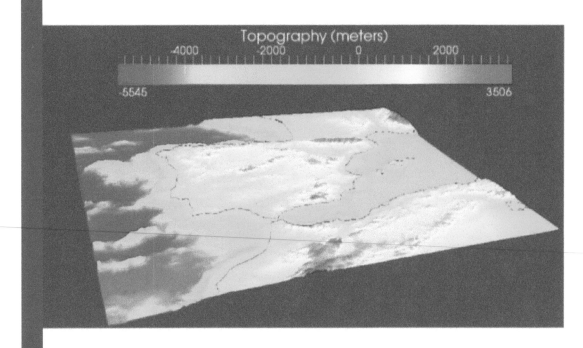

Figure 16: A topographical map using a continuous color scale to represent changing height and depth of water and land masses created with MMesh 3D. Image from https://mmesh3d.wikispaces.com/Images. CC-BY-NC-3.0.

As always, it is important to remember that there is no hard-and-fast rule, and the best choice will depend on the data. Moreover, when asking students to make visualizations, we should encourage them to try multiple strategies and see what best represents the data.

Students can learn a lot about a visualization by asking how data has been treated or collected as quantitative or as qualitative and then how those variables are represented in the graph. Sometimes multiple elements in a graph will be used to represent a single variable, such as in the bar chart of states where the bar width represented the actual population and the order on the y-axis represented the population relative to other states. Sometimes elements of a graph will represent nothing at all, a graph could just use a single color or randomly ordered bars for a bar chart.

Other times almost every possible element of a graph will be used to represent different variables, like the graph of income and life expectancy; although even that graph did not use different symbols. Some graphs work incredibly well by showing lots of complexity while others end up unreadable.

Likewise, some graphs that use a single element displaying only one variable beautifully demonstrate some deep insight while other simple graphs could easily be replaced with a table or even a few sentences.

Reading data visualizations

This chapter has focused largely on the ways in which data can be mapped to visual space and when such mappings work and when they do not. We have focused largely on the transformations and mappings that can be applied to data in order to create a diversity of visualizations. By studying the transformations and mappings necessary for a data visualization, students can discover whether a visualization succeeds and accurately represents the data.

Furthermore, through analysis, students can begin to build up a set of strategies that can be applied to any data to make visualizations. Our goal is not to deliver a lockstep set of rules but for students to think critically about how visualizations they encounter are created so that they can become savvier consumers and more thoughtful creators.

One of the best ways to learn effective data visualization is to see examples and make one's own visualizations. We have only touched on a limited number of transformations and mappings, but by exploring other data visualizations throughout the other chapters of this book and elsewhere, students will discover all sorts of options. By breaking down visualizations into smaller pieces, what a data visualization does can be understood, described, and taught.

These transformations and mappings ultimately succeed or fail in representing data based on how well they transform data to the visual space. A successful visualization makes reasonable choices for the data at hand and creates a visual space that can be read and understood. It is the spatial distribution of information that makes visualization so powerful.

We are able to see, as a result of these transformations of the data, important components and relations within the data. These transformations and mappings can range from simple counting to complex statistical functions. Likewise, they can be done by hand on small sets of data or using lots of computing power to transform huge datasets in real time. This range of possibilities and complexities make data visualization an exciting tool for teaching students of all levels about data and about any subject matter of interest, since visualization allows us to spot patterns and relations that otherwise would be inaccessible to human understanding. We should note a final danger that confronts data visualization, but has little to do with exactly what type of graph is used to present the data. As humans we are incredibly sensitive to patterns. This is what makes data visualization so powerful. When data is displayed in space, we can quickly pick out interesting patterns and relationships. Often these patterns provide us with deep insights into the nature of our world, but on occasion we can see patterns that do not really exist or are the result of random chance. Especially today, with so much data easily available, it is possible to find patterns that hold no real meaning or predictive power.

Tyler Vigen (Figure 17) has created an algorithm dedicated to searching out such random patterns in order to demonstrate how seemingly strong patterns can be found among random pairs of data. While of course it is possible that there is some relationship between the divorce rate in Maine and consumption of margarine, it is most likely that this is simply a coincidence. (See Chapter 1 for more discussion on correlation and causation.)

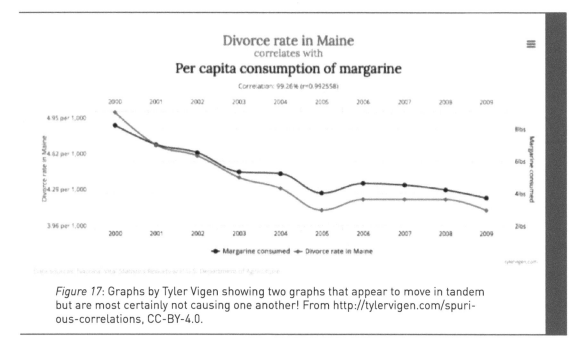

Figure 17: Graphs by Tyler Vigen showing two graphs that appear to move in tandem but are most certainly not causing one another! From http://tylervigen.com/spurious-correlations, CC-BY-4.0.

Even the most compelling and well-created visualizations should not be taken as the final truth. We should always bear in mind that we may be seeing a random coincidence.

Conclusion

Educators often hear that students can absorb visual information in less than the blink of an eye. But effective data visualizations should be seen as a chance to ask more questions rather than as something that offers a definitive answer.

» **Where does the data come from?**

» **What would the visualization look like if we had more data?**

» **What other aspects of the data would be interesting to see?**

Educators can teach students a lot about the how data is transformed into a visualization. What colors work well to convey your message? Which statistical methods were used to summarize the data? If students understand how these transformations are made, they will have a deeper knowledge of the topic at hand, and they can translate data into simple bar charts or complex interactive visualizations to enhance the understanding of others. Ultimately, it is through these transformations and mappings that data visualization either succeeds or fails to tell us something interesting about the world around us, or even more importantly to inspire us to ask more questions and investigate further.

Resources

Manovich, Lev. 2010. "What is visualization?" Manovich.net, Mar - Oct. Accessed April 17, 2017. http://manovich.net/content/04-projects/064-what-is-visualization/61_article_2010.pdf

Perry, Marc J., Paul J. Mackun, Josephine D. Baker, Colleen D. Joyce, Lisa R. Lollock, and Lucinda S. Pearsson. 2001. "Population Change and Distribution 1990 - 2000." U.S. Census. Accessed April 17, 2017. https://www.census.gov/prod/2001pubs/c2kbr01-2.pdf

7 | Data presentation: Showcasing your data with charts and graphs

Tierney Steelberg

You've run the numbers; you've got your data — now it's time to present it. You may be feeling pressure to go all out and make your data look like the intricate data visualizations you see in the news — but you can create charts and graphs right now, without breaking a sweat or needing to learn new software from scratch! You can build your argument around data that you bring together in simple spreadsheet software. It's amazing what simply focusing on the data and embracing clean, uncluttered design can do for getting your argument across.

This chapter will start by going over some tips to help you best present any data. Then it will delve into the specifics of some chart and graph types that are useful in a variety of different contexts and great to have on hand. This chapter will help you match your data (and your question) to a particular means of presentation and provide you with tips for creating compelling charts and graphs.

General rules of thumb

» **Clarity and simplicity are key.**

Remember to keep things simple: let the data speak for itself. You don't need neon colors or myriad thematic icons to get a point across. Data visualizations should be a combination of visual appeal and clearly represented information, but if you have to choose, be simple.

If you find that your chart is getting overly complicated, think about splitting it up into multiple charts. This can make the information easier to read and absorb.

» **Make it easy to read and interpret.**

Help your readers understand the point you are trying to make with your data. Start by giving your visualization an informative title. Provide a legend and labels: make it clear what symbols, colors, and sizes mean, and be consistent in their usage. Emphasize the units you are using. You can even use arrows and concise phrases to call attention to important elements of your chart.

When dealing with information sorted into categories (i.e., non-numeric information), organize values in a meaningful order (such as ascending or descending in terms of their values) to make it easy for others to compare values.

When using colors, use hues that stand out from one another or use a saturation spectrum (going from very light to very dark) of a single color, making sure your reader can easily distinguish between hues. Avoid using color combinations that are hard to distinguish for readers who are colorblind (such as reds with greens, or blues with yellows).

» **Respect visual and mathematical principles.**

When using shapes to convey data, size them proportionally according to their area, rather than their length or diameter. Separate your data into variables. A variable is a characteristic or quantity that can be counted. For example, if you are creating a bar chart comparing the total populations of different countries, the variable you're looking at is population (and the numbers for each country are the different values).

Keep things in two dimensions, preferably: 3D shapes are difficult to read and compare. The perspective that is used to create the illusion of three dimensions can also be confusing for readers by accidentally making some items feel larger or smaller than they really are.

A lot of visualizations include icons, or small pictures, as decoration. Consider leaving these out. Even when they match your data, they can distract from the point you are trying to make. They often make it more difficult to make comparisons and assess differences. Stick with plain representative shapes instead.

» **Play around with your data!**

It's easy to test out a couple different charts and see which ones do a good job showcasing your data — and which ones do not: play around with the tools at your disposal to get an idea for what feels right for visualizing an individual dataset. Excel and Google Sheets are good starting points: you can switch from chart to chart at the click of a button, and it's easy to customize general elements.

You might find things you hadn't noticed before, (trends, patterns, outliers — or even typos or errors in the data) and you'll definitely get a good sense of what charts and graphs are a good fit for your data.

» **Cite your sources.**

Finally, always give the source of your data so others can investigate for themselves. It's like providing a bibliography at the end of a paper: it's good scholarly practice, and it lets your readers know your data comes from a legitimate source.

If you created the data yourself (like with a class survey), consider providing it in its entirety. This allows readers to check your findings, and even play around with your data themselves.

Useful charts & graphs

Any graph or chart has its own strengths and weaknesses in presenting different datasets. To pick the best one, think about the story you are trying to tell or the question you are trying to answer. Consider these different chart and graph types — and their accompanying questions and suggestions — as you choose a means to present your data.

Pie charts

A *pie chart* showcases the parts of a whole or percentages of a total.

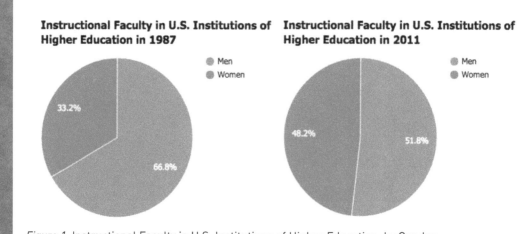

Figure 1. Instructional Faculty in U.S. Institutions of Higher Education, by Gender: Comparison of 1987 and 2011. Created with Google Sheets. Data source: National Center for Education Statistics (https://nces.ed.gov/programs/digest/d13/tables/dt13_315.10.asp).

The pie charts in Figure 1 showcase the breakdown by gender of the number of faculty members at institutions of higher education in the United States in two different years, 1987 and 2011. (See Appendix A for the data.) If x is the variable representing the number of men in the chart, and y is the variable representing the number of women, what do you notice? What information does the chart communicate?

? With x and y as slices of the pie, a pie chart answers questions like:

- What percentage of the whole is x?
- What is the composition of the whole? What elements, combined, create the whole?
- Is y's portion of the whole bigger than x's? How do x and y compare?

In Figure 1, the pie charts answer questions like:

» **What percentage of the total do women faculty members make up?**

» **How do the percentage of men and the percentage of women compare?**

Since there are two charts, both depicting the same thing in different moments in time, you can also compare them to one another.

These pie charts tell us that, while women made up one third of faculty members in the United States in 1987, in 2011 they made up almost one half of the total number of faculty members. Together, these two charts tell a more complex story than they would separately, because they show an evolution in time. In some ways, these pie charts are limited: we know only percentages, not raw values. In other ways, it is good to not have too much information because it allows the reader to focus on the most relevant information. You have to make a decision about the authentic interpretation of the data into a visualization. It would be interesting to know how the total number of instructional faculty had changed between 1987 and 2011. But if you just want to show how the ratio of male to female faculty has changed, the pie charts do an admirable job.

> **! Tips**
>
> - **Our eyes compare the angles of pie chart segments, rather than their area, so it's hard to visually compare a pie chart with more than two or three segments:** for a whole with more than two or three parts, consider an alternative for showcasing parts of a whole (like a bar chart, discussed later in this chapter) instead.
>
> - **When using percentages, the total must add up to 100%.** If you are trying to show responses from survey questions where respondents could pick multiple answers, resulting in totals of greater than 100%, then consider a bar chart instead.

Waffle charts: A pie chart alternative

A waffle chart, also known as square pie chart, can also be used to showcase the parts of a whole or percentages of a total. It consists of a large square divided into smaller squares: small squares can be colored in proportionally to the part or percentage that is being represented.

Whereas with a pie chart the reader is looking at the angles of segments in order to make a comparison, with a waffle chart the reader can analyze the area of segments or the number of individual boxes that make them up. These spatial differences are easier to assess than the differences between angles.

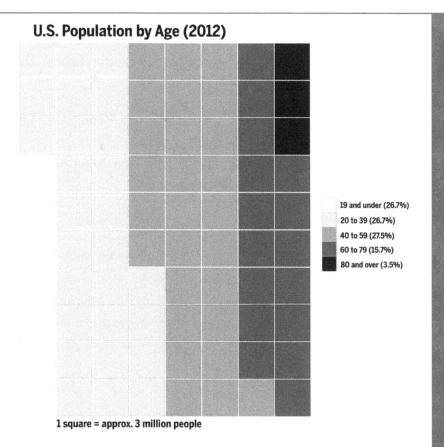

U.S. Population by Age (2012)

19 and under (26.7%)
20 to 39 (26.7%)
40 to 59 (27.5%)
60 to 79 (15.7%)
80 and over (3.5%)

1 square = approx. 3 million people

Figure 2. U.S. Population by Age (2012). Created in R (with waffle and ggplot2 packages). Data source: United States Census Bureau (http://www.census.gov/population/age/data/2012comp.html, Table 1).

The waffle chart in Figure 2 displays the U.S. population in 2012 as a whole, segmented by age groups that are each indicated by their own color. What do you think of this chart type? Does it do a good job conveying information about the breakdown of the U.S. population by age?

? **With these segments, a waffle chart answers questions like:**

- What percentage of the whole is each segment?
- What is the composition of the whole? What elements, combined, create the whole?
- How do the combinations of segments compare to each other?

In Figure 2, the waffle chart can answer questions like:

> » What percentage of the whole U.S. population in 2012 was under the age of 19?

> » What was the breakdown of the U.S. population in 2012?

> » How does the number of 40- to 59-year-olds compare to the number of 60- to 79-year-olds?

It is tricky to compare segments to one another in this chart, since the segments are quite close in size to begin with, and the chart rounds the percentage values. But you can see clearly how there are progressively fewer people in the older age brackets, as the organization is more meaningful than in a pie chart, and the waffle chart is not as crowded as a pie chart would be with five segments.

Tip

- **Waffle charts are not currently a default chart option in basic spreadsheet software, but there are tutorials online for the steps required to create them.** See Best Excel Tutorial or the *Bacon Bits* blog from Data Pig Technologies for two different methods.

Bar charts

A *bar chart* or *bar graph* displays values assigned to individual categories. Each bar represents an entire, exact value for a variable in question.

Figure 3 shows the number of male and female faculty members at institutions of higher education in the U.S. between 1987 and 2011. Here, the variable is gender. Each year gets two bars: one for the number of women and one for the number of men. The values from our earlier pie charts in Figure 1 are at either end of the chart, in 1987 and in 2011. What do you think about this chart? How does it convey information differently than the Figure 1 pie charts?

Figure 3. Number of Instructional Faculty in U.S. Institutions of Higher Education, by Gender (1987-2011). Created with Google Sheets. Data source: National Center for Education Statistics (https://nces.ed.gov/programs/digest/d13/tables/dt13_315.10.asp).

? With x as a variable, a bar chart answers questions like:

- Which category has the highest or lowest x?
- How does x vary across different categories?
- How do multiple categories compare to one another?

In Figure 3, the bar chart answers questions like:

» **Which year has the highest number of female faculty?**

» **How does the number of male faculty compare to the number of female faculty in 1991?**

» **How does the number of female faculty in 1987 compare to the number of female faculty in 2011?**

The chart in Figure 3 tells an interesting story. You can see that, while both grow, the number of female faculty grows at a more rapid rate than the number of male faculty: between 1987 and 2011, the number of female faculty has almost tripled. This chart helps you compare this information more effectively than a pie chart for each year would, since you can compare each bar to all the other bars. These bar charts provide a bigger picture than the pie charts in Figure 1: here, we see both the ratio of men to women, by comparing the two bars for a given year, and the raw numbers that show how much the number of faculty has grown between 1987 and 2011.

Note that the bar chart in Figure 3 showcases data that is continuous: the years depicted have a sequential order, so you can talk about an upward trend, or growth, in faculty members as years go by and you can observe an evolution from one set of bars to another. But bar charts do not necessarily have to showcase continuous data: they can also showcase data for distinct categories. In a bar chart showing the total populations of different countries, each country is a separate entity: you can compare the values associated with them, but you can't chart an evolution between them.

> **Tip**
> - **Bar charts in math class always start at 0, because each bar is intended to represent a whole value.** Bar charts in real life don't always do so, so when you are creating or reading a bar chart, be careful that you observe the y-axis's labels. If you would like to highlight a difference between categories and a bar chart just isn't cutting it, try a dot plot, or even a line graph (for continuous data, like data across different moments in time).
> - **Remember the rule of thumb on clarity and simplicity.** Bar charts showing more than 2 or 3 variables for each category can get crowded and hard to read: consider instead a multipanel display of separate bar charts for each variable.

A dot plot, also known as the Cleveland dot plot after its inventor, is similar to a bar chart in that it showcases values assigned to individual categorical elements — but instead of showing the entire value in the form of a bar, it plots the value as a single dot.

One advantage of dot plots is that they do not have to start at 0, so you can hone in on slight differences between elements — do not forget to clearly label your numerical axis, though! Another advantage of dot plots is that you can use them to display multiple values for each element (such as values from different years), by using different symbols and labeling them in a legend. Readers can then compare the multiple values of a single element or compare the same value type across elements.

The dot plot in Figure 4 shows amounts of money allocated to various categories of the 2009 U.S. government budget. Does the dot plot format encourage us to look at the data differently than bar chart does? If so, how?

> **? With x and y as two different variables, a dot plot answers questions like:**
> - Which category has the highest or lowest x?
> - How does x vary across different categories?
> - How do x and y vary across different categories?

The dot plot in Figure 4 answers questions like:

» **Which category is allocated the most money in the budget?**

» **How does allocation vary across different categories?**

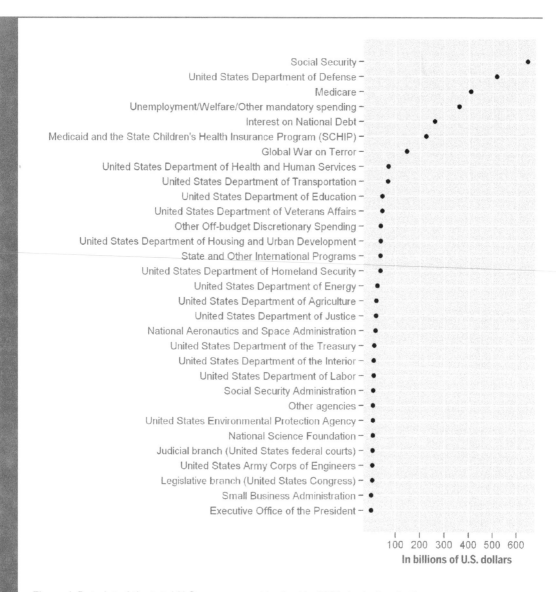

Figure 4. Dot plot of the total U.S. government budget in 2009, including both mandatory and discretionary, by Thopper, licensed under CC-BY-SA. Source: Wikipedia (https://commons.wikimedia.org/wiki/File:U.S.2009FederalExpenditures.png).

Figure 4 minimizes clutter on the chart, by using dots instead of bars, which can make it easier to compare values to one another. You can see that over twice as much is allocated to Social Security, the category with the highest value, than to interest on the national debt. You can also see that the top five or six categories are allocated quite a bit more money than the others. With a dot plot, it seems easier to observe subtle differences in the smallest values: these details might be lost in a bar chart. The dot plot could easily handle one or two more variables with very little trouble: another symbol could be used to plot values from a different year for each category, on the same line.

Tip

- **Dot plots are not currently a default chart option in basic spreadsheet software,** but there are tutorials online for the steps required to create them: they are a worthy addition to a basic repertoire of charts. See Evergreen Data for a how-to.

Maps

A *map* can be used to display a continuous spectrum of values (such as population density or the percentage of the workforce that is unemployed): this is often indicated through changes in color and shading. Color and shading can also be used on a map to help convey information about categories (like coloring states, usually red and blue, to indicate the presidential candidate preference of the states' voters).

A map can also be used to display data points on the map itself: these can be figurative (like lines indicating migration movement from area to area, or points indicating a certain number of unemployed people in a particular area) or literal (like true-to-life depictions of roads and rivers).

Tip

- **Always include a legend with your map** to explain the meaning of any colors and symbols used to convey data.

Figure 5 is a map of the United States that shows the population density of each state, using a saturation spectrum that goes from light purple for the least dense states to very dark purple for the most dense ones. A map that uses this type of proportional shading to convey values is known as a *choropleth map*. What information does this choropleth map convey?

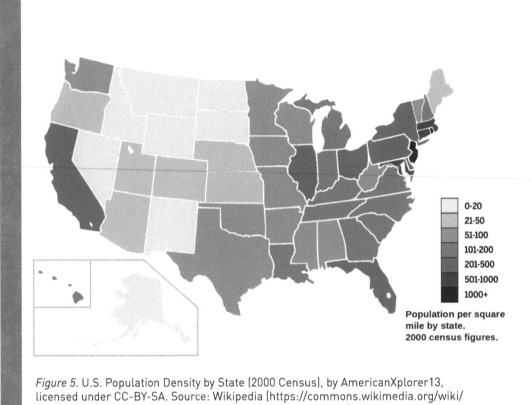

Figure 5. U.S. Population Density by State (2000 Census), by AmericanXplorer13, licensed under CC-BY-SA. Source: Wikipedia (https://commons.wikimedia.org/wiki/File:US_2000_census_population_density_map_by_state.svg).

Population density is a continuous spectrum of values, so Figure 5 answers questions like:

» **What are the most dense states?**

» **Are there patterns in the density or lack thereof?**

» **How does one state compare to another?**

You can see from their color which states are the most densely populated, and which are the least. The map is a familiar chart type: you can make deductions based on what you already know about the area (such as the locations of big cities, or of geographic features like mountains) that might affect population density. This map shows data at the state level: it could be interesting to see what population density looks like at the county level.

With x as a continuous spectrum of values, a map answers questions like:

- Where do certain values from x occur?
- Are there patterns?
- Where is x most concentrated?
- Where is x highest or lowest?
- How does one place compare to another?

With y as a category, a map answers questions like:

- Where does y occur?
- Are there patterns?
- How does one place compare to another?

With z as a data point representing color intensity, a map answers questions like:

- Are there patterns?
- Why are the z intervals broken up into unequal intervals (0-20 vs 501-1000)?

Line charts

A *line chart* or *line graph* displays data points on a graph, plotted according to a quantitative (i.e., numeric) variable and a continuous variable (often time is used). The data must be continuous or ordered so as to connect the dots with a line. Line charts depicting the evolution of something over time are also called "time series."

With y as a continuous variable, a line chart answers questions like:

- How does x evolve over time?
- When was x highest or lowest?
- Does x rise or fall in a seeming pattern?

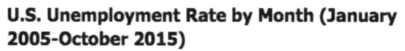

U.S. Unemployment Rate by Month (January 2005-October 2015)

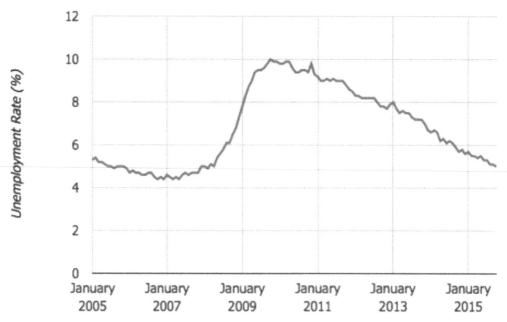

Figure 6. U.S. Unemployment Rate by Month (January 2005-October 2015). Created with Google Sheets. Data source: Bureau of Labor Statistics (http://data.bls.gov/timeseries/LNS14000000).

In Figure 6, the line chart answers questions like:

» **How did the unemployment rate evolve over time?**

» **When in this period of time was the unemployment rate highest? And when was it lowest?**

From this chart, you can see how the unemployment rate often rises and falls by small amounts from month to month. The big spike in early 2008 (between January 2007 and January 2009) can be explained using some background knowledge: that is when the recession hit. It could be helpful for this chart to add an annotation there (perhaps an arrow) to explain this sudden climb, since its cause is known.

Scatterplots

A *scatterplot* or *scattergraph* displays the values of a dataset with two quantitative, or numeric, variables. It plots every individual data point onto a single graph: the position of each point is dictated by the two variables, one on the x-axis and another on the y-axis.

When using a scatterplot, look for clusters of points, points that seem to follow a line (this implies correlation between the variables on the axes), and points that are set apart from the rest (these are called outliers).

> ## ? A scatterplot answers questions like:
>
> - Does x correlate to y?
> - What are the outliers in my data?
> - What are the patterns in my data?

The scatterplot in Figure 7 plots the total bill on the x-axis and tips received on the y-axis. Each dot is thus connected to two values: that of the total bill, and that of the tip associated with it. The line offers an annotation that helps you read the scatterplot: it shows where tips that are 16% of the total bill would be. Points above the line are tips greater than 16% of the bill, and points below it are tips less than 16% of the bill. What information does the chart help you understand? Is it effective?

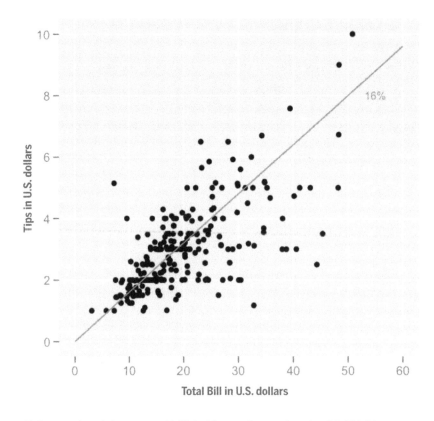

Figure 7. Scatterplot of tips vs. total bill, by Visnut, licensed under CC-BY-SA.
Source: Wikipedia (https://commons.wikimedia.org/wiki/File:Tips-scat1.png).

In Figure 7, the scatterplot answers questions like:

> » **Does a bigger bill correlate to a bigger tip?**
> » **What are the outliers in the scatterplot?**
> » **What are the patterns in the scatterplot?**

You can infer quite a bit of information from this scatterplot. There is a slight upward trend: this means that, in general, a bigger bill has a positive correlation with a bigger tip. There are some outliers in this data if you look closely. Someone tipped a little over $1 on a $33 bill, which is only a 3% tip. And someone else tipped a little over $5 on a bill that was about $7, which is a 71% tip! Points seem to cluster around a certain part of the graph: it seems like quite a few customers had bills that were between $10 and $20.

• **Correlation does not imply causation**: just because a correlation seems to exist between two variables does not mean that one causes the other.

• **If your scatterplot becomes too dense to read, consider making points opaque, or using another type of graph.**

Bubble charts

A *bubble chart* is similar to a scatterplot: data points are mapped onto a graph depending on two variables along the x- and y-axes. But a bubble chart introduces a third variable: the size of the data points, represented as bubbles, also conveys information about data elements. The bubbles can even be colored according to categories to which they belong. This can be useful when you want to visualize the potential relationships between three different variables.

The chart in Figure 8 showcases how intricate a bubble chart can be: you will probably want to go to the source and look at it more closely. Each bubble represents a country (and is helpfully labeled accordingly): a bubble's position on the x-axis is determined by the country's income per person, its position on the y-axis is determined by the percent of adults in the country infected with HIV, and its size indicates the raw number of people living with HIV in that country. The color of the bubble corresponds to the area in the world in which the country is located.

The bubble chart in Figure 8 answers questions like:

> **Are there correlations between any of the variables?**

> **Are there patterns in the data?**

> **Where are individual countries located on the chart, and what do their positions mean?**

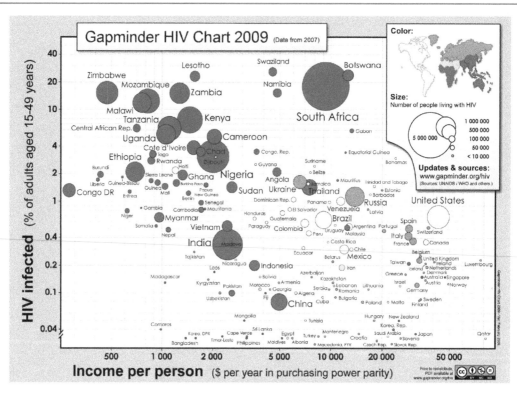

Figure 8. Gapminder HIV Chart 2009 (Data from 2007). Free material from gap-minder.org, licensed under CC-BY. Source: Gapminder (http://www.gapminder.org/downloads/gapminder-hiv-chart-2009/).

? With x as the x-axis variable, y as the y-axis variable, and z as the size variable, a bubble chart answers questions like:

- Does x correlate to y? Does x correlate to z? Does y correlate to z?

- Are there exceptions to correlations?

- What are the outliers in my data?

- What are the patterns in my data?

- What do the position, size, and color of an individual point mean for that point?

- How do multiple points compare across the board with one another?

It is hard to notice trends and patterns in this chart, since it contains so much information. Sometimes it can be more mean-ingful to read this kind of packed chart for information about individual points, rather than for overview information about the dataset as a whole. You can look at the dots for individual countries to learn more about them or to compare them to one another. But there are a few larger patterns you can glean from this chart. For example, many of the countries with the highest percentages of HIV infection are in Africa: the vast majority of the points high on the y-axis are blue. Additionally, many of the countries with high percentages of HIV infection are on the lower end for income per person (and the reverse seems true as well): this implies a correlation between the two variables.

> **! Tips**
>
> - **Bubble charts can get crowded because big bubbles can start to overlap:** use datasets that don't have too many individual elements.
>
> - **Label your bubbles so your reader can understand what element data refer to.**
>
> - **Use a legend to indicate the meaning of color and size.**
>
> - **Remember that correlation does not imply causation, as we discussed with scatterplots.**

Histograms

A *histogram* shows the distribution of a quantitative dataset. It may look like a bar chart, but it displays numeric (rather than categorical) data, and there is a mathematical logic behind the sizes of the bars. A histogram groups values into consecutive numeric ranges or intervals, also known as *bins*: the more values from a dataset fall within a particular range, the bigger its bar. The ranges are continuous, so bars do not usually have much space between them (unlike bar charts, which use the spaces between bars to distinguish between categories).

A histogram is useful because it gives a meaningful overview of data. For example, imagine you want a chart that shows the heights of students in a ninth-grade math class. It is unlikely that two people would be the exact same height, so it might be more interesting to show how many people fall into ranges of heights, rather than the exact heights of each person. You can set your own intervals, for example, 0.5 feet, and then display the people with heights between 4.5 and 5 feet in one bin, people with heights between 5.1 and 5.5 feet in the next bin, and so on. The bin gets bigger with each value that is added to it. By looking at which one is the biggest, you can see at a glance where values are most concentrated — also known as which interval of values has the highest frequency.

> **?** **A histogram answers questions like:**
> - What are the patterns in my data?
> - In what intervals do data points have the highest frequency (i.e., in what intervals are data points most concentrated)?
> - What is the distribution of my data? Does it skew a certain way?

With the overview offered by a histogram, you can immediately see if your data skews a certain way, and investigate further. Unlike box plots (up next), histograms show variation between values, since you can change the interval size of the bins.

The two histograms in Figure 9 both showcase the same data: tips given in a restaurant. But the sizes of the intervals (the bins) are different. The histogram at the top has a $1 bin width. And the histogram at the bottom has a 10¢ bin width: this allows you to see the data in greater detail. What do the two different histograms tell you about the data?

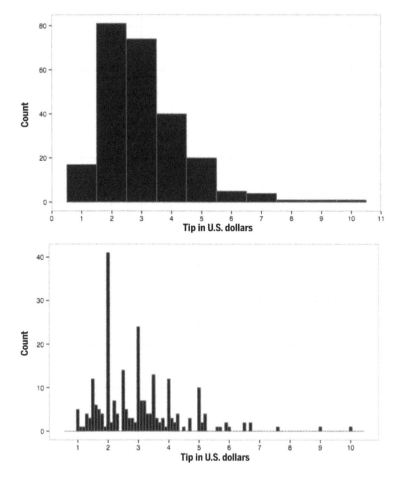

Figure 9. Histograms of tips given in a restaurant, with both a $1 bin width (top) and a 10¢ bin width (bottom), by Visnut, licensed under CC-BY-SA. Source: Wikipedia (https:// en.wikipedia.org/wiki/File:Tips-histogram1.png and https://en.wikipedia. org/wiki/ File:Tips-histogram2.png).

The two histograms in Figure 9 answer questions like:

» **What are the patterns in the tips?**

» **In what intervals do the most tips fall?**

» **What is the distribution of the data?**

Both bin widths used by the two histograms reveal different patterns in the data. The histogram with the $1 bin width demonstrates very clearly that the data skews to the right (i.e., to smaller rather than larger tips — since that's where the highest frequencies are on the graph). It shows that the range with the highest frequency is $1.5 to $2.5. The histogram with the 10¢ bin width shows an interesting pattern: tips that are round dollar amounts have higher frequencies. It also shows more precisely what range has the highest frequency: it is the $1.95 to $2.05 range.

> **!** **Tip**
> - **Play around with your histogram's breakpoints — the interval size of the bins in which your data is placed (in the heights example, interval size could be 1 foot, 0.5 feet, or even 0.25 feet):** by changing the way you display your data, you can learn more about its distribution. You will notice that histograms that are too detailed and histograms that are not detailed enough are difficult to read and convey very little useful information about the dataset. Laerd Statistics gives a helpful rundown of this (with some example images) under "Choosing the Correct Bin Width."

Box plots

A *box plot*, also known as a box-and-whiskers or merely a whisker plot, shows the distribution of a quantitative dataset. It uses a dataset's quartiles to create a box that can provide overview information about the dataset. Quartiles are the three values that divide a dataset into four equal parts. The middle quartile is more commonly known as the median: it is the value that divides a dataset into two equal parts (as in, there as many values above the median as there are below it).

In a box plot, the quartiles are represented as lines that form a box, with the median as a line dividing the box in two. The upper and lower extremities of the dataset are represented as lines emanating from the box (these are the whiskers): the ends of the lines show the maximum and minimum of the dataset, respectively. Outliers are points that fall more than one and a half times away from either end of the box plot: these outliers are traditionally represented as individual points outside of the box plot. The whole box plot is shown on a graph, so values can be located quickly and easily.

Like histograms, box plots can be helpful for getting a very general overview of your dataset: you can see if your data skews a certain way (by gauging the range between quartiles), and investigate further.

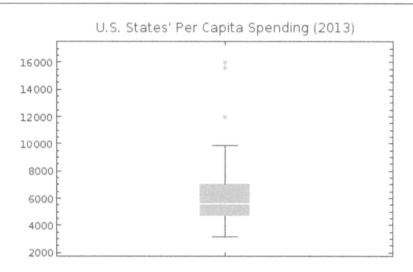

Figure 10. U.S. States' Per Capita Spending in 2013. Created with Google Sheets and g(Math) for Sheets. Data source: The Henry J. Kaiser Family Foundation. (http://kff.org/other/state-indicator/per-capita-state-spending/).

The box plot in Figure 10 showcases the distribution of a dataset of individual U.S. states' per capita spending in 2013. The median is the white line bisecting the orange box. The orange dots toward the top of the graph are outliers. What do you notice about the distribution of this dataset? Does the box plot seem like a helpful way to get an overview of a dataset?

? **A box plot answers questions like:**
- What is the median of my dataset?
- What is the distribution of my data? Does it skew a certain way?

This box plot answers questions like:

> » **what is the median of per capita spending by state?**
> » **what is the distribution of the data?**

The median sits low in the box: this means that the data skews toward the bottom, which is to say toward lower per capita spending. The data has quite a wide range: the lowest value is around $3,000 and the highest (which is one of three outliers) is about $16,000 — that's a range of $13,000! It would be interesting to compare multiple box plots, each showing states' per capita spending for a different year, to see if and how the range and skew of the data might change.

Tips

- **Multiple box plots can be mapped onto a single graph** to show distribution of several datasets at once and draw quick comparisons between them.

- **There is an add-on for Google Sheets called "g(Math) for Sheets"** that allows you to create box plots with ease. Unfortunately, you can only plot a single box plot onto the graph you create.

Conclusion

Next time you need to create a chart or graph, think about these examples and the kinds of questions they provoke. Consider the rules of thumb from the beginning of the chapter, and how you might put them into practice. Try out a few different types of charts and graphs with your data before you decide on one. Experimentation is key to seeing new patterns and envisioning new ways of representing your data.

The other key to successful data presentation is to learn from other people's charts and graphs. Notice visualizations as you come across them in your daily life (or, even better, seek them out) and think about the questions they answer and the way they are used. Think deeply: what stories do they tell? are they misleading? what do you like about them, and what might you do differently? The critical eye that you develop will help you make more compelling charts and graphs yourself.

Once you have created a visualization that you like, check your work against the questions and rules of thumb in this chapter, and you'll be on your way to communicating your data effectively!

Resources

Abela, Andrew W. 2006. Choosing a good chart. Extreme Presentation (blog), September 6. Accessed April 19, 2017. http://extremepresentation.typepad.com/blog/2006/09/choosing_a_good.html

Cleveland, W. S. 1993. *Visualizing data*. Summit, NJ: Hobart Press.

R Core Team 2015. R: A language and environment for statistical computing. R Foundation for Statistical Computing, Vienna, Austria. Accessed April 19, 2017. https://www.R-project.org/.

Robbins, N. B. 2004. *Creating more effective graphs*. Hoboken, NJ : Wiley-Interscience.

Tufte, E. R. 1983. *The visual display of quantitative information*. Cheshire, CT: Graphics Press.

Vital, Anna. (2015, March 6). How to think visually using visual analogies. Anna Vital (blog), March 6. Accessed April 19, 2017. http://anna.vc/post/112863438962/how-to-think-using-visual-analogies .

Yau, Nathan 2008. How to read and use a box-and-whisker plot. *FlowingData* (blog), February 15. Accessed April 19, 2017. http://flowingdata.com/2008/02/15/how-to-read-and-use-a-box-and-whisker-plot/

Yau, Nathan. 2009. "9 ways to visualize proportions – a guide". *FlowingData* (blog), November 25. Accessed April 19, 2017. http://flowingdata.com/2009/11/25/9-ways-to-visualize-proportions-a-guide/

Yau, Nathan. 2010. "11 ways to visualize changes over time – a guide". *FlowingData* (blog), January 7. Accessed April 19, 2017. http://flowingdata.com/2010/01/07/11-ways-to-visual¬ize-changes-over-time-a-guide/

Yau, Nathan. 2013. *Data points: visualization that means something*. Indianapolis, IN: John Wiley & Sons.

Appendix A

This table represents data from the National Center for Education Statistics on the gender breakdown of faculty members in higher education between 1987 and 2011.

Number of Instructional Faculty in U.S. Institutions of Higher Education		
Year	Men	Women
1987	529,413	263,657
1989	534,254	289,966
1991	525,599	300,653
1993	561,123	354,351
1995	562,893	368,813
1997	587,420	402,393
1999	602,469	425,361
2001	644,514	468,669
2003	663,723	509,870
2005	714,453	575,973
2007	743,812	627,578
2009	761,035	678,109
2011	789,197	734,418

Instructional Faculty in U.S. Institutions of Higher Education, by Gender. Data source: National Center for Education Statistics

8 | Deconstructing data visualizations: What every teen should know

Susan Smith

Emily wakes up to the sound of her cell phone alarm, thinking about what lies ahead for her at school as a high school senior. Her phone screen lights up with today's celebrity news, texts from friends, and calendar reminders of school assignments. Before she puts her feet on the floor, she posts to her Facebook page and checks the day's news, laden with images, graphs, and charts. In her first period environmental science class, the textbook requires her to decipher a chart depicting climate change in order to project the consequences of continued warming. During her free period she decides to research her father's recently diagnosed heart disease, as she's feeling anxious about the family discussion last evening. After school she's in charge of reporting her lacrosse team's stats to the school newspaper, then remembers she needs more acne medicine, and checks online reviews and data to see which one is most effective. Before she leaves school, friends reminded her to register to vote in the upcoming primary, but she is unconvinced that young voters can really make a difference, so she consults her state's polling data.

Each of these activities involves data analysis and reading data in visualized form, some of it rather sophisticated. Today's information universe is vast, and there is too little time to scrutinize data, especially when it is embedded in colorful graphics with a convincing message. Data visualization has long been used by academic researchers to summarize their findings, but more recently publishers and commercial marketing firms have embraced the use of visualization to impart information in new ways that are attractive and space-efficient (Centaur Communications 2010). These graphics draw the reader in, provide an instant takeaway, and are easy to share on social media. In order to *read* these charts, graphs, and statistics, today's teen needs a toolkit for data literacy that requires a critical eye and a keen understanding of the creator's intentions.

How do we move beyond a simple check of the sponsoring website that published the information? When data and graphics have different creators, how do we evaluate the infographic – holistically or piecemeal?

As educators, we must model what it means to be a critical consumer of data visualizations and other visual representations of data while at the same time giving our students a few rules of thumb to help simplify the process in their everyday lives. We can promote healthy skepticism by helping students learn how to effectively *question* what they view. Students love to critique things; we can teach them a framework to do this constructively. By doing so, we can help them grapple with uncertainty and use their questions to spur further investigation. Evaluating data visualizations across the curriculum as well as providing opportunities for students to create their own visual depictions of real world data are important additions to 21st-century information literacy skills.

You may be thinking, *Why can't I just leave data literacy to math and science teachers?* We know post-secondary students will likely contribute to the creation of data in their discipline and must become proficient at content-specific data visualizations. The challenge in high school is to both scaffold for these advanced academic skills as well as to prepare students to intelligently consume visualized data in their everyday lives. To this end, analyzing graphs and charts "in the wild" teaches them to identify misleading or ambiguous representations. Surveys of college faculty reveal that while students master the use of chart- and map-making tools quickly, they do not know what makes a *good* visualization (Carlson and Johnston 2015).

In a 2012 Pew study on teens and technology, media expert Sam Punnet observed, "[A]ll communications [in the teen world] must be short, visual, and distracting/entertaining" (in Anderson and Rainie 2012). Data visualizations fit this bill; they tell a story in a compact combination of words and images. Data are often embedded in infographics to lend credibility; after all, numbers do not lie ... do they? Complicated infographics containing data visualizations require students to evaluate graphical techniques. In a world where visual information is preferred by consumers and marketers alike, students need to leave high school able to *read* data visualizations as powerful sources of information across disciplines, both in and out of the classroom.

How can you help students gain data literacy skills if the discipline you teach doesn't typically include data? Keep an eye out for teaching materials, collect subject-relevant examples embedded in media coverage of current events, scrutinize your textbook with a fresh eye for data and charts, offer visuals as an alternative to textual information, and consult resources in this book for professional development in this area. In the meantime, we can identify some simple evaluation tactics to add to our toolkit. This chapter will help you think more like a designer, extend basic information literacy skills, and add some new heuristics so you can de-mystify data visualizations for your students.

Think like a designer

Data visualization expert Edward Tufte (2006) suggests that every designer makes moral and intellectual choices in the creation of an infographic, and in consuming them we must hold the creator(s) responsible for those decisions. Every visualization involves a series of intentional choices, and while we can never fully appreciate each, it is helpful to *read* all graphics with this in mind. Every visualization is a picture with a message; students must think in terms of the designer's agenda or perspective, e.g., *Why was this data, and the story it tells, depicted in a series of bar graphs rather than a pie chart, and why the use of bright, bold colors?* As consumers, we must actively engage with each graphic; as teachers we need to model this in each discipline.

Infographics and data visualizations represent a burgeoning new field of marketing. Companies spend 62% of their content marketing dollars on infographics, up 15% over a year ago (Content Marketing Institute 2016). An estimated 84% of Internet communication will be visual by 2018, according to *Reuters* (Lopes 2014). In the world of marketing, designers work with their clients to craft a visual message consistent with the company's mission. Similarly, political campaigns depend on infographics to quickly communicate their track record to voters on issues like job creation. In this case, graphics are often designed to make the reader feel aligned with the candidate, and every detail — from the range and unit of data selected, to the color palette used, to the font type used for text labels — is carefully selected to support the message. A graph of the same data may look very different if produced by BarackObama.com rather than WashingtonPost.com.

One site is intended to persuade you to agree with a candidate's policies, and the other's goal is primarily to inform from an objective standpoint. As readers, it's our job to decipher the message, given the perspective of its creator(s), rather than to merely react to the image and accept the data visualization at face value. As teachers, we need to help students to develop this fluency.

Extending information literacy skills

Information literate students already learn how to evaluate text sources. They can leverage this knowledge to deconstruct infographic data visualizations. Using techniques similar to those employed for the evaluation of text sources (in which we prompt students to consider who created it, on what authority, over what period of time, and reflecting what point of view) teachers must consider the following when teaching about visual information:

» **Provide students with time to look and think about the message, and begin to generate their own questions.** Unlike a purely textual source, there are many layers to visualized data, including text, graphics, data, proportion, and color. What is seen initially, changes with time and focus given to each element. When students generate their own questions about the data, they engage with the graphic.

» **Graphics, and the datasets within, may originate from different (or multiple) sources.** Students need to interrogate how and when data was collected, analyzed, and ultimately displayed; the answers are essential to judge the veracity of an infographic.

» **Look for the source of the data, not the URL where the infographic may have been found.** Basic website evaluation techniques usually include deconstructing URLs and investigating the domain. Such common practices give rise to black-and-white *rules* for students such as "All .gov sites can be trusted" or ".edu sites are all created by scholars." However, where a data visualization is published (or re-published) on the web may be unrelated to who generated the data or the agenda they suggest. For example, while respected universities often produce datasets and infographics, they may be funded by an outside interest or be republished on blogs or online journals. "Following the money" may uncover the story behind the story.

A few basic rules of thumb

While mastering all the design and statistical principles necessary to evaluate visualizations is daunting, we can lead students through their deconstruction.

A key question to ask is, "What is the story, and who are the storytellers?" Every infographic seeks to tell a story using images or icons and sparse text, laid out cleverly to convey a message. It is important to consider both your first impression (the thesis) as well as deeper questions about each element. Question the story: Are the claims clear, reasonable, and accurate?

What can we ask about the graphs, charts, and images? How can we better understand the choice of visualization?

What does the data really mean?

Having examined the story and those telling it, we now turn our attention to the data itself. Americans often accept data at face value; we – and our students! – tend to accept numbers as irrefutable "facts." When students don't know much about the claim being made, it seems overwhelming to try to evaluate the data. Like a textual search, there is a need to build context in order to evaluate. The graphs and charts contained in an infographic

Who

- Who has created the visual components (often a graphic designer)? What can you find out about his or her credentials that suggests expertise in the issue being described?

- Who collected, analyzed, and published the data?

- What perspective or objectives might the creator or organizational sponsor represent?

What

- Try to summarize the thesis — or big takeaway — of this graphic. What does the creator want you to think? Is the goal to persuade, sell, or inform? Who is the storyteller?

- Is there an alternative explanation?

- What information is missing?

- Is the claim plausible based on what you know? Can you do an Internet search and find a trusted source to corroborate the findings?

When

- When was the chart or graph created? Is it different from the publication date of the visualization and/or the article/post in which the visualization appears?

- When was the source data collected? Is it reasonably current? If not, consider the implication of using old data to make new claims.

Where

- Where did the data come from? Was the data collected by a research team at a university? A non-profit? What else have they published on this topic? Does knowing the source change the context?

- Where is the data visualization published; does it suggest an agenda?

Why/How

- How might I better understand this topic? What context or background information is required?

- How does the author or organization's perspective affect the interpretation of the data?

reflect a constellation of choices, and this is where we must focus our evaluation. Page 199 provides some questions to discuss with students, and Appendix B provides a sample infographic accompanied by a sample student conversation using those questions.

Numerical information

When analyzing data, we can ask many questions of the numbers themselves. Here are some useful strategies to keep in mind:

» **Correlation of two sets of data should not be used to imply cause and effect.** For example, the fact that autism and ice cream consumption both increase over some period of time does not imply that ice cream consumption causes autism. This may be the simplest yet one of the most valuable data literacy skills.

» **Can you quickly verify some benchmark statistics** (Best 2013), e.g., population, distance, birth or death rates that can help provide context for the data and numbers in a visualization? Providing students with a short list of statistics related to the subject of the infographic can make this easier.

» **Do the numbers seem too big or too conveniently rounded?** Big, round numbers are often inexact guesses (Best 2013).

» **What is being measured over what period of time?** Are the units of measure consistent, or are different units used to describe a single phenomenon? Does it seem implausible based on what you know? Odd units or preposterous claims should be questioned.

» **Check the y-axis on the graph.** We are used to seeing graphs in math class where the intersection of the x- and y-axes begin at zero. In the wild, this may not be the case, so students need to consciously check the labels on graphs, particularly the y-axis. A y-axis that does not begin at zero is not inherently incorrect – it could be that truncating the range of numbers is space-efficient or that there are no data points that correspond with numbers close to zero. On the other hand, graphics with non-traditional or unexpected y-axes can raise questions: Was the range of data selectively chosen, perhaps to cherry-pick a short-term trend to support an argument? Would you feel differently about the trend if a longer time period was depicted, or a wider range of numbers? Were the intervals selected to support the creator's intended conclusion?

» **Be cautious when looking at percentages, percentile, and percent change.** As noted in Chapter 1, these terms sound similar but have distinct meanings.

Methods

An infographic's raw data and the organization or researchers that produced it may not always be included, but some additional searching may lead to these kinds of details.

» **Can you locate the sample size (expressed as n=x)?**

» **Is the methodology for data collection available, especially information on how the sample was gathered?** Was it randomized, meaning the researcher's data collection accurately depicts a larger population or

dataset? Beware of generalizations made using small samples (n<25). For more on sampling, see Chapter 1.

» **Are the intervals regularly or irregularly spaced?** *Logarithmic graphs* are used to depict change over time, and feature an accelerated rate of change using unevenly spaced intervals. They can be useful when a few data points are skewed away from the bulk of the data or when depicting percent change (rather than absolute). Absolute graphs feature regularly-spaced intervals (the same distance is present between each). Beware of charts comparing data graphed on an absolute scale with those using a logarithmic scale.

» **Is the data cherry-picked?** Are date ranges or time boundaries specifically chosen because they demonstrate a desired result? If you looked at a different or broader interval, would the data look very different? For more on intervals, see Chapter 6.

» **Beware of the word *average*.** Many people assume that average means the arithmetic mean (adding up all numbers and dividing by the quantity of numbers), but the author may mean median or mode, which can distort the raw data. For more discussion on averages, see Chapter 1.

» **Ask questions of text and labels**
  - Does the title convey a thesis or put forth an argument? Does this match your "read" of the data?
  - Can you spot emotionally-laden words: rhetoric (words like freedom-fighter or terrorist) and hyperbole (claims like the most, the largest, or the best) or is the language neutral and purely descriptive?
  - Do font size or color connote importance (size) or caution (red, orange)? Were either used to intentionally mislead? Read the fine print for important details that the creator may have tried to de-emphasize.
  - Are all values clearly labeled using consistent units? Do the labels clarify or confuse? Are the terms defined, e.g., the definition of *family* versus *household* when used to collect income data.

Layout

Helping students understand the organization and flow of elements in an infographic can aid in improving comprehension.

Here are some questions you may ask of your students.

» **Is this the best way to visualize this data?** If not, can you find it graphed another way or find the original dataset and lay it out differently? See Figure 2 for some common charts and when to use them (Maguire 2016).

» **What does the color choice tell us?** How do the colors used make you feel? Red usually signals trouble, or at least emphasis. Are the colors communicating emotion that is supported by the data? Or distracts from or over-emphasizes it?

» **Is the graphic layout designed to emphasize or de-emphasize some of the data?**

» **Does the relative size of elements/icons accurately represent the data?** Respective icon size should reflect data not emphasis; the area of two-dimensional shapes should be proportional to values.

For a sample conversation about layout, see Appendix C.

Practice, practice, practice

Short lessons, peppered throughout the high school curriculum, will make evaluation of visualized data a habit of mind. Plan collaborative lessons with other teachers to scaffold learning throughout the year, for example:

» **Conduct a whole-class evaluation of a single infographic;** assign groups to evaluate one of the categories.

» **Display a lesson-relevant image as a warm-up exercise,** coupled with a checklist to complete or a required post to an online class discussion. Introduce a small subset of the criteria shown in this chapter at a single sitting so that students gain evaluative experience and confidence over time.

» **Assign groups to evaluate one of a set of related infographics on a single topic** and have each share what their evaluation revealed. Be sure to include "what's missing?" as a prompt.

» **Include an infographic requirement to a research paper** and require a critical annotation to explain why it was chosen as a source.

» **Post the chart in Appendix D and remind students that the selection of a visualization style can be critical in assisting readers' comprehension.**

Conclusion

Every opportunity we provide students to critically evaluate infographics improves their data literacy. Ultimately – and with practice – students will transfer the critical eye we require in the classroom to the myriad graphics they confront in their everyday lives.

Resources

Anderson, Janna, and Lee Rainie. 2012. *Main Findings: Teens, Technology, and Human Potential in 2020*. Washington, D.C.: Pew Research Center. Accessed May 3, 2016. http://www.pewinternet.org/2012/02/29/main-findings-teens-technology-and-human-potential-in-2020/.

Best, Joel. 2013. *Stat-spotting: A Field Guide to Identifying Dubious Data*. Berkeley: University of California Press.

Carlson, Jake, and Lisa Johnston. 2015. *Data Information Literacy: Librarians, Data, and the Education of a New Generation of Researchers*. Purdue Information Literacy Handbooks. West Lafayette, IN: Purdue University Press.

Centaur Communications Limited. 2010. "Data Visualization: Facts and Figures." *New Age Media*, September 2.

Content Marketing Institute. 2016. *B2C Content Marketing: Benchmarks, Budgets, and Trends— North America*. Cleveland, OH: Content Marketing Institute. Accessed May 1, 2016. http://contentmarketinginstitute.com/wp-content/uploads/2015/10/2016_B2C_Research_Final.pdf.

Lopes, Marina. "Videos May Make Up 84 Percent of Internet Traffic by 2018: Cisco." Edited by Andre Grenon. Reuters.com. Last modified June 10, 2014. Accessed May 1,

2016. http://www.reuters.com/article/us-internet-consumers-cisco-systems-idUSKB-N0EL15E20140610.

Maguire, Sara. 2016. "No Fuss Chart Design." Business2Community.com. March 26. Accessed April 4, 2017. http://www.business2community.com/content-marketing/no-fuss-chart-design-cheat-sheet-01494593

Tufte, Edward R. *Beautiful Evidence*. 2006. Cheshire, Conn.: Graphics Press.

If you have five minutes:

- **Create a warm-up exercise with an infographic related to the content you are teaching.** Post a journal prompt for students: "What do you think the thesis is for this infographic?"

- **Screen an infographic for 1 minute, and then have students describe in writing or orally how the color, font, or layout of the infographic made them feel.** Have them describe their first impressions.

- **Screen an infographic from a news article or popular science topic.** List 4 possible "messages" and place them in a 4-Corners Game (see Figure 1). Ask students to move to the corner that best represents the message they took away from the infographic.

If you have 30 minutes:

- **Ask students to compare two infographics on the same topic.** Break into groups to discuss which is more effective and why.

- **Ask students to select an effective infographic from among 3-5 chosen for evaluation (representing varying levels of accuracy).** Focus the evaluation on 3 criteria, e.g., data visualization (chart choice), color, and text labels.

If you have one class period:

- **Hold a debate on a topic where only infographic evidence is allowed.** Model how to search for infographics using "Images" in a search engine. Break the class into groups and have them debate both sides of an issue in pairs, using infographics they find and evaluate, then present as evidence of their stance.

- **Using the criteria outlined in this chapter,** ask students to present a critical summary of a single infographic, either found by them or selected by you.

4-Corners Game

Front Left	Front Right
To inform	To educate
To entertain	To deceive
Back Left	Back Right

Figure 1: The 4-Corners Game

UNDERAGE DRINKING:
NOT YOUR CHILD?

Most 12- to 17-year-olds do not drink, but the percentage who use alcohol and report drunkenness increases by grade.

Having a friend who drinks is an early warning sign that strongly predicts your child's future drinking levels.[1]

PAST-MONTH ALCOHOL USE AND DRUNKENNESS REPORTED BY 8TH-, 10TH-, AND 12TH-GRADE STUDENTS[2]

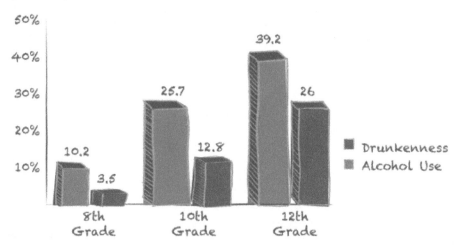

Get informed. Get involved. Help prevent underage drinking.
https://www.StopAlcoholAbuse.gov

[1] http://pubs.niaaa.nih.gov/publications/Practitioner/YouthGuide/YouthGuide.pdf
[2] http://www.monitoringthefuture.org//pubs/monographs/mtf-overview2013.pdf

Figure 2: Source: https://www.stopalcoholabuse.gov/resources/infographics/share.aspx?info=13

Who created this?

- **Substance Abuse and Mental Health Services Administration (SAMHSA)** is the lead government agency for StopAlcoholAbuse.gov, the web portal for the Interagency Coordinating Committee on the Prevention of Underage Drinking (ICCPUD)

- **Data comes from MonitoringTheFuture.org's 2014 report on adolescent drug abuse.** Monitoring the Future (MTF) is a non-governmental organization (NGO) that conducts and publishes results from an annual "long-term epidemiological study that surveys trends in legal and illicit drug use among American adolescents and adults as well as personal levels of perceived risk and disapproval for each drug. The survey is conducted by researchers at the University of Michigan's Institute for Social Research, funded by research grants from the National Institute on Drug Abuse, one of the National Institutes of Health." [Wikipedia]

- **Perspective or agenda?** Produced by a government agency that seeks to reduce teen drug use.

What is the message or thesis?

- **Teen drinking increases from grades 9 thru 12.**

- **Having a friend who drinks predicts likelihood that a student will use alcohol.**

- **Seems like the storyteller wants to educate parents about underage drinking.** Audience is parents.

- **What information is missing?** Maybe it would be helpful to know if the data represents urban/rural, low income/high income, students with low or high GPAs, etc. This data is from a 2013 survey; does it represent an increase or decrease from previous years?

- **Does this information make sense?** Can you corroborate the findings elsewhere? Responsibility.org, drugabuse.org, and other sites all refer to this report. Seems like this is a respected source.

When was the chart or graph created? When was the source data collected? Is it different from the publication date of the visualization?

- **No publication or copyright date is listed for the graphic.**
- **The data in the MonitorTheFuture.org report was collected in 2013; the report was published in 2014.**
- **The data seems reasonably current.**

Where did the data come from? Was the data collected by a research team at a university? A non-profit? What else have they published on this topic? Does knowing the source change the context?

- **University of Michigan's Institute for Social Research** conducts the MTF survey each year (1975-2013) on a range of drug use by adolescents.
- **This lends credibility to this infographic** because it is conducted by a major research university and sponsored by several government agencies.

How might I better understand this topic? What context or background information is required? How does the author or organization's perspective affect the interpretation of the data?

- **Read the "Alcohol" section on page 37 of the MTF report** to understand how "drunkenness" and "alcohol use" are defined in this study.
- **Read the "Study Design and Methods" section on page 3 of the MTF report** to answer questions about how many students were surveyed, what sampling methods were used, and what specific questions were asked.
- **University researchers would be likely to use a scientific approach** rather than having a specific agenda on this topic.

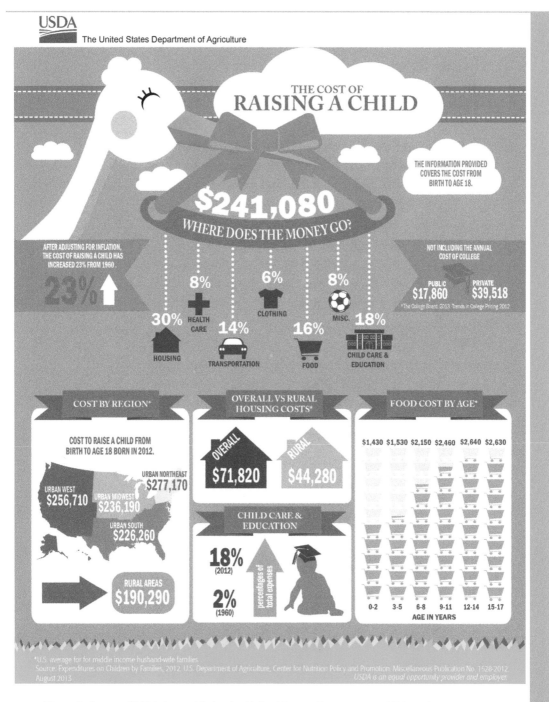

Figure 3: August 2013 infographic by the United States Department of Education showing the anticipated cost of raising a child from birth to age 18. Source: https://www.cnpp.usda.gov/sites/default/files/expenditures_on_children_by_families/CRC2012InfoGraphic.pdf

Activity: Evaluating an infographic's layout

Consider questions like these when evaluating the aesthetic choices in "The Cost of Raising a Child."

1. **Is this the best way to visualize this data?** Could the components of the $241K be displayed to better differentiate between the high cost of housing vs. the relatively low cost of clothing?

2. **Consider questions like these when evaluating the aesthetic choices in "The Cost of Raising a Child."** How does the the color pink make you feel? The rosy-cheeked stork? Is this just about girls? Could cost of raising a girl vs. boy differ?

3. **What stands out?** Does the designer want to focus on some data more than others? Why is the 23% increase since 1960 in such a large font? Why are college costs included when the graphic supposedly depicts costs only from birth to age 18 and most students are in college beyond age 18?

4. **Do the icons accurately represent the data?** Does each shopping cart depict the same cost? Should the urban and rural house icons be the same size?

Type of Chart	Best for...	
Pie Chart	Showing the relative proportion of variables as parts of a whole. Beware of many small "slices," especially without labels. Pie charts make comparisons difficult.	
Bar Graph (horizontal or vertical)	Illustrating discrete quantities of a number of outcomes. Must include labels and legends.	
Line Graph	Showing change in a variable over time. Labels and units of measure must be clear.	
3D Graphs (any type)	Nothing! 3D graphics are inherently difficult to interpret without error.	

9 | Designing your infographic: Getting to design

Connie Williams

The joy of building an infographic as a classroom-assigned project lies in the engagement that it can bring to both the teacher and student. Students begin to make connections to topic questions they created, researched, defined, and understood. Teachers see students making these connections and get excited. When working together, students can dig deeper to discover how to take content they've learned and present it to others so their audience understands the insights they've uncovered in their investigations. As you've seen in other chapters, infographics capture essential questions. The way students answer those questions is presented as collated evidence in infographics, backing up the insights they've gained.

Infographics, similarly to memes, are rendered to give the reader a sense of serendipity mixed with a sense of recognition of the absolute truth about something. Much as Debbie Abilock (2013) explains, "infographics that merge design, data, and a good essential statement or question create a sense of unease or 'friction' in the reader so that something that may be inherently known is now supported." As you look at samples of infographics throughout this book, you will notice when you read a successful infographic that either enhances a position you already hold or helps you to understand a new or difficult concept, you are engaged and possibly eager to carry the discussion further. Likewise, when students find that they have asked a real, essential-to-them question, they will work hard to make connections they can then present in visual form which helps them show it off.

At first glance, it may seem like an infographic is today's word for poster. I disagree. Creating an infographic requires students to think beyond *the poster*. Students have produced posters since their early grades, and teachers have required that student posters demonstrate they've gathered information the teacher feels is important. For example, most poster assignments contain similar elements:

» **topic overview**

» **brief history**

» **key figures**

» **key locations**

» **key experiments and/or important events**

» **a conclusion**

These are displayed on poster board — or more frequently, online — and include images and captions. Teachers check for student understanding when asking students to present their newly discovered knowledge. The use of an information poster allows for critical analysis of display choices made for needed elements in a pleasing presentation and allows teachers to assess content knowledge — an important assessment for sure.

There is value in assigning the information poster. They offer advantages by teaching students how to pull out those facts, images, and text that exhibit important information about their chosen topic. In assessing these posters, we look at the end product for an understanding of the event, person, or idea by analyzing what we think are important facts displayed in a pleasing way. In an infographic, we want to see a distillation of an argument or claim rather than an explanation.

Assessment of an infographic takes place throughout the process itself and culminates in the teacher evaluating the success of the topic understanding and the choice of elements and design to best express that understanding. Both content knowledge and arguments based on that knowledge are important and useful in the classroom. As teachers it is important that we identify the product we actually want and the amount of time we are willing to invest in teaching the necessary, and very transferrable, skills needed to create a successful infographic.

By assigning students to create an infographic, we are requiring them to dig deeper into the content to make important connections that show the topic content in new, different, or challenging ways. By creating an *argument,* or an *insight*, that entices the reader to discover what the creator sees and understands within their argument, students actually *begin* a dialog with their reader.

Steps for teaching an infographic lesson

While it sounds like more effort than many teachers might like to take, assigning an infographic as a project is not only worthwhile, it *ramps up* poster knowledge from content knowledge to synthesis: a goal we all seek. Teachers can manage this instruction by assessing content knowledge through tests, essays, class activities, before (or while) students conduct their research for the infographic. When it's time to assess the infographic, teachers already know where individual students stand with their content knowledge and can focus their final infographic assessment based on a rubric centered more on design choice, essential questions, how the evidence supports the claim, and what dialog *begins* with the reader. Skills such as locating and evaluating information, note-taking, designing, citation, and question-asking are all incorporated into this process and have been assessed during the process. When a student has been given the OK to proceed with the design, the teacher knows that he has completed all the necessary steps prior to sitting down at the design table. These are all important, transferrable skills to any research-based product, so direct instruction here creates learning that is important for this necessary research skill set.

The steps needed to identify important data, analyze it, and apply it as support or refutation to an essential question are discussed in other chapters in this book. Let us look at the steps our students, with research in hand, could use to visualize their essential question into an infographic. Students will need the following materials:

- » **a packet of sticky notes for each student or group**
- » **at least one piece of paper, 11x17" or larger**
- » **student notes, outlines, and drafts**

The steps include pre-organizing the infographic, creating storyframes, creating a rough draft, formative assessment, work-shopping the infographic, reflecting on the infographic, and determining final revisions. Other resources that might help are *Smashing Magazine*'s article "The Do's And Don'ts Of Infographic Design" (https://www.smashingmagazine.com/2011/10/the-dos-and-donts-of-infographic-design/) and "8 Types of Infographic" on the NeoMam Studies website (http://neomam.com/blog/the-8-types-of-infographic/).

Step 1: Pre-organization: What's the "story"?

Once students have their research completed and an idea of what the essential statement or question might be for their topic presentation, they are ready to begin thinking about which data points will best serve as evidence for their statement, and what kind of design will best support, and more importantly, enhance that evidence. Having learned that there are many different *frames* to present data such as pie charts, bar charts, or timelines, students look over the possibilities and determine what will best tell their story. If a story is about the steps it took to gain women's suffrage, then a timeline might be the frame of choice. But if a story wants to show that women's suffrage brought about changes in fashion, the student (or student group) could decide to cover many instances of change (e.g., bloomers and short hair). It could be framed as a comparison (between a woman from 1800 and one from 1920), or conceptually as a metaphor (for example, the journey to complete suffrage rolling and roiling on the waves of popular opinion). The first step to any infographic is: "What is my claim?" or "What is my story?"

At this stage, students have completed research and have collected numerical data (either in number form or visualized in charts, maps, or graphs), text (such as quotes or memes), and/or images (or, at a minimum, a sense of the types of images they would like to locate). This combined information may — or may not — be the data that completes an argument. Students should have lots of data to choose from so they can *play* with it to see which data tells which story — combinations of different data change the story. Students look at the data they have in hand and choose the data they think might create the argument they think they are making. They write these data bits onto sticky notes and place them next to their big paper for easy access.

Now is the time for the teacher and librarian to assess the data to see if the student is ready to move on to visual design. Here are some questions to consider:

» **Does the student have appropriate data to support his or her stated question/statement?**

» **Does he or she have enough?**

> » **Does the student have citations completed so that teachers, and other readers can verify the information?**

> » **Can the student explain the meaning of these data pieces?**

Assessment can be informal, with the teacher meeting with each student to see what has been chosen. Assessment can be formal too, via an in-class essay using only the materials students bring with them to class. The essay requires students to give background to the topic and place the topic within an historical, cultural, scientific, or other context as determined by the class subject area.

Step 2: Create storyframes

Once students have settled on a claim and/or a story, they are ready to storyboard their ideas and test several to see which of those designs might best help them tell their story. They can do this by using storyframes.

When making a movie or audio performance, writers *storyboard* their program. Laying out each scene with dialog, the expected placement of people, props, and set allows the crew to anticipate how to set up shots, where to light, where to stand and determine what the dialog is and how it's delivered, etc. (For examples of storyboards from movies like *Psycho* and *Star Wars*, visit http://screencrush.com/movie-storyboards/). In the world of online creation *wireframing* is a way to do a similar thing: determine image placement, graphic design, and coloring. An important piece to consider first in this process is the *flow* of the argument — and deciding what kind of frame best *holds* the story of that argument. For our infographic instruction, Debbie Abilock and I wrote a *KnowledgeQuest* article to help teachers and librarians think about infographic assignments (Abilock and Williams 2014).

My ideas for this chapter complement the article, merging storyboarding and wireframing to create a *story-frame* process. Storyframing — the juxtaposition of the concepts of *storyboard-*

ing and *wireframing* — is an important step in helping students think through where, how, why, and in what sequence to place certain design elements on their page. It creates the backdrop that best illustrates their ideas. Thus an infographic that tells the story of war's high death toll might *frame* it illustratively within a peace sign or along a road from battle to battle as the data shows higher mortality.

While there are many steps to creating an infographic, all of which are outlined elsewhere in this book, this step of storyframing is crucial. Review the sample infographics formats with the class, asking each student or student group to pay attention to the kinds of design frames that may be useful for their own infographic.

Release students to their groups or individual work and ask them to imagine their finished design: "What kind of understanding should their reader glean?" Give them the Question Design Matrix (see Appendix A in this chapter) as a worksheet to help them think through the many pieces that can make up a design. Asking the question from the matrix: "What kind of frame might work?" and then playing with different design frames, gives students the opportunity to play out different scenarios.

Again, using the structural components as outlined in Chapter 7, students begin to think about which design is the best to hold (or frame) the work. They can turn in to the teacher two or three design possibilities (for example, Topic 1: women at work; data showing women making less than men in the same job; frame of a see-saw with a woman on one side and man on the other. Topic 2: something about inequality, something along the lines of: the ups and downs of women's rights).

The teacher can direct student work at this point with questions to get him or her thinking more deeply and looking for connections: "I see that this chart tells us the amount of money that women make in comparison with men, and I wonder which of these other pieces of data help us understand the bigger picture. Which one in particular might be most useful in doing that?" Teachers can also continue to assess for content knowledge at this point and give students credit for work accomplished in understanding key subject matter concepts. Assessing all along the way for both content and participation helps to keep students on task while allowing the teacher the ability to keep content front and center over the easier *dazzle* of creation. It keeps us all honest to keep honing in on how particular data points tell stories and why they are important. For example, "Can we see how the outcome of an event changed because of the discovery, and application of medicine?"

Step 3: Rough draft: "playing" with the data

At this point, students still have not approached the online digital tools they will be ultimately using. So often, when we want our students to produce something (a presentation, video, audio file, etc.) utilizing online tools, we want to get right to it, thinking that it is the tool that engages them. Watching students center on their 'aha' of the content shows us the real engagement comes from discovering new ideas and re-framing them into the stories they now understand in a way they didn't before; and making connections to their own vision spurs them on to wanting to create an interesting presentation.

Students place a working title on their sheet of paper. Place one data bit (a chart, number, factoid, or sketch) on a single sticky note. Then place it on the side of the large paper. Repeat until each data piece is represented by a sticky note and stashed on the margins of the paper. If students get lost or frustrated, have them return to their Question Design Matrix and review the question: "What is my compelling "aha!" argument?" Taking a different look at a frame can also help to re-track frustration. If a student has been working with a timeline frame and finds herself unable to create the argument effectively, suggest a time out to remove all the sticky notes from the page. Pencil in a different layout style (perhaps a comparison, flow chart, or even a background image representing the topic, such as a helmet to represent war or a Ferris wheel that shows the circular nature of life and death in literature). Let loose afresh with the data and see if it now fits better. Only through non-threatening, easy-to-discard-and-replace materials can students take the risk to try and try again.

This is the most important part of the creation process: once students know what they want to *explain* or *argue* or *hypothesize*, they can determine which bits of data, visuals, and text tell the story. This takes time and experimentation. This is when students decide that the structure of their visualization is going to be a compare/contrast or timeline. They then lay their sticky notes on the draft drawing and add in the elements such as arrows, circles, or other items. Asking again and again, "Is this factoid the one that shows my reader the gist of my story?" "Will it allow students to mix/match/add/delete items that don't assist in the storytelling?"

When they start this process online, they rarely participate in the process of asking questions, re-tooling titles to find the one that truly synthesizes the message or play with their data. What happens online centers on the design creation using the offered tools. Before we can design with the cool tools we have to go through the thinking process of the content. Often, there is a huge learning curve with the online tool and so students tend to want to fit data points into what the tool has to offer. What works is to go to the tool after the thinking has been done. There will be changes made, but the scaffold will be there to work with the creation tool — and using it in its best form.

At this point, student attention is on the content, the idea, and the story. The hands-on, with paper and sticky notes, provides a physical, visual way for students to imagine the meaning of their work. I have seen it again and again: a student group will have what they think is a complete idea, and someone (maybe the teacher, maybe another student who sees the work in a gallery walk) asks: "What changes if you move this data in relation to this other data?" The creators often take a moment to think about it and most often go back to the drawing board to re-think their vision, change their title, or look at the data in a different way.

While we often start with a pre-conceived idea of what an info-graphic will look like, the end result *after* play time is often quite different. We may end up with an argument that is quite distinct from the initial thinking. This is a KEY point in time. It's the moment when the student also experiences the "aha." This is when students discard data, decide on the message, and then move data around into patterns that tell the story.

Step 4: Formative assessment: Instructor feedback

Now, the flow is beginning as students take the data they have in hand and begin to apply it. Teachers can take this opportunity to evaluate the data they've chosen as part of the process of evidence evaluation. As mentioned above, teachers can use this time for formative assessment through questioning and/or observation. But this is an excellent time for assessing for content requirements. If each student has a different project topic, but they all fall under the unit content (e.g.,Civil Rights – with individual student projects on Rosa Parks, Jim Crow, *Plessy v Ferguson*) teachers can assess by:

- » **requiring an in-class essay** – ask students to write about how their particular topic created change during the years being studied in class.
- » **teacher check-in on the notes/data** – give points for notes that show up in the sticky note pages; check for depth and breadth.

Sadie's story

A Columbian Exchange assignment asked my students to think about what happens when very different cultures meet up. When Sadie first chose this topic and finished her preliminary research, she felt pretty confident that she understood that what Columbus brought to the New World was a more "technologically advanced" culture that would enhance what the native cultures they met had. She outlined what each culture met for the first time, and began her design.

Using the storyframing activity, Sadie noted on each sticky note a sample of an item from each culture. She began to play around with what those items might mean. Placing sticky notes with items like guns, money, clothing, blankets, food on the map in Europe, then placing sticky notes with items like gold, furs, and food items on the map of the Americas, she began moving them around when she would ask herself, "Did this item make it back to Europe? Once it got there, what happened to it — to the culture that embraced it?"

Likewise, she asked the same of the European items and their impact on the native cultures. She consulted her notes, and returned to research some more. Her conversation changed when she added in items like disease, language, cultural artifacts, and tools. What she thought she understood about the meeting of cultures ("the powerful European culture brought all the "new stuff" to the native culture that was primitive) changed when she expanded her research to look at the impact of particular items on the European culture.

Moving the sticky notes, experimenting with assigning different data pieces to each note, adding with shapes like arrows, Venn diagram circles, and deciding on an overall design concept help her to create her newly discovered argument: Exchange of culture, objects, and values flows both ways.

STORYFRAMING IN ACTION

» **citation checks** – definitely a requirement – librarians can help to verify format, etc. Require annotations for each citation.

» **in-class test on the class topic.**

If the infographic assignment is to highlight something from the Civil Rights, the test might be on the Civil Rights movement in general. It might include a short essay on the specific topic the student has researched or impressions from other infographics the students have observed in their gallery walks – see below.

If a teacher is assigning an information poster – then he/she will most likely want to see lots of data points. Remembering that an information poster is designed to exhibit highlights from a topic in a clear and creative manner, having facts and images that cover the salient points of the topic is important. If the assignment is to bring concepts together into a metaphor, or a point of view argument, or other synthesis of a topic, as is required for an infographic, then there might be less data shown. Thinking through to an "aha" requires students to imagine the task and build an argument that informs, persuades, explains, or questions a concept or event. Laying out the anticipated topic allows them to question if they have narrowed down their topic enough in order to understand which of the many data bits they have in hand are meaningful to a particular thought, idea, or argument, or if they need to re-look at their question and tweak it in some way.

Because teachers have already assessed the quantity and quality of data acquired, it is now OK for students to discard or delete unnecessary factoids and other data. Many a compelling infographic contained a minimum of facts in favor of highlighting an important connection or a single piece of irony.

Again, holding students accountable for each step along the way assures the teacher students are working with the material thoughtfully while they are learning the research process itself. By this time, students have:

» **participated in class instruction** prior to the assignment, gaining the big picture of the unit to be studied;

» **asked themselves many questions** about their topic and researched the answers;

» **created notes** that include facts, figures, images, ideas, and quotes that help them understand why or how their topic is important;

» **participated in a "scholarly conversation"** with their resources by annotating their citations and checking in on the usefulness (or not) of their resource;

» **taken in-class objective tests,** in-class essays, discussions, and other assessments for content;

» **created mock infographic for others to see.**

Now it's time to *workshop* their work by allowing students to participate in look/see activities and conversing with other about their work.

Gallery walks, brief presentations, and small group conversations allow students to try out their arguments on others to see if they have successfully stated what they wanted to before committing themselves to a design. This, too, is an important step that should not be skipped, because it helps students note where their project topic fits into the big picture of your unit. Conversations need to include:

- » **When did specific events take place?**

- » **What are the implications of one topic upon another —** e.g., where in the timeline of the 1950s/ '60s Civil Rights activism did the March on Washington fall? Did Rosa Parks' action influence the March or vice versa?

- » **How do those actions relate to each other?**

These sorts of insights and conversations can be taken back to individual student works so that they can be seen with new eyes — and maybe a whole new insight.

There are several ways to share student work:

- » **If this is a group project, choose one person to stay at the table with the project displayed on the table.** The other group members will spend about five minutes at each of the other tables to view the displays, as questions of the student sitting there, and offer suggestions. A checklist of questions can be displayed on the board. After all the rotations have been completed, students return to their home table and report back to each other on their observations. The student who stayed behind explains any critiques he/she received from others. The group can make any changes if desired. This can be done informally and quickly, or it can be another assessment piece with each group participating in a "write around" at each table where the newcomers to the table write comments/questions about the piece.

- » **Display all the projects on the wall.** Place butcher paper beneath each project so students can write questions or critiques. Alternatively, pass out sticky notes that students can write on and place on the work itself.

- » **Have each group give a quick presentation** to the whole class showing their project in progress and answering questions about it.

Regardless of which activity is chosen, gallery walks allow for students and teachers to touch base and ask questions. Work with students before gallery walks and set guidelines for specific questions they might ask or items they might look for as they observe and speak with their fellow students.

Questions — whether for determining a topic, assessing learning, or just checking in — are continuous and probing. As a *drop-in* reflection tool, questioning can give one more opportunity to become sure of their direction. Teachers can take a moment to bring the class back to a focus point at any time during this process and spend a few minutes having the students ask questions about their projects such as:

> » **Do I see a pattern that best suggests my goal of persuading teachers that school should start at 10:00 a.m.?**
>
> » **What kind of image best shows off "23 percent of workers"?**
>
> » **What caption best explains the graph that correlates mosquito bites and childhood death?**

As students share their drafts, the teacher can respond with the question, "What is the goal of your infographic?" A student who asks, "What caption best explains the graph that correlates mosquito bites and childhood death?" might answer, "My goal is to get as many kids as possible in my school to contribute to a fund to buy mosquito nets." The teacher then can use that as a prompt to generate discussion that models the brainstorming process that happens during the pencil and sticky-note storyframing stage.

Again, with any of these activities, the teacher can informally or formally assess the process, check-in with the data and evidence, and check for understanding.

Checking in with others to see what they take away from the infographic can help the creators make any needed changes before committing to a more finished draft. Others might see connections that the creators missed and upon reflection, the creators might like these new connections better.

Step 6: Reflection

As we get pressed for time, reflection can often be pushed aside. We might get frustrated because of time barriers, but significant learning can happen when students think back on their info-graphic-creation process. Reflection can be done individually, in small groups, or as a class, but it should be done regardless of the amount of time you'll need. Reflecting in a journal allows for teacher oversight and prompting (as well as another point for assessment) while small or whole class discussion adds that dimension of group insights that goes missing with pencil to paper writing. Both provide useful information that solidifies decisions and makes students ready to move on to creating their info-graphic digitally.

Step 7: Final revisions

With a completed storyframe in hand, students are ready to build their infographic, beginning to incorporate the next layer of design strategies: color, shape, light, and depth. Consider the ideas put forward in Chapters 6 and 7 to inform how color, shape, and light can enhance student infographics.

While, of course, you could have students do an infographic with colored pencils, markers and foam core, keep in mind that we are not advocating that these are the only methods for the actual final draft. After the entire storyframe process is complete, introduce your students to tools like Easel.ly, Piktochart.com, and

Canva.com for web-based, easy-to-use graphic options for creating an infographic.

Conclusion

Structured effectively, the infographics process generates discoveries that make it all worthwhile because the product can engage many kinds of talents and interests. If students have had time to look at many examples of infographics, and through class discussion or small group work explored how data works, how memes exploit our emotions (for good or not-so-good reasons), how media persuades, and other data literacy processes, then the ability to make a compelling infographic of one's own can be engaging.

If we're lucky, infographic design encourages them to continue past their assignment into a real interest. Curating information has its own merits in teaching the skills of locating information, analyzing it, deciding what is important and what is less so, designing the story arc, the text, and the images to best tell the story. In designing an infographic, we not only use those skills but also help students understand why and how sources differ, think about points of view, reflect on their world and the world around them, and refine an idea that tries to answer a specific question.

I have been fortunate to be a part of the learning process in many of our health classes over the past few years. The assignment "Create an infographic designed to convince teens about the dangers of STDs" was designed to teach the research process as well as make connections with real issues in sexuality that teens need to know. In one class, students were madly getting ready to create infographics that might be invited to be posted in our local health clinic. One group discovered that the process of building a story — and one that might convince another teenager about the downside of STDs — could be quite frustrating. Their topic regarding condoms was easy to research. They had good data and solid ideas of why condoms are useful in preventing STDs. But they could not come up with a title or a frame that matched their goal of convincing teenagers to think through their options before having sex.

They persevered, and they came to an "aha" moment as they discussed the title. Stymied by the thought of creating a great title, they spent much time dismissing several as too mundane: "Condoms are Important" or "Be Safe, Use a Condom." They wanted something to grab attention.

Then, as teenagers often do, they started getting goofy and throwing out ideas, each, I'm sure more ridiculous than the previous. At some point their title emerged. They eagerly set to work on their draft, and created their frame and set their sticky notes where they wanted them. The design, a series of data points about STDs and condom use centered on the perplexed face of a teen under the title: "Don't Be Silly. Wrap your Willie".

Was the teacher aghast? A little. Were we unsure about its propriety? Yes. Was it effective? You bet. Their point was made, and it certainly wasn't boring. In the gallery walk, other students paid attention and spent a bit more time reviewing this design, because they made a connection — that wacky title set their school expectations askew. Their fellow students were thrilled to respond to their infographic with positive and negative, but thoughtful, feedback.

These students, in dismissing the boring, the traditionally informative, and the most obvious titles, for the weird, off-kilter, but captivating title that captured the essence of what their message (or argument) was, discovered that through discussion, fact-gathering, consideration, and yes, silliness and play, they could hone in on what their message truly was rather than settle for just providing information. Their assignment was to instigate change. They were on the road to understanding how design, data, and a compelling, eye-catching title work together to synthesize their message.

Resources

Abilock, Debbie, and Williams, Connie. 2014. "Recipe for an Infographic."
   Knowledge Quest 43(2), Nov./Dec., 46-55.
Abilock, Debbie. 2013. "Essentially a Multimodal Argument," August 22.
   E-mail received by the author.

Audience	My interest/my problem	Choices/ possibilities for design frame	Thinking
Who is the audience for my project?	What is my compelling "aha!" argument?	What kind of frame might work?	What kinds of information do I need in order to answer my question?

Working question:

Audience:

My argument:

My frame:

Further thinking:

Audience	My interest/my problem	Choices/possibilities for design frame	Thinking
Who is the audience for my project? Audience: **rock-and-roll musicians, music appreciation students, teachers, dulcimer players**	What is my compelling "aha!" argument? **Dulcimer music is just like other kinds of music!**	What kind of frame might work? My frame: **outline of a dulcimer or musical note (the musical note could be made to look like a timeline)**	What kinds of information do I need in order to answer my question? **Books about musical instruments** **History of rock-and-roll book or website**

Working question: **How successful could the dulcimer be as a part of today's rock and roll/alternative music scene?**

Audience: **High school classmates**

My argument: **the dulcimer is a fantastic instrument for alternative music. There are many musicians that have used it in their songs successfully**

My frame: **Comparison between Beatles and Ravi Shankar then, dulcimer and rock today?**

Further thinking: **data that shows musicians who have used dulcimers in their music, timeline style; OR historical info on the dulcimer OR data info that shows the range of the dulcimer**

10 | Using data visualizations in the content areas

Jennifer Colby

Why is delivering content through data visualizations important for motivating different learner types, developing literacy skills, delivering content, addressing standards, and improving performance on standardized tests?

"A picture is worth a thousand words" is a phrase that applies to any visualization. Sharing real-world data visualizations with students is informative and fun — it sparks interest and generates discussion. A graph, chart, table, or infographic packs a lot of data in a small space.

By analyzing graphs, charts, tables, and infographics students gain insight, identify patterns, and uncover new meanings while developing literacy skills. Student comprehension is enhanced through good data visualizations and students develop inquiry skills demanded by today's standardized tests.

This chapter considers how incorporating different texts into instruction can motivate students in all content areas. Examples of data visualizations and lesson tips are provided across content areas. Sample data visualization questions from high school level standardized tests are discussed to help educators understand how important data literacy skills are to performance on these tests. How does this look in your classroom? Let's find out.

Why is data visualization instruction important in the classroom?

Students learn best when motivated. My 15-year-old son can explain all aspects of a virtual world video game he's been involved with for hours (if I let him). Yet, he insists on a 15-minute break for every 30 minutes of homework. Why can he focus with no *brain break* while gaming but cannot study U.S. history for more than 30 minutes? It's simple: he's not interested in U.S. history. He's not motivated.

High school students can often recite endless facts about popular movies, a YouTube channel, or Kobe Bryant's last game, but they don't have a lot to say about *Romeo and Juliet,* earth science, world history, or personal finance. Elizabeth Moje (2006) hypothesizes that students' motivation to obtain information shapes their ability to make sense of a text. If a student is not interested in a text, she argues, the student will not be interested in decoding, comprehending, or expressing information from that text. Moje asks whether the literacy skills obtained in a student's out-of-school literacy pursuits can transfer to in-school contexts where academic literacy skills are required. Motivating texts can encourage struggling students to employ known reading strategies that they might not already employ while reading a traditional text.

Students may not have the inherent motivation to decode, comprehend, and express information. Yet, a text itself can motivate or demotivate. Students can regain interest in any content area by reading a motivating text. A student's perceived value of a text determines its usefulness, which in turn engages the student's interest. Moje explains that students' preferred out-of-school texts "(a) represent aspects that feel real... in terms of age, geography, and ethnicity/race of the protagonists, (b) impart life lessons, (e.g.,resilience/survival, inspiration) (c) offer utility/practical knowledge, and (d) allow [students] to explore relationships" (p. 13). This is great news! By providing students with *useful texts*, i.e., data visualizations that offer practical knowledge, we are engaging (and sometimes re-engaging) content-area interest. We know students constantly engage themselves with visual information, so why not use data visualizations as a more intriguing entry point into content?

Many struggling students can benefit from using multiple texts to supplement a more traditional text (Moje 2006). Did you catch that? The intent of incorporating data visualization into content areas is not to *replace* traditional texts, but to *supplement* traditional texts. We do not want you to abandon the linguistic challenges of traditional texts. Data visualizations are tools to scaffold instruction and can be incorporated to differentiate instruction to meet the needs of varying types and levels of learners in our classrooms. Alternative texts such as tables, charts, graphs, and infographics can help struggling readers better understand traditional texts while piquing content-area interest.

Data literacy skills can be the same as literacy skills

Incorporating data visualizations into content areas is not all about statistics and probability (thank goodness). Considering the three key visualization types (chart, graph, or infographic) as new kinds of text, we can gather information the same way we gather information from a traditional text. Increasing a student's data literacy increases a student's literacy. Strategies that apply to decoding, comprehending, and expressing information in a traditional piece of text apply to any type of data visualization.

Minding the GAP

Student comprehension increases when using a strategy of the Reading Apprenticeship Framework, "Mind the GAP" (WestEd 2017). GAP is the acronym for genre, audience, and purpose. Students can "Mind the GAP" as a simple strategy to begin to understand any data visualization.

Consider using this strategy with an infographic:

» **G (genre)** – Students can determine why an infographic (the genre) was used to represent the information visually. Why is an infographic, with its combination of numerical, statistical, and text snippets, the best format?

» **A (audience)** – Audience can be determined by reviewing the source of the data, the creator of the text, and the means in which it is published. Who is the creator envisioning the reader or viewer of this work to be?

» **P (purpose)** – Purpose is determined by extracting the text's data and studying it. Is it meant to inform or persuade?

In addition, simple strategies such as "Think Alouds" (teachers and students verbally expressing their comprehension of the text as it is read aloud) and "Talk to the Text" (written or digital text annotation as it is read through) can be applied to any data visualization to find the claim and its supporting evidence to achieve comprehension (Greenleaf 2014). These lend themselves to an ongoing conversation about how and what students are thinking when they read. Later in this chapter we will provide some examples of how data visualizations as text can deliver (and/or enhance) traditional content in the core curriculum areas and provide some lesson tips for "reading" visualizations.

Students develop real-world skills of interpreting information when data visualizations are incorporated into any content area. As a society, we are bombarded with charts, tables, and graphs. If we are unprepared to evaluate and interpret the data used to create a visualization, we are unable to learn from (or question) it. Consider associated data visualizations help us to better understand and decode articles in magazines and newspapers because they provide us with a quick summary of the data contained within the article. All a reader needs then is a basic understanding of statistics to be able to evaluate the information presented in a graph, chart, or table "with a more critical eye" (Gilmartin and Rex 2016, 5). Understanding the "language" of data visualizations helps our students interpret, analyze, and question information presented in multiple formats.

Example: *Romeo and Juliet*

There are many opportunities to mine data from traditional math and science textbooks. But what if we take text we do not traditionally think of as visual and make it so? Let's consider William Shakespeare's *Romeo and Juliet.* Quick — who dies in the play, how do they die, and in which order? Most of us read Shakespeare's play at some point in high school, but remembering the sequence is as big a challenge today as it was back in our freshman year.

The key to student understanding is giving students the opportunity to gather information from supplemental texts as well, because many students cannot comprehend the action of *Romeo and Juliet* just by reading the unfamiliar prose. There are many ways to comprehend the tragedy inherent to *Romeo and Juliet* – including movies, audio recordings, and *No Fear Shakespeare* – but we can also use visualizations to help our students gain memory hooks upon which to map their knowledge of an extended text. We've actually been using visualizations for decades in our classes. Graphic organizers, drawing rising/falling action in plot lines, even diagramming sentences have all been part of the ELA toolkit. Modern visualizations just take this to the next step. Let's look at how this information can be presented visually for better understanding. Consider this data visualization, "The *Romeo and Juliet* Death Clock" by Mya Gosling (2015):

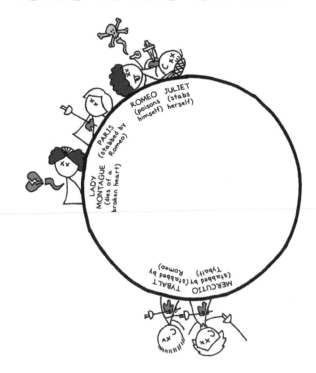

THE ROMEO AND JULIET DEATH CLOCK

c 2015 Mya Gosling; used with permission. Available from http://goodticklebrain.com/home/2015/8/26/the-romeo-and-juliet-death-clock .

Because the deaths are presented graphically, we can interpret this visualization and immediately determine:

» **how many people die**

» **who dies**

» **at what point they die in the story**

» **how they die**

» **and even their countenance upon dying (those aren't ears ... they're smiles)**

Looking at the graphic, how long did it take you to decipher those main plot points? How much time would it take to decipher the same main plot points from reading the text? This is a unique visualization. Gosling has created death clocks for just about every Shakespearean tragedy on her web site (goodticklebrain.com). Many students could quickly and easily interpret this visualization to add to their understanding of the text. This is not to suggest that data visualizations should replace traditional content — data visualizations should enhance traditional content.

At the end of this chapter, Appendix A provides a sample template for constructing data visualization conversations in your classroom. Appendix B brings another *Romeo and Juliet* infographic to ELA courses, while Appendices C-E preview other visualization activities across content areas that will help you think expansively about how to employ them in your curriculum.

Addressing national standards

When developing classroom curriculum, we must consider the applicable national standards. Let's consider how the learning goals for college-and-career-ready students of the Common Core State Standards (CCSS) can be achieved through the integration of data visualizations into your content area. There is a link at the back of this book to a list of national standards that mention data and statistical literacy.

CCSS Learning Goals for English, Science, and Social Studies (College and Career Ready)

Using data visualizations as companion texts to traditional texts can help students discern key components they otherwise may have overlooked. A student's level of comprehension can be misrepresented if the information is only presented in a wordier text. This is especially true for English language learners. Necessary skills are outlined for students who are college and career ready in the CCSS English Language Arts Introduction. While not part of the numbered standards, these capacities provide a description of students working toward meeting the standards while frequently displaying these skills. Incorporating data visualizations as companion texts can help develop the following CCSS capacities in our students (CCSSI 2017b).

Demonstrating independence

Think of the information students are exposed to through social media platforms like Twitter, Instagram, Pinterest, Tumblr, Facebook, Reddit, and dozens of others. A simple Internet search for the "top 10 social media platforms" will give you a better understanding of the most popular "news" sources on the Internet. How are these "news" sources different from pre-social media news sources? The answer is simple — most social media sources are not vetted.

The Internet is full of inaccurate and unauthoritative information. But it gets worse — every "fact" is passed on from one social media account to another with no regard for the source or the accuracy of the information it contains. Students should be armed with the ability to comprehend and evaluate "complex texts across a range of types and disciplines" so they're able to "construct effective arguments and convey intricate or multifaceted information" (CCSSI 2017b). In short, our students need to be able to gather, evaluate, expand on, and articulate information to demonstrate comprehension.

Possessing a strong knowledge of content

Of course, we want our students to build strong subject content knowledge, but this content can come from varying texts, not just classroom textbooks. Students build strong knowledge by establishing "a base of knowledge across a wide range of subject matter by engaging with works of quality and substance" (CCSSI 2017b). Content knowledge can be gained through purposeful research and study of great data visualizations (as explained with the previous examples of content-area infographics). Students can then create their own data visualizations to share with others.

Responding to the varying demands of audience, purpose, task, and discipline

Our students are bombarded with information every minute of every day. A quick way to share information is through tables, charts, and graphs presented in authoritative daily news sources. In the analysis of these types of data visualizations, students must respond to the varying CCSS-aligned demands of audience, task, purpose, and discipline set forth by the creator of the visualization. Data visualizations give students a great opportunity to discern the target audience and whether the text is meant to inform or persuade.

Comprehending and critiquing

Everyone has opinions and everyone is exposed to others' opinions. Through the analysis of data visualizations, students comprehend new information to help "understand precisely what an author or speaker is saying" (CCSSI 2017b). Students must determine and question the audience, purpose, and intent set forth by the creator of the visualization as they evaluate its credibility, accuracy, and effectiveness. Understanding the claim of the text and how it is (or is not) supported is crucial to student comprehension. Students can also critique student-created data visualizations.

Valuing evidence

Many conversations start with, "I was listening to," or "I saw on," or "I read online," but rarely is the specific source remembered. We also sometimes tweak or exaggerate our evidence to better support our argument. Students must learn to cite specific evidence from a text/data visualization. Relevant evidence must be clearly presented to support their argument. They must also be able to constructively evaluate and assess others' use of textual evidence.

Using technology and media capably and strategically

Students must use technology and digital media "thoughtfully to enhance their reading, writing, speaking, listening, and language use" (CCSSI 2017b) as they integrate what they learn from traditional texts with what they learn online. They must understand the strengths and limitations of the technological tools and digital mediums they choose to use and interact with. Creating data visualizations using tech tools gives students a great opportunity to determine which tool best delivers their message.

Understanding other perspectives and cultures

As more and more school curriculums reflect a world focus, students can develop an understanding of other perspectives and cultures by appreciating "that the twenty-first century classroom and workplace are settings in which people from often widely divergent cultures and who represent diverse experiences and perspectives must learn and work together" (CCSSI 2017b). The health and safety of our world depends on students' active knowledge-gathering about those next door *and* across the globe. Students must be able to effectively communicate

with people of diverse backgrounds and critically and constructively evaluate others' varied points of views. Considering data
visualizations created in other countries (look, for example, at
international newspapers) gives students insight into other perspectives.

CCSS Learning Goals for Mathematics (Standards for Mathematical Practice)

Incorporating data literacy content into the mathematics curriculum helps students better understand how statistics and
probability shape the information we are presented with daily
and how the intent of a visualization can shape our understanding of content. Students can show understanding by creating
their own data visualizations to justify a claim and then comparing their work with others' work. Incorporating data visualizations
can help develop skills that address several CCSS math standards
in our students.

CCSS.MATH.PRACTICE.MP1: Make sense of problems and persevere in solving them

Students need entry points to begin to develop understanding
of mathematical concepts. Introducing current, content-relat-
ed data visualizations help generate student interest in problem
solving. Interested students are better able to make meaning of
a problem in order to analyze it, make conjectures from it, plan
solutions for it, and consider analogous problems, while asking
themselves, *Does this make sense?*

CCSS.MATH.PRACTICE.MP2: Reason abstractly and quantitatively

Students need to understand quantities and their relationships in
many different contexts. Numbers represented visually (e.g., data

visualizations) help students to decode the numerical information. Asking questions about the meaning of symbols, such as,
"What is involved?" and "How many are there?" are necessary to
gain competency in computation. Data visualizations not only
provide the decontextualized information (symbols), but can also
be easily contextualized (subject/content) to develop a better understanding of the visualization's purpose and meaning.

CCSS.MATH.PRACTICE.MP3: Construct viable arguments and critique the reasoning
of others

Developing questions about content and analyzing that content
leads to discovering and justifying answers. By using inductive
reasoning to identify and predict a trend in a graph, table, or
chart, students can learn how to question and critique arguments
by identifying the information's flaws and strengths.

CCSS.MATH.PRACTICE.MP4: Model with mathematics

Data is and can be collected for just about anything. Students
can compare what they already know to what they see to make
new conclusions. Creating new data visualizations with newly
student-collected information can confirm or deny an existing
argument. Students can interpret data already being collected in many schools (i.e., the number of disposable trays used
in the cafeteria per day, the number of library patrons counted
per day, the number of water bottles saved per day by using the
filtered water fountain) to determine whether the data makes
sense or not based on assumptions they already have about their
school. Students should "routinely interpret their mathematical
results in the context of the situation and reflect on whether the
results make sense, possibly improving the model if it has not
served its purpose" (CCSSI 2017a).

There are many data visualization tools available to students, from simple graph paper to online statistics portals for finding and generating data visualizations from collected data. Students must choose the appropriate tool for the appropriate purpose. They must "use technological tools to explore and deepen their understanding of concepts" (CCSSI 2017a).

CCSS.MATH.PRACTICE.MP6: Attend to precision

Communication is successful only if it is precise enough to understand. Communicating through the presentation and creation of data visualizations (with appropriate and consistent labeling) can help students examine and present claims with accuracy and efficiency.

Data visualizations can do all that?

Many national standards can be addressed with content delivery through data visualizations. Don't be overwhelmed. As with any new idea for curriculum delivery, applicable standards can be easily identified through a simple comparison of lesson goals and the content material that supports them. The "hard work" of identifying applicable standards has been done for you, so now it is your job (as a curriculum expert in your content area) to match the standards with your content and determine how you will deliver it to students. It isn't hard – just think of data visualizations as variations of any traditional text that you are already using to deliver your content.

Though incorporating data visualizations is not only applicable to the mathematics curriculum, many of the statistics and probability concepts in math relate directly to how students decode, comprehend, and express information drawn from data visualizations. It is important that students have an understanding of the basic mathematical concepts presented in a data visualization. So many different types of data visualizations exist (and can be created) to express information from any content area. It may seem surprising that there are just as many English standards that can be addressed by content delivery through data visualizations as there are for math (if not more).

We know that standards are simply guidelines for excellent teaching, and to be excellent teachers we must continually reflect on and revise our content and its delivery. It is not necessary to include data visualizations in every lesson (as it is not necessary to address every standard in every lesson), but it is important to provide varied modes of content to ensure access to knowledge for different types of learners.

A 2015 study of secondary school students found that the preferred learning style was visual (45.7%), followed by auditory (21%), tactile (18.3%), and kinesthetic (15%) (Laxman, Govil, and Rani 2015). These findings support the incorporation of more visual learning experiences into the curriculum. Knowing our students' preferred learning style best determines how we deliver content. Incorporating data visualizations such as charts, graphs, histograms, and infographics into any content area will lead to a better understanding of concepts and subjects that our visually-oriented high schoolers have previously found very difficult to understand (Laxman, Govil, and Rani 2015).

How does developing data literacy skills help students with standardized testing?

Today's standardized tests require students to gather information from many different types of sources. Even within a single question there can be multiple modes in which information is presented. It is important for students to not skip over a data visualization because it is "just a picture." Visualizations need to be "read" and understood. As we know, data visualizations can present information more quickly and more clearly than blocks of texts. Understanding how to read these "texts" can increase comprehension speed. As students better understand how to read, interpret, and comprehend data visualizations they will perform better on standardized tests that integrate graphs, charts, and tables into questions.

ELA testing

For the purposes of ELA testing, students do not need to understand how the data was collected or to determine the reliability of the data. Therefore, students do not need to apply the "Mind the GAP" strategy to data visualizations on these tests.

Students do need to be able to

- » **extract information from multiple forms of text**
- » **make sense of that information,** including synthesizing information found in text with that found in graphics
- » **determine how this information best answers the question.** In fact, some questions require the student to "interpret graphics and to edit a part of the accompanying passage so that it clearly and accurately communicates the information in the graphics" (College Board 2017a).

What does that look like? Take a look at https://collegereadiness. collegeboard.org/sample-questions/reading/6 . This sample, which includes sample questions 6-8, is deemed appropriate for both SAT and PSAT practice. Students must interpret the bar chart and read the 526-word companion passage to answer the questions.

According to the College Board's preparatory materials (College Board 2017b),

>   **The objective of the questions in this sample is to "reasonably infer an assumption that is implied in the passage."** This is a common objective for many questions on the SAT. Students need to find evidence in multiple forms of text (in a short amount of time) to answer the questions.

>   **Students have 65 minutes to complete the Reading test.**

>   **There are 52 questions in the test.**

This gives students an average of *1 minute and 15 seconds* in which to process and answer each question. Therefore, building up students' *comprehension speed* and *ability to shift quickly between data and text* is critical to their success.

For a sample ELA lesson you can use with your students with sample test questions and data visualization, please see Appendix F. For additional preparatory materials, the College Board (developer of the PSAT/SAT) provides free access to sample questions in all tested content areas at https://collegereadiness.college-board.org/sample-questions/. Additional free online SAT practice is available through Khan Academy at https://www.khanacademy.org/sat. Many state tests provide access to online portals for students to practice sample questions. Consider accessing these resources to provide quick, daily classroom practice.

Science and standardized testing

Science standards still vary widely by state, but knowing how to draw meaning from graphed data is likely to appear on high school standardized tests. Appendix G provides sample teaching ideas related a released test question from the California Standards Test in Biology. In the sample, students must interpret the chart, a combination histograph/bar chart/scatter plot, to answer the question. This question requires students to find information from within an unfamiliar type of graph. Students must consider not only the length of each "bar," but also the shape of the bar (in regard to its width at a specific point).

Additional subjects and standardized testing

A lesson to help high school students approach sample test questions for the California Standards Test in U.S. History is available in Appendix H. Appendix I provides ideas for approaching visualizations in math.

Differentiation in testing

Before we move to the next section of this chapter, a quick word about how to approach data visualization test questions with your students with disabilities. Be aware that students with disabilities and/or English language learners may qualify for standardized test accommodations. To be compliant with the Every Student Succeeds Act (ESSA), all states must provide alternative assessments to students if deemed necessary by an individual student's individualized education plan (IEP) requirements (Advocacy Institute & Center for Law and Education n.d.). Check with your State Board of Education to determine the availability of alternative assessments and to determine how data visualizations are incorporated into those assessments.

So, now are you ready to incorporate data literacy instruction into your content area?

This chapter demonstrates how data literacy integration motivates different learner types, develops literacy skills, delivers content, addresses standards, and improves standardized test performance. All information needs to be questioned and reflected on before we can make an informed decision. Incorporating data visualizations into these conversations about "real world" issues sparks interest about and enthusiasm for classroom content.

To develop literacy skills among our diverse learners, we need to be flexible in how we deliver content. We can do this by utilizing a variety of teaching modalities, providing information that will overlap with information our students already have, and by reiterating and reinforcing information throughout a unit or during the course of a year (Friedman 2012, 11-15).

Integration of data visualizations into existing classroom lessons can help students to read, analyze, comprehend, and create information while addressing national standards. This type of integration better prepares our students to be able to extract information from multiple forms of text, in order to evaluate it and determine how the information best answers questions posed on standardized tests. These test questions contain claims (with supporting evidence) presented in charts, images, graphs, diagrams, tables, and text blocks. This data, in all forms, must be interpreted and understood in a prescribed amount of time to ensure success on all standardized tests.

Integrating data literacy into classroom learning is NOT about replacing your content, changing your teaching style, or dumbing things down. Integrating data literacy into your classroom is about supplementing your content, amplifying your teaching style, and developing inquiry learners. Because having the power to gain knowledge and make informed decisions means students understand data and where it comes from, are able to extract data from charts, graphs, tables, and other types of visualizations, and can present data as evidence to make a claim. Numbers representing any type of statistic can be used in any content area — from the breakdown of a college student's budget, to water pollution, to the Olympic medals won over time, and even to theatrical deaths. Data representation can take place in many forms from traditional texts to data visualizations. Data is information and information helps our students to better understand content.

Resources

Advocacy Institute and Center for Law and Education. n.d. "Our Kids Count: ESSA & Students With Disabilities." The Advocacy Institute. Accessed March 26, 2017. http://www.advocacyinstitute.org/ESSA/SWDanalysis.shtml.

California Department of Education. 2009. "Released Test Questions: Introduction – Biology." California Standards Test. Accessed March 26, 2017. http://www.cde.ca.gov/ta/tg/sr/documents/cstrtqbiology.pdf.

College Board, The. 2014. "Founding Documents and the Great Global Conversation." The College Board. Accessed March 26, 2017. https://collegereadiness.collegeboard.org/pdf/founding-documents-great-global-conversation.pdf.

College Board, The. 2017a. "Key Content Features." The College Board. Accessed March 26, 2017. https://collegereadiness.collegeboard.org/sat/inside-the-test/key-features

College Board, The. 2017b. "Sample Reading Test Questions." *Official SAT Study Guide*. College Board. Accessed March 26, 2017. https://collegereadiness.collegeboard.org/pdf/official-sat-study-guide-ch-12-sample-reading-test-questions.pdf

College Board, The. n.d. "Sample Questions: Introduction." The College Board. Accessed March 26, 2017. https://collegereadiness.collegeboard.org/sample-questions.

Common Core State Standards Initiative (CCSSI). 2017a. "Standards for Mathematical Practice," Common Core State Standards Initiative. Accessed March 26, 2017. http://www.corestandards.org/Math/Practice/.

Common Core State Standards Initiative (CCSSI). 2017b. "Students Who are College and Career Ready in Reading, Writing, Speaking, Listening, & Language." Common Core State Standards Initiative. Accessed March 26, 2017. http://www.corestandards.org/ELA-Literacy/introduction/students-who-are-college-and-career-ready-in-reading-writing-speaking-listening-language/ .

Dee, Johnny. 2013. "*Romeo And Juliet*: Everything You Need To Know - Infographic". *The Guardian*. Accessed March 26, 2017. http://web.archive.org/web/20140513090230/http://www.theguardian.com/culture/picture/2013/oct/11/romeo-and-juliet-infomania .

Greenleaf, Cynthia. WestEd. 2014. "Apprenticing Adolescents to Academic Literacy in the Subject Areas: The Reading Apprenticeship Instructional Framework." Reading Apprenticeship/WestEd, Mar. 20. Accessed March 26, 2017. https://readingapprenticeship.org/wp-content/uploads/2014/04/Apprenticing-Adolescents-to-Academic-Literacy-in-the-Subject-Areas-The-Reading-Apprenticeship-Instructional-Framework.pdf .

Friedman, Bruce D. 2012. *How to Teach Effectively: A Brief Guide*, 2nd ed. Chicago: Lyceum Books.

Gilmartin, Kathleen, and Karen Rex. 1999. "Student Toolkit 3: Working with Charts, graphs, and Tables." The Open University. Accessed March 27, 2017. http://www2.open.ac.uk/students/skillsforstudy/doc/working-with-charts-graphs-and-tables-toolkit.pdf.

Gosling, Mya. 2015."The Romeo and Juliet Death Clock," Peace, Good Tickle Brain (blog). August 26. Accessed March 27, 2017. http://goodticklebrain.com/home/2015/8/26/the-romeo-and-juliet-death-clock .

Laxman, Singh, Punita Govil, and Rekha Rani. 2015. "Learning style preferences among secondary school students." *International Journal of Recent Scientific Research* 6 (5), 3924-3928. 3924-3928. http://www.recentscientific.com/sites/default/files/2411.pdf .

Moje, Elizabeth Birr. 2006. "Motivating texts, motivating contexts, motivating adolescents: An examination of the role of motivation in adolescent literacy practices and development." *Perspectives* 32 (3), 10-14). Accessed March 26, 2017. http://305089.edicypages. com/files/MotivatingTextsMotivatingContextsMotivatin-gAdolescents.pdf.

Nester, Hannah. n.d. "Infographic: 10 Things You Should Know About Water." Circle of Blue. Accessed March 26, 2017. http://www.circleofblue.org/2009/world/infographic-ten-things-you-should-know-about-water/.

Sweetser, Shannon. 2010. "22 Mind-Blowing Infographics on Education," *Socrato! Learning Analytics Blog*. November 4, Accessed March 26, 2017. http://blog.socrato. com/2-mind-blowing-infographics-on-education/.

Rost, Lisa Charlotte, and Alyson Hurt. 2016. "How The Olympic Medal Tables Explain The World." *The Torch* blog/NPR.org, August 6. Accessed March 26, 2017. http://www.npr.org/sections/thetorch/2016/08/05/488507996/how-the-olympic-medal-tables-explains-the-world.

WestEd. 2017. "Reading Apprenticeship." WestEd. Accessed March 26, 2017. https://www.wested.org/project/reading-apprenticeship/.

Appendix A: Tips for integrating data visualizations into any content area

If you have 30 minutes,

Share these rules of thumb of the Reading Apprenticeship "Mind the GAP" strategy with students before they begin analyzing an infographic:

- Consider the genre, audience, and purpose of the data visualization. Every text:
  - » is created to embrace a specific **genre**.
  - » is directed toward a specific **audience**.
  - » has an intended **purpose**.

If you have one class period,

Then ask students to:

- Determine the claim of the text.
- Determine how it is presented. Is it meant to inform or persuade?
- Identify the evidence that supports it and engage students in conversations that address the rules of thumb above, using the "Mind the GAP" terms of genre, audience, and purpose.

If you have multiple class periods,

Then ask students to compare the information found in a traditional text to information in a data visualization by:

- Providing students with a more traditional text (textbook, novel, article, etc.) and an infographic related to that text.
- Asking students to find the information presented in the data visualizations within the traditional text to determine if the facts are represented accurately in the infographic. This can be accomplished through talking to the text, close reading, and/or using the search tool COMMAND+F (on a Mac) or CTRL+F (on a PC) to search for words and phrases in an electronic version of a text.
- Asking students to compare how claims are made and supported by each type of text.

If you have an entire unit,

Have your students create an infographic by:

- Looking around your school/community to find out how data is already being collected or considering the data presented in a required text.

- Considering the purpose/goal of the data collection.

- Finding existing data or collecting new data.

- Analyzing the data to determine what it means.

- Determining the best method to convey the data.

- Generating data visualizations.

- Presenting and critiquing student-created data visualizations.

Appendix B: Integrating an infographic about *Romeo and Juliet* into the ELA classroom

Visit "Infomania Fact-checking the famous: *Romeo and Juliet*." While originally published in December 2016 by *The Guardian* online, this is now archived at http://web.archive.org/web/20140513090230/http://www.theguardian.com/culture/picture/2013/oct/11/romeo-and-juliet-infomania .

This infographic does not document the deaths in *Romeo and Juliet* but instead pulls data from the text to compare the author, themes, main characters, and references to current events and movies. It's not just a poster about the tragic story of two star-crossed lovers: it's the research process in visual form.

Before you ask your students to create their own infographics, a useful activity is to unpack an existing infographic to help students understand its intent, what claims it makes, and its success in doing so.

If you have 30 minutes,

Use the Reading Apprenticeship "Mind the GAP" strategy outlined in Appendix A.

If you have one class period,

Ask students to:

- **Determine the claim of the text**. This text is providing information about William Shakespeare, his original play of *Romeo and Juliet*, subsequent and varied incarnations of *Romeo and Juliet* throughout the years, and modern *Romeo and Juliet* connections.

- **Determine how the text is presented.** Is it meant to inform or persuade? The intended purpose of this text is to inform the reader. It's labeled as a fact-checker, but it also includes some veiled humor. Ask: *to what extent is this an appropriate source of information for a scholarly analysis of Romeo and Juliet?*

- **Identify supporting evidence and engage students in conversations about the rules of thumb to "Mind the GAP".**
  - » **Genre:** This text is visually representative of an infographic. Infographics are visual documents composed of text blocks, images, graphs, quotes, timelines, and statistics.
  - » **Audience:** By looking at the sources of information at the bottom of the text, students can determine if the information is from a reliable and authoritative source. This helps determine if the intended audience is a scholarly reader or a casual fan. A visual scan can also help determine the intended audience. The infographic's look and language are informal. Therefore, the audience is anyone interested in the play.
  - » **Purpose:** The intended purpose of this text is to inform the reader, not persuade. This infographic is not trying to convince the reader that *Romeo and Juliet* is the best play ever written … or even trying to persuade the reader to read *Romeo and Juliet*. It is merely providing information about William Shakespeare and about the play over the years.

If you have multiple class periods,

Compare the information found in a more traditional text to information in a data visualization by:

- **Providing students with Shakespeare's original *Romeo and Juliet*.**
- **Asking students to compare the infographic's content to that of the traditional text to determine if the infographic represents the play accurately.** This can be accomplished through talking to the text, close reading, and/or using the search tool COMMAND+F (on a Mac) or CTRL+F (on a PC) to search for words and phrases in on a website or PDF version of the play.
  - » **Compare** basic facts such as how old the protagonists are, the length of their relationship, how they died, and more.
  - » **Search for language.** Shakespeare's plays provide students with a great opportunity to go on word searches to find uses of his unique language. For

example, students can search for the word "bump" to determine how many times it is used, where it is used, by whom, and what it means in context. You can then discuss how "bump" used today may or may not have a different definition or connotation.

» **Visualize word frequency.** From the activity above, students gain data they can use to graph word frequency in the original text.

» **Track words over time.** Students can use the Google Books Ngram viewer to chart a Shakespearean words usage or popularity over time (https://books.google.com/ngrams).

- **Asking students to compare how claims are made and supported by each of the text types.** For example, evidence of one of the tragedy's themes (the forceful nature of romantic love) can be found in the original text and in the infographic. Ask students to provide supporting evidence in both texts to determine if the infographic accurately represents the theme.

If you have an entire unit:

Refer to the unit-length strategies in Appendix A.

Appendix C: Integrating an infographic about water into the science classroom

Visit "Ten Things You Should Know About Water" at http://www.circleofblue.org/2009/world/infographic-ten-things-you-should-know-about-water/ .

 If you have 30 minutes,

Use the "Mind the GAP" strategy outlined in Appendix A.

If you have one class period,

Ask students to:

- **Determine the claim of the text**. This text highlights the value of water, how it is used, and how easily it can become polluted.

- **Determine how it is presented**. Is it meant to inform or persuade? This text is meant to convince the reader that water is a valuable and scarce resource.

- **Identify supporting evidence and engage students in "Mind the GAP" conversations:**

  » **Genre** – This text is visually representative of an info-graphic as defined in Appendix B.

  » **Audience** – By looking at the sources of information at the bottom of the text, students can determine if the information is from a reliable and authoritative source. This helps determine if the intended audience is a scholarly or casual. Students can also go to the Circle of Blue website (http://www.circleofblue.org) and look at the organization's "About" page. This will help students understand if this organization has a political agenda, constituency, or point of view. A visual scan of this infographic helps determine the intended audience. The look and language is formal, yet it is still approachable and understandable for most high school readers. The intended audience is anyone who can understand the science behind the claims being made.

» **Purpose** – The purpose of this text is to provide information in such a way that the reader becomes persuaded that water should be conserved. The title of the infographic is a discussion starter to determine if the text is meant to inform or persuade. Why should the reader know these facts about water? What's the purpose for sharing these ten pieces of evidence? Should water be conserved? If so, why?

If you have multiple class periods,

Compare the information found in a more traditional text to information in the data visualization by:

- **Providing students with textbook information or a pertinent article for use as comparison**. Or, in the case of this specific infographic, students can compare the text on the Circle of Blue website to the visualization.

- **Asking students to find the visualized information within the traditional text to determine if the facts are represented accurately in the infographic**. Students could also search online to find other reliable sources that confirm or disprove the infographic's information. This can be accomplished through talking to the text, close reading, and/or using the search tool COMMAND+F (on a Mac) or CTRL+F (on a PC) to search for words and phrases in a digital document. For example, how much of Earth's water is used for agriculture? What percentage of Earth's water is salt versus fresh? How much water is used to produce different products? etc.

- **Asking students to compare how claims are made and supported by each type of text.** For example, students could study the water cycle within a traditional text to make inferences and connections as to why the infographic claims may or may not be accurate and supportable in reference to what they already know (or are learning) about the natural processes of Earth.

If you have an entire unit,

Refer to the unit-length strategies in Appendix A.

Appendix D: Integrating an infographic about the Olympics into the social studies classroom

Visit "How The Olympic Medal Tables Explains The World" at http://www.npr.org/sections/thetorch/2016/08/05/488507996/ how-the-olympic-medal-tables-explains-the-world .

 If you have 30 minutes,

Refer to the 30-minute "Mind the Gap" strategies in Appendix A.

If you have one class period,

Ask students to:

- **Determine the claim of the text.** This visualization claims that the number of medals a country wins (or doesn't win) in an Olympic games correlates to an event in history.

- **Determine how it is presented.** Is it meant to inform or persuade? This text is meant to inform the reader. Upon discerning the share of Olympic medals won by each country, the reader is then supposed to make connections to historical, political, and social events to determine why a country's medal tally during a specific Olympics reflects what was occurring in that country (or the world) at that time.

- **Identify supporting evidence and engage students in "Mind the GAP" conversations.**

  » **Genre** – This text is a series of bar charts (or bar graphs). A bar chart is a visual display of data presented in a series of bars of different heights (proportional to the data they represent) plotted over time. A bar chart is a type of data visualization.

  » **Audience** – By looking at the sources of information at the bottom of the text, students can determine if the information is from a reliable and authoritative source. This helps determine if the intended audience is a scholarly reader or a casual reader. Because the source of the text is "Sports Reference," the reader can infer that this text is first intended for those interested in sports. Students can also go to NPR's website (http://npr.org), and look at the organization's "About" page. This will help students understand if this organization has a political agenda and a particular following that the site caters to. A visual scan of this infographic can also help to determine the intended audience. The entire look of the data visualization is formal yet easy to understand. This is intended for high school (and possibly middle school) students and above who are interested in making connections between sports and world history.

» **Purpose** – The purpose of this text is to inform. The text makes connections between sports and world history — a perfect discussion starter for those who otherwise may not be interested in world history.

If you have multiple class periods,

Compare the information found in a traditional text to information in a data visualization by:

- **Providing students with textbook information or a pertinent article to compare to this infographic.** Or in the case of this specific infographic, students can compare it to the accompanying text on the NPR website (http://www.npr.org/sections/ thetorch/2016/08/05/488507996/how-the-olympic-medal-tables-explains-the-world).

- **Asking students to find the information presented in the data visualizations within the traditional text to determine if the facts are represented accurately in the infographic**. This can be accomplished through talking to the text, close reading, and/or using the search tool COMMAND+F (on a Mac) or CTRL+F (on a PC) to search for words and phrases in an electronic version of a world history textbook or article, or on a website. For example, students could go back to the source, Sports Reference (sports-reference.com), and determine if the website information regarding the number of medals won per country per Olympic Games has been transposed accurately in the bar charts.

- **Asking students to compare how claims are made and supported by each type of text.** For example, students can search their world history textbook for key events occurring around the world or within the specific countries of the United States, Russia, China, and Germany in the past 100 years. They can then compare this information to the information presented in the bar charts, discern why such events would affect each country's performance at an Olympic Games. A comparison between the NPR article (URL above) and the easy-to-comprehend visualization can help diverse types of learners better understand the intent of the word-dense article.

If you have an entire unit,

Knowledge of founding documents is crucial to student success on the SAT. The Reading Test and the Writing and Language Test of the SAT asks students to read and answer questions about "works that explore challenging ideas, offer important insights, reveal new discoveries, and build deep knowledge in numerous disciplines" (College Board 2014).

Social studies content lessons may already incorporate these kinds of documents — consider the extra insight that could be gained by making them visual. Ask your students to create data visualizations of founding documents such as the U.S. Constitution. Assign students sections of the U.S. Constitution and guide them in identifying data from the document (i.e. age/residency requirements, term lengths, voting majorities, Electoral College representation, amendments, etc.) with which to create data visualizations. (Refer to Chapter 9 for strategies for building high-impact infographics with students.)

For more ideas, refer to the unit-length strategies in Appendix A.

Appendix E: Integrating an infographic about budgeting into a math classroom

Visit "Breakdown of Average Student Budget" (#5 at http://blog. socrato.com/2-mind-blowing-infographics-on-education/).

 If you have 30 minutes,

Use the "Mind the GAP" strategy outlined in Appendix A.

If you have one class period,

Ask students to:

- **Determine the claim of the text**. This text's claim is to present a breakdown of today's average college student's budget and to compare it to a 1915 college student's budget in today's dollars.

- **Determine how it is presented**. Is it meant to inform or persuade? This infographic is informative, but it also may effectively persuade students to save for college!

- **Identify supporting evidence and engage students in "Mind the GAP" conversations:**

  » **Genre** – This text is visually representative of an infographic as defined in Appendix B.

  » **Audience** – By looking at the information sources at the bottom of the text, students can determine if the information is from a reliable and authoritative source. This helps determine if the intended audience is scholarly or casual. Because the sources include a professional tax and accounting firm, government statistics, and a professional survey company, the reader can infer that this text is first intended for those interested in finances. The infographic's title, "Breakdown of Average Student Budget," also identifies the text's intended audience — college-bound students and their parents. The reader must look at the text more closely to discern that this budget breakdown is indeed that of the average college student. A visual scan of this infographic can also help to determine the intended audience. The entire look of the infographic is polished yet easily understood.

>> **Purpose** – This text's purpose is to inform. The text breaks down a college student's budget to highlight proportional spending and decision making. This infographic would be a good discussion starter for students in a personal finance class (and their parents) to provoke a conversation about financial responsibility.

If you have multiple class periods,

Compare the information in the infographic to a more traditional text by:

- **Providing students with related formulas and concepts from a math textbook to compare how the same formulas and concepts are represented in this infographic.** Concepts might include averages, percentages, adjustment for inflation, comparisons, etc.

- **Asking students to find the information presented in the data visualizations within a traditional text to determine if the infographic's information is accurate.** For example, students can look for inconsistencies in how the infographic represents the data (for example, in the pie chart breakdowns) to better understand why that kind of visualization was used and suggest how it could be better explained or represented. Why do the smaller pie chart percentages not add up to 100? How is it explained (or not) in the infographic?

- **Asking students to compare how claims are made and supported by each text type.** For example, students could determine the amount of money they will have available to spend in college and then break down that budget into the infographic's categories and percentages. The infographic's claim that the average student's budget is 40% discretionary could lead to conversations about financial inequities between students. Searching the sources for the current information (this infographic is from 2009) could help students make an updated version.

If you have an entire unit:

Refer to the unit-length strategies in Appendix A.

Appendix F: Using a sample assessment question for an ELA classroom

Please access https://collegereadiness.collegeboard.org/ sample-questions/reading/8 for this activity.

 If you have 15 minutes,

Ask students to review the bar graph and draw out as much information as they can. For example, you might encourage them to ask:

- What question needs to be answered?
- What is the graph's purpose, according to its title?
- What is measured in the bar graph according to the labels on the x- and y-axes?
- What is the significance of the varying heights of the bars?
- What is the significance of the downward trend of the bars as the graph moves from left to right?
- What is the significance of the darker gray bar?

If you have one class period,

Ask students to compare how claims are made and supported in each text in the sample problem. To answer question 8, students need to choose from a list of claims to discern which claim is best represented by the graph and the information (evidence) it contains that supports the claim. Students should also consider information from the companion text to answer the sample question. The information (or evidence) provided in both texts will support a specific claim. Students should look at the length of the bars representing the cities mentioned in each answer choice to determine which claim the graphs supports. After doing so, students can identify choice "C" as the correct answer.

Appendix G: Using a sample assessment question for a science classroom

Please access http://www.cde.ca.gov/ta/tg/sr/documents/cstrtqbiology.pdf and find question 73 (p. 25) for this activity.

If you have 15 minutes,

Ask students to discern the information found in the visualization. For example:

- What question needs to be answered?
- What is the purpose of the graph, according to the title?
- What is being measured on the graph, according to the labels on the x- and y-axes?
- What is the significance of the varying lengths, widths, and shapes of the "bars"?

If you have one class period,

Ask students how claims are made and supported in the graph. For example, after students understand how the information is presented in the graph, they need to apply that knowledge to choose the correct answer. This may be an unfamiliar graph type to many students, so letting them know that all the information they need exists in the graph will help ease their anxiety. By looking at the question, they can infer that they need to focus on the segment of the graph labeled "Cretaceous" to determine which group demonstrated the greatest biodiversity. Limiting the focus to just that segment helps eliminate confusion. The students can then see that all the different animal groups have varying widths in this segment. The lizard group has the widest shape at that point, so the correct answer is choice "D."

Appendix H: Using a sample assessment question for a social studies classroom

Please access http://www.cde.ca.gov/ta/tg/sr/documents/ cstrtqhssmar18.pdf for this activity.

 If you have 15 minutes,

Ask students to discern the information found in the data visualization. For example, students should determine:

- What question needs to be answered?
- According to its title, what is the purpose of the table?
- What do the numbers in the table represent?
- How do the numbers in the table correlate to a sector?

If you have one class period,

Ask students to compare their pre-existing knowledge to the evidence in the graph to support a claim. In this case, all the information necessary to support a claim (or answer the question) is NOT provided in the table. Students need to consider their pre-existing knowledge of world history to identify which factor created the trend the table represents. Since the table title identifies "Employment Figures," we can determine that the numbers under the three sector headings represent people (in millions according to the table). The student needs to already understand the history of the factors listed in the answer choices in order to choose the factor that is most responsible. Students must already know that advances in technology during the first half of the 20th century (i.e., the assembly line) spurred production and increased demand for manufactured goods, thereby creating more jobs for more people. Students also need to understand that the U.S.'s involvement in World War II (in the 1940s) spurred demand for weaponry, also creating more jobs in manufacturing. It is necessary for students to have this prior knowledge and be able to interpret the table in order to choose the correct answer, "A". That's a lot of pre-existing knowledge to bring to the table (pun intended)!

Appendix I: Using a sample assessment question for a math classroom

Please access https://collegereadiness.collegeboard.org/ sample-questions/math/calculator-permitted/20 for this activity.

 If you have 15 minutes,

Ask students to discern the information found in the data visualization. For example:

- What question needs to be answered?
- What is the purpose of the scatter plot according to its title?
- What is being measured according to the labels on the x- and y-axes?

If you have one class period,

Ask students to compare how claims are made and supported in the graph. Students first need to understand what type of graph this is. This graph, a scatter plot, plots the values of two variables along two axes. The resulting pattern of points reveals a correlation between the two variables. The straight line in the scatter plot runs through the center of the points and is called the "line of best fit." To answer this question, students need to read the graph and then use their pre-existing knowledge of mathematical formulas to determine the closest value to the average yearly increase in the number of manatees. By looking at the horizontal x-axis in comparison to the line of best fit, the student can determine that growth occurred from about 1991 to about 2011. This is the time period the question is concerned with. By looking at the vertical y-axis in comparison to the line of best fit, the student can determine that the number of manatees grew from about 1,000 to 4,000 during this time period. This indicates a population increase of about 3,000 manatees. The student needs to determine the average yearly increase over the 20 years the graph represents. The student should then divide 3,000 manatees by 20 years to determine that choice "C" is the correct answer.

11 | Teaching data contexts: An instructional lens

Debbie Abilock

In textbooks, data often appears next to text that provides context and guidance about how to interpret that data. In the real world, however, disaggregated data often appears disconnected from any text that students might look to for explanation. Bits of data are snagged, aggregated and displayed, often with little context (Weinberger 2007). We encounter them as infographics, unattributed news, data factoids, Google "answers" and even T-shirts (Figure 1). Educators can just accept these "answers" or they can apply an instructional framework of information literacy reasoning (ACRL 2016) to data and treat them as opportunities for inquiry.

Figure 1: Data presented on a t-shirt at a baseball game. Copyright Debbie Abilock, used with permission.

A statistic doesn't speak for itself, by itself. As readers, we contextualize statistics to make meaning or evaluate an argument. As authors, we extract and manipulate statistics from data sources to use as evidence within an argument. As the Association of College and Research Librarians' *ACRL Framework for Information Literacy* (2016) points out, information is constructed and contextual. Sources reflect the "creators' expertise and credibility, and are evaluated based on the information need and the context in which the information will be used ... [V]arious communities may recognize different types of authority. It is contextual in that the information need may help to determine the level of authority required." The same is true of data. As you have seen elsewhere in this book, we must train ourselves to think of numerical data not as truth but as a reflection of the world in which the data was defined, collected, and discussed.

The following scenarios follow a school librarian who is focused on including data literacy in her instruction, specifically framing it within an understanding of data *context*. By no means are her responses the only possible ones; they depend on the data that's both available and relevant to the expertise of the students, the goals of the teacher, and our own inclinations and understandings.

Scenario 1: Area: Why context matters

A student needs the area of Alaska for a project he's doing about the impact of glaciers on global warming. Because he is in the early phases of research, his librarian recommends that he use the open Web to gain easy-to-read, easy-to-access basic information. He uses the search terms [size of Alaska] in an early Google search (note: the brackets are a convention representing the search box but are not characters entered into the search box). Google's algorithms can now predict the likely kind of information the searcher desires (likely because the word "size" is part of the query) and offer an immediate answer in lieu of a link to a potential answer (see Figure 2).

Figure 2: Google search result for [size of Alaska]

Alaska must be a pretty big state, he thinks. Another quick search confirms that it's the largest ... but why are three area numbers listed in the Wikipedia chart: total area (his number), land area, and water area (Figure 3)? He assumed that he'd get a single number answer — a fixed and immutable "area" statistic. He asks the librarian if he should use the total area, which includes water bodies like inland lakes, rivers and even the territorial waters around the land, or the land area which, in the case of Alaska, includes glaciers — that are melting.

This question is important to the student because glaciers are water ... but also solid, like land. The librarian knows that everyday words may imply quantities, counting and measuring but that students may not grasp their significance.

The librarian explains to the student that certain everyday words like area imply a measurement or quantity but, because it is used in various situations, its definition may be ambiguous or imprecise. In this case geologists, geophysicists and other scientists are precise about the area measure they are using (e.g., land or water), so that they can compare the appropriate numbers with others who are measuring glacial recession. Since the whole class will encounter the same ambiguity in area measurements, the librarian decides that this nuance merits greater attention and begins to curate specific information that will help students understand which number to use and why.

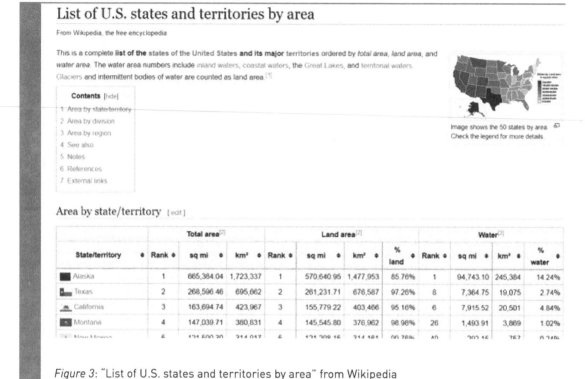

List of U.S. states and territories by area

From Wikipedia, the free encyclopedia

This is a complete list of the states of the United States and its major territories ordered by *total area*, *land area*, and *water area*. The water area numbers include inland waters, coastal waters, the Great Lakes, and territorial waters. Glaciers and intermittent bodies of water are counted as land area.[1]

Contents [hide]
- 1 Area by state/territory
- 2 Area by division
- 3 Area by region
- 4 See also
- 5 Notes
- 6 References
- 7 External links

Image shows the 50 states by area.
Check the legend for more details.

Area by state/territory [edit]

State/territory	Rank	Total area[2] sq mi	km²	Rank	Land area[2] sq mi	km²	% land	Rank	Water[2] sq mi	km²	% water
Alaska	1	665,384.04	1,723,337	1	570,640.95	1,477,953	85.76%	1	94,743.10	245,384	14.24%
Texas	2	268,596.46	695,662	2	261,231.71	676,587	97.26%	8	7,364.75	19,075	2.74%
California	3	163,694.74	423,967	3	155,779.22	403,466	95.16%	6	7,915.52	20,501	4.84%
Montana	4	147,039.71	380,831	4	145,545.80	376,962	98.96%	26	1,493.91	3,869	1.02%
New Mexico	5	121,590.30	314,917	5	121,298.15	314,161	99.76%	49	292.15	757	0.24%

Figure 3: "List of U.S. states and territories by area" from Wikipedia

An instructor curates to help students develop context or background specific to their needs and the learning goal. Curation is not just linking to a bunch of sources about climate change or glaciers. Google does that. For a librarian to curate for a project means having a conversation with the teacher about the learning goal and the students' needs, then evaluating and selecting from the "glut" of sources just those which provide the context needed for the students' investigation. Curation is a targeted instructional strategy librarians can use to build just-in-time background (Abilock n.d.).

Examples of quantifiers found in everyday contexts

- all
- area
- distance
- every
- fewer
- heavy
- light
- many

- more
- much
- none
- progress
- some
- trend
- volume

Knowing that other schools might also study the effects of climate change on Alaskan glaciers, the librarian taps into social curation tools and searches curated curricular resources built by librarians for use in their academic, special library and school communities (Valenza et al. 2014). The results are abundant, to say the least, so she runs her thinking by the teacher. She proposes limiting this initial curation to specific pages from the U.S. Geological Survey, the major source of U.S. earth science data. Her final list (below) is highly selective and annotated to clarify why each site is relevant and important:

» **Definition from the U.S. Geological Survey's Glaciology Project (http://www.usgs.gov/climate_landuse/clu_rd/ glacierstudies/massBalance.asp)** This site explains how the area and thickness of glaciers are calculated. The USGS' Glaciology Project measures how glaciers respond to climate change in order to both predict and prepare for the impact of glacial changes. Read their description of the significance of this glacial mass research to climate change study (http:// www2.usgs.gov/climate_landuse/clu_rd/gla- cierstudies/ benchmarkGlaciers.asp).

» **Visual explanation from Researchers at the Centre for Quaternary Research at Royal Holloway, University of London (http://www.antarcticglaciers.org/ modern-glaciers/introduction-glacier-mass-balance/)** This site charts explaining glacier mass balance and graphs showing trends of mass balance over time written by a glaciologist as part of her commitment to education.

» **Arctic Sea Ice Thickness Maps Data from the Center for Polar Observation and Modeling (CPOM) (http://www.cpom. ucl.ac.uk/csopr/seaice.html)** CPOM compares satellite radar signals that bounce off ice vs. water and, together with ice concentration and types data, can produce accurate thickness measurements in near-real time. For additional insight on how satellites can be used to measure glaciers, see http://www.indiaenvironmentportal.org.in/files/file/Arctic%20sea%20ice%20warm%20winter.pdf.

» **Glacier Mass Balance Data from the National Snow and Ice Data Center (https://nsidc.org/data/ g10002)** Historical data from 1945-2003 is available for download. The National Snow and Ice Data Center (NSIDC) manages data and supports research about the cryosphere.

She plans to do a mini-lesson to introduce these sources, then help students find data in CPOM and NSIDC related to their selected glaciers. The teacher, who is much more interested in getting into the action-research project, will use the U.S. Climate Resilience Toolkit framework (https://toolkit.climate.gov), a source that the librarian found, to help the class define the problems, develop solutions based on what they've learned, and decide on actions they might take.

In this first scenario, the librarian recognizes that the student believes he is searching for an unambiguous term that stood for a single number. Rather than treat this as one student's confusion, the librarian reframes the misconception in a way that can help the entire class recognize that scientists collect specifically-defined measurements over time in order to see trends, make predictions and take action. Her just-in-time curated resources focus on the area measurements that students need for their class' science project. Her annotations explain why these sources are relevant and authoritative, modeling the critical thinking she wants students to use when evaluating other sources for the project. Collaborative planning between the teacher and librarian take into account their respective strengths and goals.

Strategies

- **Listen for verbal quantifiers.** These are contextual clues to opportunities for data literacy instruction.

- **Identify relevant curators**. Reach out for help from social media curators and collaborative curation venues with demonstrated expertise in this particular topic in order to develop your own background and recognize the most useful resources for this specific research.

- **Understand student learning goals.** Understand the purpose of the assignment so that your sources are highly relevant rather than "just-in-case" general pointers.

- **Annotate curated sources.** Write descriptions that evaluate the data context and assess their authority for this topic, as these become models for the students' own evaluative thinking.

For state or country reports, ask students to find the area in square miles (or square kilometers) using Google search results, Wolfram Alpha, a government source or other appropriate sources. What reasons might account for differences? (For more guidance, please see https://www2.census.gov/geo/pdfs/reference/GARM/Ch15GARM.pdf .)

Here are examples of results for Alaska:

Area in square miles	Source
570,640.95	**United States Census** (http://www.census.gov/quickfacts/table/LND110210/00,02)
663,300	**Google** (https://www.google.com/search?q=area+of+alaska&ie=utf-8&oe=utf-8)
661,957	**Alaska Government publication** (p.8) (http://labor.alaska.gov/research/pop/estimates/pub/popover.pdf)
665,400	**Wolfram Alpha** (https://www.wolframalpha.com/input/?i=area+of+alaska)

Here are examples of results for Great Britain:

Area in square miles	Source
84,440	**Wolfram Alpha** (https://www.wolframalpha.com/input/?i=area+of+Great+Britain)
88,745	**Google** (goo.gl/PFYucQ)
80,823 (given as 209331.1 sq. km)	**United Nations** (http://islands.unep.ch/ICJ.htm#943)
94,525	**Nations Encyclopedia** (http://www.nationsencyclopedia.com/economies/Europe/United-Kingdom.html)

Scenario 2: Population: How data is constructed and contextualized

American history classes are studying shifts in people's views about immigration. The teachers plan to contrast the colonial immigrants' attitudes toward the indigenous Native American population with U.S. citizens' responses to recent immigrant groups.

The librarian knows that the teachers want students to infer historical attitudes from primary sources like letters, journals, diaries, and drawings that they've used before. She realizes that she has an opportunity to add data as another type of primary source: a census and a survey. She plans to ask students to draw inferences about societal attitudes by comparing them over time.

 Examples of primary source data by discipline

- **Humanities** – text mining from unstructured data in archives and manuscripts
- **Social sciences** – tabulated data collected from surveys, polls, census
- **Natural sciences** – tabulated data collected from clinical trials, controlled studies

She reasons that students should learn about the U.S. Census data because it's the main source of U.S. population data. Besides providing the population counts that are used to determine the number of seats each state has in the House of Representatives, the results are used "for many important but overlooked political, economic, and social decisions that end up affecting our daily lives" (U.S. Census Bureau, "Why it's important" n.d.).

Although *statistics* from public opinion polls are reported ubiquitously today, she is less certain about how to find the *primary sources* of public opinion survey *data* from which particular statistics are extracted. Many LibGuides from colleges and universities point to the SDA Archive, which uses the General Social Survey (GSS) and the American National Election Study (ANES), two major sources of public opinion research in the United States. However, after trying to search them herself, she decides that they are too complex for high school students. Instead she discovers the beta GSS Explorer (https://gssdataexplorer.norc.org/), which students can easily use to search, extract, analyze, and even visualize statistics from their longitudinal public opinion surveys run since 1972.

At the social studies departmental meeting she proposes that she teach students to use a public opinion survey and the census to trace public attitudes. She'll use Alaska as a model, reserving the thirteen original colonies and their states for the students' own research. She quickly shows teachers how to search the U.S. Census to find population figures, starting with American Indians and Alaskan Natives in Alaska's 2010 census figures (U.S. Census Bureau, "Quick Facts: Alaska," n.d.). Then, using five slides, she explains how the Census's evolving definitions of "Indian" mirrors the societal shifts in attitudes toward race and immigrants:

» **Slide #1** Definition #1: The 1787 Constitution established the census to allocate the number of representatives from each state and determine how taxes would be divided among the states. Initially Indians weren't included for either purpose — *they were not considered federal or state citizens because they didn't pay taxes* — so they weren't counted.

» **Slide #2** Definition #2: The American Indian wars and large-scale removals exacerbated distinctions between tribal membership vs. citizenship for the U.S. Marshals, the 1860 census counters, because they were told to count Indians — but only those *who had "renounced tribal rule."* (See Figure 4.)

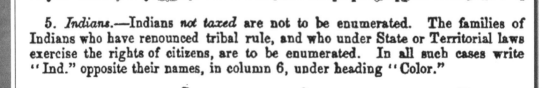

5. *Indians.*—Indians *not taxed* are not to be enumerated. The families of Indians who have renounced tribal rule, and who under State or Territorial laws exercise the rights of citizens, are to be enumerated. In all such cases write "Ind." opposite their names, in column 6, under heading "Color."

Figure 4: Instructions on counting Indians for the 1860 census (U.S. Census Bureau 1860).

- » **Slide #3** The census takers were instructed to *exclude Indians on reservations, those that were roaming unsettled areas and any Indians living in Alaska* (Collins 2006). Although people thought that Indians had clear physical characteristics, the census had no instruction on how to identify them, especially those that were of mixed race living within the general population. No surprise that the marshals found it difficult to count everyone.

- » **Slide #4** Definition #3: The 1890 census instructed that "all Indians" were to be counted — except *neither Aleuts nor Eskimos were included as Indians* until Alaska became a state (1959).

- » **Slide #5** Definition #4: When the government began mailing the census to homes (1960), people were asked to *self-identify as Indian*. However, *people of Hispanic origin self-identified as Indian* in large numbers in the 2010 census, muddying the definition still further (U.S. Census, "Instructions" n.d.; Decker 2011).

She demonstrates how to use Pew's language timeline to pinpoint when racial terms were added or changed in census questions (Pew Research Center for Social and Demographic Trends 2015b). Then she suggests that, when historical periods and immigrant groups are discussed in class, teachers refer to that timeline and prompt students to consider why the government would want to count that group, in that way, at that time.

When classes are ready to look at contemporary attitudes, she will devote another library period to having students read a historical analysis of attitudes toward immigrants that researchers derived from opinion-polling archives (DeSilver 2015). During a third library period, she'll help students create accounts at the GSS Explorer in order to select and visualize statistical data, evaluate survey methods, and discuss their reflection of attitudes. In a fourth library period, she will ask students to contrast a census with a survey as a formative assessment. In particular, they'll use a Pew Research survey, looking for potential bias or distortions in the types of questions, then compare it with the proposed data collection plan for the next decennial census (Pew Research Center for U.S. Politics and Policy 2016; Cohn 2015).

After both the science and social studies projects are finished, she'll want to give students a short online quiz in which they compare the kinds of primary sources used in science vs. social science. For now, she'll use the C3 social studies standards during library class (see Figure 5) to build their specific awareness about the forms of primary source data that various social scientists use to answer questions in their particular field.

Wrap-up

In this second scenario, the librarian recognizes that the history teachers have overlooked data as a type of primary source. She uses the U.S. Census, a comprehensive longitudinal public data aggregation of U.S. demographic and economic information, because of its importance in government policy decisions as well as in the electoral process. Since students often encounter surveys and polls in popular culture, her goal is to have students distinguish between a survey (which samples a representative subset of the population to make estimates about the entire population) and a census (which aims to gather data from every person in a country). In addition to her explicit focus on how changing definitions and question wording impact data collection and interpretation, she embeds this sequence of lessons within her longer-term scope and sequence plans to integrate vertically across grades and to make curricular connections across disciplines.

WAYS OF KNOWING	CIVICS/ GOVERNMENT POLITICAL SCIENTISTS SAY...	ECONOMICS ECONOMISTS SAY...	GEOGRAPHY GEOGRAPHERS SAY...	HISTORY HISTORIANS SAY...
DIMENSION 2				
DATA SOURCES NEEDED TO ADDRESS QUESTIONS	Government policies, policy pronouncements, political poll results, statistics, leadership efforts, political behavior; observations of local conditions, interviews; news reports	Statistics and lots of them in as real time as possible (labor, capital, credit, monetary flow, supply, demand)	Spatial and environmental data; statistics, map representations, GIS data to measure observable changes to the planet; indicators of territorial impact	Accounts from the recent recession and from hard economic times in the past, both firsthand and synthetic, as many as can be found (oral history, diaries, journals, newspapers, photos, economic data, artifacts, etc.)
KEY CONCEPTS AND CONCEPTUAL UNDERSTANDINGS NECESSARY TO ADDRESS QUESTIONS (non-exclusive examples)	Theories of political behavior, rationality, self-interest, political parties, power flow, government, fiscal policy; relationships between the state and markets; constitutional limits on government, debates about those limits; evidence (to make claims)	Application of different types of economic theories to gauge inflation/deflation, labor shrinkage, capital contraction, asset/liability analyses from banking sector; changes in supply and demand; evidence (to make claims)	Theories of human land/resource use; spatial representation, scale, degree of distortion, map symbols, specialized GIS symbolic systems and representations; evidence (to make claims)	Theories of human behavior, thought, perspective, agency, context, historical significance; historical imagination; moral judgment; evidence (to make claims)
KEY STRATEGIES AND SKILLS NEEDED TO ADDRESS QUESTIONS (non-exclusive examples)	Reading statistics from polls, conducting polls and interview research; reading subtext into policies/pronouncements; reading power flow and blockage, converting such data into evidence to make arguments and claims that answer sub-questions	Capability to read statistics critically, for assessing agendas behind statistical representations; conducting survey research; capability to convert statistics into meaningful arguments and claims that answer the sub-questions	Cartography including using map symbol systems, critical reading and thinking, capability of using statistics to represent spatial change, capability to use statistical and spatial (often digitized) representations to make arguments and claims that address sub-questions	Critical reading and thinking, analysis and synthesis, reading subtext and agency in older sources; statistics; converting verbal, written, photographic, oral, artifactual accounts into evidence to make arguments and claims that answer the sub-questions

Figure 5: Dimension 2 of the C3 Framework showing the kinds of data needed to address disciplinary research questions and the specific reading strategies needed (National Council for the Social Studies 2013). Citation: National Council for the Social Studies (NCSS), The College, Career, and Civic Life (C3) Framework for Social Studies State Standards: Guidance for Enhancing the Rigor of K-12 Civics, Economics, Geography, and History (Silver Spring, MD: NCSS, 2013).

Strategies

- **Teach source literacy within a discipline.** (Murphy 2016). By contextualizing historical data as a type of primary source, data literacy gains recognition beyond math classes.

- **Compare types of data collection methods** (e.g., census vs. poll) to understand the context of a statistic.

- **Plan one-shot library lessons as beads on a necklace.** Use big-picture knowledge of the school curriculum to contextualize one-shot data literacy lessons in long-term learning sequences built on information literacy goals.

- **Teach key data sources as models.** Choose a substantial source of data and articulate why you've chosen it. Your goal is not merely to teach "how to use" a particular dataset or a digital tool. Rather students learn that, in every field, certain key data sources can help them develop a deeper understanding of their research topic.

Try this

While some countries collect data about race, ethnicity or religion, it illegal in others to ask questions about these topics in a census (INSEE 2015). Look for opportunities in language classes or global studies where students could look at the social and cultural contexts of census data in other countries.

Scenario 3: Pandemics: The emotional context

Students' fears about catching Ebola or the Zika virus have spiraled as reports about deaths and birth defects flood the news. The combination of unusual symptoms, impact on infants, and limited prevention information, along with emotionally-charged graphic descriptions of transmission and high death rates, are a sure recipe that an "availability bias" that will color how students respond to data reported in the news. Availability bias is a psychological term referring to how the mind can give greater weight to the newest or most familiar information. When data is presented as odd (unique or unusual) and memories are recent and filled with anxiety, one is likely to overestimate the likelihood of something bad happening.

A teacher and the librarian decide to do a health unit to help students manage these gut-level responses. They want students to slow down their thinking, so they decide to add moments of "friction" to the lesson (Seroff, Bergson-Michelson, and Abilock 2015). By doing so, they hope students will learn to step back from knee-jerk emotions to perform a more dispassionate evaluation of news about disease outbreaks and quantify their risks analytically. There is particular urgency in learning this because dissemination of information about epidemics in social media has preempted the traditional role of health officials who normally issue warnings on authoritative websites with full explanations of symptoms, risks and prevention plans (see, for example, the World Health Organization (WHO) and its Disease Outbreak News alerts posted at http://www.who.int/csr/don/en/). Indeed, a recent study found that tweets, not official WHO Disease Outbreak News (DONs), broke the Ebola story to over 60 million people over a three-day period (Odlum and Yoon 2015).

The teacher and the librarian acknowledge that they, probably like their students, are unclear about the differences between commonly-used terms like epidemics and pandemics, so they look for background information from the Centers for Disease Control and Prevention (CDC), the major source of health data about Americans:

> The amount of a particular disease that is usually present in a community is referred to as the baseline or *endemic* level of the disease. This level is not necessarily the desired level, which may in fact be zero, but rather is the observed level. In the absence of intervention and assuming that the level is

not high enough to deplete the pool of susceptible persons, the disease may continue to occur at this level indefinitely. Thus, the baseline level is often regarded as the expected level of the disease (CDC 2012).

Occasionally, the amount of disease in a community rises above the expected level. *Epidemic* refers to an increase, often sudden, in the number of cases of a disease above what is normally expected in that population in that area. *Outbreak* carries the same definition of epidemic, but is often used for a more limited geographic area. *Cluster* refers to an aggregation of cases grouped in place and time that are suspected to be greater than the number expected, even though the expected number may not be known. *Pandemic* refers to an epidemic that has spread over several countries or continents, usually affecting many people (CDC 2012a).

The teachers decide to focus on infectious diseases like Zika and Ebola, rather than including non-contagious epidemics like diabetes and obesity. Their first thought is to prompt students with headlines about epidemics that include or imply statistics, but locating a sufficient number proves to be too laborious. Instead they locate a fear-based infographic that received quite a bit of traction when it was released (https:// www.good.is/infographics/ infographic-the-deadliest-disease-outbreaks-in-history).

Students pick a disease from the infographic — one that either worries or interests them — and then team up by their chosen disease. Groups will deconstruct the data given in the infographic and compare it to information about the disease from other sources. Knowing that students' free-text searches will return all sorts of random data bits, the teacher and librarian decide to limit students' searches to two sources of reasonably comparable data about pandemics:

» **The Centers for Disease Control and Prevention** contains a rich range of data with a focus on Americans, ranging from simple statistics in FastStats (http://www.cdc.gov/nchs/fastats/) to raw datasets on diseases and conditions (http://www.cdc.gov/DiseasesConditions).

» **The World Health Organization,** the major international source of disease data, publishes Global Health Observatory by country (http://www.who.int/gho/en) and by topic (http://www.who.int/topics/en).[1]

To be sure that all groups collect similar information, the instructors create a spreadsheet-like matrix to contain the data found by each group (http:// noodle.to/pandemic). To maximize their efficiency while researching and recording data, the teachers add the following links to the matrix:

» **A link to the infographic**

» **A source for historical census data**

» **Links to the CDC and WHO information about infectious diseases**

» **Definitions of key terms students will encounter: endemic, epidemic and pandemic**

Since they want students to also evaluate the visual display of the data in the infographic, they include a column for a statistic called the Case Fatality Rate (CFR), which quantifies the deaths among cases.

In data literacy, it is essential that students understand how to select comparable numbers. For example, the Zika outbreak in

---

[1]Both the National Center for Health Statistics (NCHS) and the World Health Organization (WHO) are developing easy-to-use online tools that allow users to examine vital statistics data interactively and create their own tables within the tool, as well as export data for use in other formats. Since these major sources for public health data are likely to be valuable for future research projects (e.g., maternal and child health, nutrition, dental care, substance abuse, noninfectious diseases), school librarians might want to explore them now and follow their evolution.

Brazil that began in April 2015 ought to be matched with data from the same period (2015-2016), some of which is likely to be an estimate. They show students a matrix of Brazil's population data collected from various sources (goo.gl/0p4Se1) and remind them to avoid a "precision bias," a cognitive predisposition to assume that the most precise number they find is *de facto* the most accurate.

During a class discussion, they consider other evaluation criteria for Brazilian population statistics. Should they use http://Worldometers.info, which seems to update in real time but is clearly an estimate? Should they use some average of the population data from the same year(s)? Perhaps they should use the Brazilian Census figures because they're "official" government numbers?

Ultimately, they decide to use data from The World Bank because it standardizes Brazil's aggregated data from global, national and regional sources so that it's comparable with other countries' data. The online interface allows them to visualize the data on maps or in graphs, view it in tables or download it as datasets. Students also find the Bank's country office contacts in Brazil and Washington D.C. and the names of a specific team focused on combatting Zika in Latin American that they might email with questions. The availability of expert help, the comparable numbers from identifiable sources, and the prospect of experimenting with varied visualizations outweigh the students' initial preference for data sites that offer easier access and simpler results.

As students start to compare U.S.-focused information with global data, they realize that there are differences in the case fatality ratio (CFR), which is the risk of death expressed as a percent based on the proportion of people who die from a disease outbreak out of those who are infected. CFR will differ based on regional or local conditions and health care systems. For example, while measles is currently under control (endemic — and therefore not much of a worry) in countries like the U.S., it is the leading cause of death among children in India, Nigeria and Pakistan (CDC 2015).

Once the teams complete the matrix, each group presents their findings to the class, comparing them with what was displayed in the infographic. As they present, the teacher makes connections to other measures of morbidity, such as the number of Brazilians who die from other causes like heart disease and cancer. This helps students contextualize the scope of the outbreak (CDC 2012a).

Next the teachers want the class to practice using data selectively from the matrix as evidence in an argument. To help students appreciate how the same data can be used to support very different conclusions, they show a *New York Times* interactive graphic that models using the same job numbers for different arguments (http://www. nytimes.com/interactive/2012/10/05/business/economy/one-report-diverging-perspectives.html). The class discusses how drawing different conclusions from the same data can be done with complete honesty; it's not always a signal of intentional manipulation.

The librarian reinforces this idea by explaining one experiment reported in *Nature* in which 29 scientific teams looked at the same information about soccer games and answered the same question: "Are dark-skinned players more likely to be given red cards than light-skinned ones?" The scientists came to widely disparate conclusions; some saw no difference between light- and dark-skinned players while others saw a strong trend toward giving more red cards to dark-skinned players. The study concludes that each team's inferences were contextualized by their expertise and background:

> Teams approached the data with a wide array of analytical techniques, and obtained highly varied results. Next, we organized rounds of peer feedback, technique refinement and

joint discussion to see whether the initial variety could be channeled into a joint conclusion. We found that the overall group consensus was much more tentative than would be expected from a single-team analysis (Silberzahn and Uhlmann 2015).

As students become more comfortable with data literacy skills, they approach ambiguities in exercises like these with greater confidence and are open to understanding that data is neither infallible nor arbitrary — human interpretation plays a key role.

Teachers assign the "Infographic Design Matrix" to help students identify their audience (Abilock and Williams 2014). As a final task, each student will select some statistics from the matrix to support a unique visual argument — to display either on a PowerPoint slide or, if they have time, as an infographic — using some of the statistics they have collected. Teachers caution students to resist "anchoring," another cognitive bias in which students accept the first piece of evidence as "truth" and measure all other information against that first data bit. The teacher and librarian hope that this selection process reinforces students' understanding that data is being used as evidence rather than as immutable facts.

Wrap-up

In this scenario, the librarian and teacher decide to look at a visual display of decontextualized data — what we commonly call "data in the wild." Since infographics are so prevalent online, they want students to both deconstruct and, at least partially, to construct their own visual display of data using a typical genre. They explain to students that, to make comparisons easier, they are controlling both the sources of data and the format in which statistics are collected. They offer students a limited choice so that students will be able to compare and discuss comparable results. Initially students work in groups but, to ensure accountability, they eventually choose data that is relevant to a specific audience in order to craft a compelling argument. Throughout the project, the teacher and librarian continually refer to ways in which data is constructed and contextualized — by cognitive biases, content creators, a purpose and an audience.

! Strategies

- **Pick emotionally charged statistics to teach cognitive biases.** Use data about highly charged current topics to raise students' metacognitive awareness of their emotional responses and intuitive but faulty judgments. Then add "friction" to slow down students' thinking and develop the analytical strategies they need to learn in order to manage their emotional reactions.

- **Teach students to read data genres.** Build awareness of the constraints and affordances of infographics and other graphic representations of data by deconstructing and constructing them as genres.

- **Scaffold lessons with manageable datasets to put student attention on thinking with data.** Curation can be informally linked from a collection document, providing controlled exposure to data "in the wild" through manageable sets of statistics. Explain that choices are limited to facilitate comparisons.

- **Teach nuances of data analysis.** There are honest differences among experts about the meaning of data. By encouraging students to bring different deductions and interpretations to the same set of statistics, you resist stereotyping data analysis as a process of always identifying disinformation or discovering propaganda.

Try this

Explore data context. Context can mean both the genre in which numbers are found (e.g., chart, spreadsheet, infographic, or text) as well as the *content described* by the numbers. Expose students to spreadsheets of data that compare political, social or economic aspects of countries. When seemingly comparable numbers appear in the same spreadsheet, students make superficial comparisons simply because the numbers seem related. In UNICEF's single spreadsheet (http://data.unicef.org/topic/child-protection/child-labour/, in "Access the Data" section), Afghanistan and Chile have similar data on percentages of child labor by country. However, the circumstances within each country, as well as the absolute numbers of children, are vastly different. In Afghanistan, most children work in agriculture, in their homes, in forced hazardous brick production or in illicit activities. In Chile, most are in retail businesses or commercial sexual exploitation. In Chile, a prosperous country, there is a significant government push to eliminate the worst forms of child labor, an initiative that Afghanistan, a poor nation, would find much more difficult to implement.

Strategies for teaching context in the wild: Find a problem, build a rule

Both the explicit guidelines that can help novices learn to vet the credibility of new content and the tacit "rules of thumb" that they subconsciously use to evaluate familiar content are part of the "context" we bring to data literacy. Typically, each of us makes unconscious decisions in many, daily situations where we have to make a choice (Gigerenzer 2007). We use mental shortcuts, called heuristics, to speed decision-making. These unarticulated "rules" — which may begin with formally stated recommendations but then transition into tacit, intuitive behaviors — allow us to function efficiently without stopping to think through each choice we make, each action we take, and each detail of a problem we encounter.

These shortcuts are generally good enough. We happily perk along unconsciously using these rules — until they don't work. When we recognize that we are stuck, we will bring the rule into consciousness (metacognition) and consider revising it. Good instructional design aims to bring these rules to light by putting challenges in front of students so that they reexamine their assumptions, learn from their errors and revise simplistic algorithms.

The general problem with relying on unconscious rules of thumb is that they reinforce cognitive biases. And, while a set of explicit data literacy "rules" may provide guidance for beginners, such lists are not productive in the long run. Students will change rule-based behavior only when cognitive dissonance provokes a shift in their thinking. As Kuhn (2000) asserts, "Strategy training may appear successful, but if nothing has been done to influence the metalevel, the new behavior will quickly disappear once the instructional context is withdrawn and individuals resume meta-level management of their own behavior."

Another possible teaching strategy is to use discussion and re-flection to uncover the useful tacit knowledge within rules of thumb (Polanyi and Sen 2009; André et al. 2002). Initially we can ask students to become aware of their unconscious rules by completing the following sentence:

"When I see...then I do..."

so that they identify and then describe a specific and condition-al decision strategy that they employ in a particular situation. In the process of explaining a rule, students may verbalize strate-gies that their peers have not considered. Or they may be able to convert a vague rule of thumb into a just-in-time checklist, which is what Gawande argues is necessary for critical decision-making in highly charged situations like an operating room or the cock-pit of a falling plane (Gawande 2010). One opening instructional move, then, is to have students develop their own checklists targeted to places where it's essential to make critical decisions about data evaluation or data visualization. For example, we may teach a novice to look where zero falls on the y-axis of a graph. Over time, however, a student may revise that to a more nuanced checklist:

> » **Don't assume that the y-axis begins at zero.**
> » **Look for labels on the y-axis.**
> » **Look at the increments on the y-axis to help you know if a change is significant or not.**

Of course, experts also have rules of thumb that we can learn from; these are valuable procedures and processes that emerge from their years of experience within a discipline or field. One set of processes specifically related to data literacy is described by a professor of sociology and criminal justice as "statistical benchmarks." As mentioned throughout this text, these are validated statistics (such as the size of the U.S. population) that can help us judge whether new population statistics we encounter are significant (Best 2013). While we may not have the disciplinary expertise to provide students with benchmark strategies for every topic, we can model a process that involves noticing a problem with odd data, unearthing our tacit assumptions, faulty procedures and unconscious misconceptions and then developing more accurate strategies to evaluate data in the wild. Let's explore what this might look like in the following four short scenarios.

Example 1: Evaluating data in the context of a visualized benchmark

Scenario: *The Internet's Own Boy*

The Internet's Own Boy is a documentary film about programming prodigy and open-access activist Aaron Swartz. In the film, public domain advocate Carl Malamud agrees to work with Swartz to download and provide free access to what are, in fact, public records. Indeed, the Public Access to Court Electronic Records (PACER) database makes inordinate profits on what should be freely accessible court records (E-Government Act of 2002; *Internet's Own Boy* 2014 31:33 min). As a result of their activism, PACER agrees to provide free access to 17 libraries across the country. Malamud exclaims: "One library for every 22,000 square miles!" Does this make any sense, even in a quick mental check that requires only a few seconds?

Finding a relevant statistical benchmark

When I saw this film, I referenced a quick benchmark from my toolkit: the fact that the 48 contiguous states make a very rough rectangle about 3,000 miles from east to west and perhaps about 1,000 miles from north to south: an area of about 3 million square miles. 3 million square miles divided by 17 locations? It's instantly clear that there are far too few locations for the majority of Americans to reach easily, even without figuring in Alaska and Hawaii. Another way I could have approached this would have been to use the benchmark that we have 50 states. 50 states divided by 17 locations means around one location for every three states: again, not very accessible for most Americans. A third way to approach this would be to have the actual total area of the United States in mind as a statistical benchmark. According to the U.S. Census, the total land and water mass of the United States (including Hawaii and Alaska) is 3,805,927 square miles (U.S. Census 2012). Again, it's very quick to see that 3.8 million divided by 17 is very poor coverage.

Reasoning using the statistical benchmark

So the average area covered by each of those 17 libraries would be about 3.8 million square miles divided by 17 libraries, which is a little over 220,000 square miles. It's beginning to look like that

22,000 figure is off by a full order of magnitude and might be attributable to a decimal point error.

Example 2: Evaluating data in the context of a common misconception

Scenario: *The Martian*

The film *The Martian* (2014) tells the story of a manned mission to Mars that goes awry because the crew leaves one man for dead. NASA realizes he's still alive and pulls out all the stops to bring him home. Under tremendous pressure to launch a rescue ship and worried about the astronaut's mental as well as physical health, Vince Kapoor (Chiwetel Ejiofor) says, "He's *50 million miles away from home, he thinks he's totally alone, he thinks we gave up on him — I mean, what does that do to a man, psychological-ly? What the hell is he thinking right now?*" (2015, 34:10 min). Is that 50 million mile distance from Earth to Mars credible within the context of the film's story?

Uncovering a data misconception with students

From their first picture book about the solar system to endless examples in media, students have been exposed to distorted images of the planets, their orbits and distances. Help students develop a better idea of the actual distances using a video show-ing a scale model of the solar system on a dry lakebed in Nevada (https://vimeo.com/139407849).

Reasoning through a data misconception with students

Many students have already learned that Earth's average distance from the sun is about 93 million miles, and a quick Web check confirms that Mars' average distance from the sun is about 142 million miles. So it's obvious that the screenwriters probably just subtracted one figure from the other to arrive at 50 million miles. In fact, the two planets orbit the sun at different speeds and come that close to each other only on rare occasions when their positions in their orbits lined up on the same side of the sun. They do not remain the same distance apart throughout their orbits. Indeed, the Mars Mission Director's exclamation would have been more dramatic (and more credible), if he had relegated the stranded astronaut to a position twice as far from home!

Example 3: Answering a data question by making an analogy to a known data context

Scenario: Historical data on the Black Death

Recently I asked an epidemiologist how we could teach students to figure the case fatality ratio — remember that's the number who die out of the number who get infected — for the Black Death. She acknowledged that historical population numbers, infection rates, and death rates are *very rough estimates.*

Finding a known context and using it as an estimated proxy

She shared a strategy that public health workers use to assess outbreaks of diseases that have a historical trail. *Yersinia pestis*, the bacterium responsible for the Black Death, the Plague of Justinian, and the Third Plague, continues to cause plagues in Africa and Asia today (CDC 2015). Therefore, to estimate a historical disease impact like the Black Death's case fatality ratio she uses the modern case fatality ratio assuming no treatment, since there were no antibiotics during the 14th century.

By applying current-day CFR estimates for plagues to Black Death, we can guess that the CFR ranged from about 50% (for the bubonic form) to almost 100% (for the pneumonic form). Of course, CFRs are a moving target. In both historical and modern times, the bubonic plague affects the old and infirm in the first wave, but death rates drop significantly as immunity builds and the weak are wiped out — and so the CFR declines.

Example 4: Questioning a data claim by building background context

Scenario: Unemployment figures

"We have 93 million people out of work. They look for jobs, they give up, and all of a sudden, statistically, they're considered employed" (Jacobson 2015). This seems like an enormous and very serious problem — and it's repeated often, more recently upped to 94 million. People assume that "out of work" means "unemployed," that is, 93 million people *want to work and are looking for a job but can't find one.*

Finding a context

Two statistical benchmarks for students to remember are the current population of the U.S. (about 325 million) and China (about 1.3 billion). If we go to the Bureau of Labor Statistics (BLS), a good source of government information about jobs, we find that the U.S. unemployment rate is currently about 5% (BLS 2016). If 93 million people represents 5% of the U.S. population, the total U.S. population would have to be almost 2 billion people. That doesn't make sense — even the population of China is only somewhere over one billion!

The BLS issues a monthly press release on the number of *unemployed* people — currently about 8 million (BLS 2016). In fact, 93 million people are not "out of work" (i.e., unemployed) but rather they are "out of the workforce." Most of this number consists of people of working age who aren't looking for jobs — students, disabled people, housewives/househusbands, early retirees — anyone who could theoretically work. Ask students to think about whether the recurring choice of the phrase "out of work" or "out of the labor force" in these claims involves ignorance or intent to deceive.

By gathering examples like these from popular culture, politics, and the media, we can support students as they recognize and wrestle with real-world data challenges.

Conclusion

Throughout this chapter we have modeled teaching strategies to scaffold students' growing understanding and ability to evaluate data in the wild. By contextual framing, we can address students' grab-and-go approach to data and create moments of friction (Abilock 2016) at which point they are intrigued enough to reassess their assumptions about numbers as indisputable and fixed. Ambiguity drives inquiry. Investigations of data context result in data insights. As educators, we can choose when our students are ready to tackle this ambiguity and, by doing so, achieve higher levels of data comprehension.

Abilock, Debbie. n.d. "Curriculum Curation." OER Commons. Accessed April 24, 2017.
https://www.oercommons.org/courseware/module/11007 .

_____. 2016. "How Can I Teach Students to Think of Numbers as Evidence Rather
than Answers?" *School Library Connection*, March, 40-41.

Abilock, Debbie, and Connie Williams. 2014. "Recipe for an Infographic."
Knowledge Quest 43(2), November/December, 46-55. Accessed April 19, 2017. http://
files.eric.ed.gov/fulltext/EJ1045949.pdf .

André, Malin, Lars Borgquist, Mats Foldevi, and Sigvard Mölstad. 2002. "Asking for 'Rules
of Thumb': A Way to Discover Tacit Knowledge in General Practice." *Family Practice*
19(6), December, 617-22. doi:10.1093/fampra/19.6.617 .

Association of College and Research Libraries. 2016. "Framework for Information
Literacy for Higher Education." ALA. Accessed April 19, 2017. http://www.ala.org/acrl/
standards/ilframework .

Best, Joel. 2013. *Stat-spotting: A Field Guide to Identifying Dubious Data*. Updated and
expanded ed. Berkeley: University of California Press.

Bostok, Mike, Amanda Cox, and Kevin Quelay. 2012. "One Report, Diverging
Perspectives." *New York Times*, October 5. http://www.nytimes.com/
interactive/2012/10/05/business/economy/one-report-diverging-perspectives.html .

Bureau of Labor Statistics. 2016. "The Employment Situation - April 2016." News release,
May 6. Accessed April 19, 2017. http://www.bls.gov/news.release/pdf/empsit.pdf.

Centers for Disease Control and Prevention (CDC). 2012a. "Section 11: Epidemic Disease
Occurrence." Accessed April 24, 2017. http://www.cdc.gov/ophss/csels/dsepd/ss1978/
lesson1/section11.html .

_____. 2012b. "Lesson 3: Measures of Risk." Accessed April 24, 2017. http://www.cdc.
gov/ophss/csels/dsepd/ss1978/lesson3/section2.html .

_____. n.d. "Moving Faster than Measles and Rubella." Infographic. Accessed April
19, 2017. http://www.cdc.gov/globalhealth/immunization/infographic/measles.htm .

_____. 2015. "Plague." Accessed April 24, 2017. http://www.cdc.gov/plague/ .

Cohn, D'Vera. 2015 ."Census Considers New Approach to Asking about Race – by Not
Using the Term at All." *FactTank* (blog), Pew Research Center. Accessed April 19, 2017.
http://www.pewresearch.org/fact-tank/2015/06/18/census-considers-new-approach-
to-asking-about-race-by-not-using-the-term-at-all/ .

Collins, James P. 2006. "Native Americans in the Census, 1860–1890." *Prologue
Magazine*, 38(2), Summer. Accessed April 19, 2017. http://www.archives.gov/
publications/prologue/2006/summer/indian-census.html .

Column Five. 2011. "Outbreak: The Deadliest Pandemics in History." Infographic. GOOD.
Accessed April 19, 2017. https://www.good.is/infographics/infographic-the-deadliest-
disease-outbreaks-in-history#open .

Decker, Geoffrey. 2011. "Hispanics Identifying Themselves as Indians." *New York Times*,
July 3. Accessed April 19, 2017. http://nyti.ms/18KBMlo .

DeSilver, Drew. 2015. "U.S. Public Seldom Has Welcomed Refugees into Country."
FactTank (blog). Pew Research Center, November 19. http://www.pewresearch.org/
fact-tank/2015/11/19/u-s-public-seldom-has-welcomed-refugees-into-country/ .

E-Government Act of 2002. 107–347 107th Congress. Accessed April 24, 2017.
https://www.gpo.gov/fdsys/pkg/PLAW-107publ347/pdf/PLAW-107publ347.pdf .

Gawande, Atul. 2010. *The Checklist Manifesto: How to Get Things Right*.
New York: Metropolitan Books.

Gigerenzer, Gerd. 2007. *Gut Feelings: The Intelligence of the Unconscious*.
New York: Viking.

Internet's Own Boy, The: The Story of Aaron Swartz. Directed by Brian Knappenberger.
2014. Beverly Hills, CA: Participant Media, 2015. DVD.

Jacobson, Louis. 2015. "Donald Trump Says U.S. Has 93 Million People 'Out of Work,'
but That's Way Too High." Politifact, August 31. Accessed April 19, 2017. http://www.
politifact.com/truth-o-meter/statements/2015/aug/31/donald-trump/donald-trump-
says-us-has-93-milion-people-out-work/ .

Kuhn, Deanna. 2000. "Does Memory Development Belong on an Endangered Topic List?" *Child Development* 71(1), January/February, 21-25. doi:10.1111/1467-8624.00114.

The Martian. 2015. Directed by Ridley Scott. 2015. Beverly Hills, CA: 20th Century Fox, 2016. DVD.

Murphy, Nora. 2016. "How to Develop Strong Source Literacy: Practice!" *Voices from The Hill* (blog). January 1. Accessed April 19, 2017. http://blog.fsha.org/develop-source-literacy/ .

National Council for the Social Studies (NCSS). 2013. *The College, Career, and Civic Life (C3) Framework for Social Studies State Standards: Guidance for Enhancing the Rigor of K-12 Civics, Economics, Geography, and History.* Silver Springs, MD: NCSS,. http://www.socialstudies.org/system/files/c3/C3-Framework-for-Social-Studies.pdf .

National Institute for Statistics and Economic Studies (INSEE). 2016. "Ethnic-based Statistics." INSEE, September 16. Accessed April 19, 2017. https://www.insee.fr/en/information/2388586 .

Odlum, Michelle, and Sunmoo Yoon. 2015. "What Can We Learn about the Ebola Outbreak from Tweets?" *American Journal of Infection Control* 43(6), June 1, 563-71. http://dx.doi.org/10.1016/j.ajic.2015.02.023 .

Pew Research Center for U.S. Politics and Policy. 2016. "Campaign Exposes Fissures Over Issues, Values and How Life Has Changed in the U.S." Pew Research Center. Accessed April 19, 2017. http://www.people-press.org/2016/03/31/campaign-exposes-fissures-over-issues-values-and-how-life-has-changed-in-the-u-s/ .

Pew Research Center for Social and Demographic Trends. 2015a. "Chapter 7: The Many Dimensions of Hispanic Racial Identity." In *Multiracial in America: Proud, Diverse and Growing in Numbers*, 98-109. Ed. Kim Parker et al. Washington, DC: Pew Research Center. Accessed April 17, 2017. http://www.pewsocialtrends.org/2015/06/11/multiracial-in-america/ .

Pew Research Center for Social and Demographic Trends. 2015b. "What Census Calls Us: A Historical Timeline." Pew Research Center, June 10. Accessed April 22, 2017. http://www.pewsocialtrends.org/interactives/multiracial-timeline/ .

Polanyi, Michael, and Amartya Sen. 2009. *The Tacit Dimension.* Chicago: University of Chicago Press.

Seroff, Jole, Tasha Bergson-Michelson, and Debbie Abilock. 2015. "Friction: Teaching Slow Thinking and Intentionality in Research." NoodleTools, Accessed November 15, 2015. https://www.noodletools.com/debbie/literacies/information/friction.pdf .

Silberzahn, Raphael, and Eric H. Uhlmann. 2015. "Crowdsourced Research: Many Hands Make Tight Work." *Nature* 526(7572), October 7, 189-91. doi:10.1038/526189a.

United States Bureau of the Census. 1994. "Chapter 15 Area Measurement/Water Classification." In *Geographic Areas Reference Manual*, 15-1-15-11. Washington, DC: Department of Commerce, 1994. Accessed April 24, 2017. https://www2.census.gov/geo/pdfs/reference/GARM/Ch15GARM.pdf .

United States Census Bureau. n.d. "Census Instructions." https://www.census.gov/history/www/through_the_decades/census_instructions/ .

. n.d. "1860 Instructions." Accessed April 24, 2017. https://www.census.gov/history/www/through_the_decades/census_instructions/1860_instructions.html .

_____. n.d. "Quick Facts: Alaska." Accessed April 24, 2017. https://www.census.gov/quickfacts/table/PST045216/02 .

_____. 2012. "State Area Measurements and Internal Point Coordinates." Accessed April 24, 2017. https://www.census.gov/geo/reference/state-area.html .

_____. n.d. "Why It's Important." Accessed April 24, 2017. http://www.census.gov/2010census/about/why-important.php .

Valenza, Joyce Kasman, Brenda L. Boyer, and Della Curtis. 2014. *Library Technology Reports.* 50(7), October. Chicago, IL: ALA TechSource. Accessed April 24, 2017. https://journals.ala.org/index.php/ltr/issue/view/200 .

Weinberger, David. 2007. *Everything Is Miscellaneous: The Power of the New Digital Disorder.* New York: Times Books.

World Health Organization (WHO). 2017. "Zika Virus and Complications: Questions and Answers." Accessed April 24, 2017. http://www.who.int/features/qa/zika/en/ .

If you have five minutes:

- Point out the quantifiers in an assignment or research question.

- Use one of the scenarios in the final section of this chapter with your students.

- Ask students to bring in printouts or collect screenshots of data to add to a physical or virtual bulletin board.

If you have 15 minutes:

- Choose a student's example (see above) or find a current statistic for discussion in class. Ask questions about the context or brainstorm a statistical benchmark that might make it possible to evaluate the number provided.

- Show students two visualizations of the same statistic and ask which one makes more sense to use for the topic they're researching or argument they're building and why.

If you have 30 minutes:

- Demonstrate how to assess a data source they might use to research their topic. Then ask students to critically annotate a second source from a list you've curated. The resource at http://www.oercommons.org/ courseware/ module/11007/overview provides additional insight and guidance.

If you have a class period or more:

- Ask students to compare two sources of data related to an ongoing topic.

- Integrate a data source into an existing research project.

Susan D. Ballard

Helping students to become data literate is a challenge on many levels, but none is so compelling as this: how do we make data interesting and meaningful to them? One answer may lie in contextualizing data skills in the world and interests of our students by having them do research themselves following the action research model.

Knowing that modeling is an impactful teaching strategy (Coffey n.d.) and recognizing the role of affect in the information seeking process (Kuhlthau 1993), we can better address this dilemma by employing action research (AR) to both improve our own practice and skills set and provide an authentic example to students of how we use data to solve real-world problems. The visible and intentional use of action research will also help to increase our credibility with students who struggle with the inquiry process. When we show them that we have taken the plunge, too, we can state with confidence that we understand what they are going through!

In this chapter, you'll learn the stages of action research and how to apply them to pursue your own areas of interest. Once you've become comfortable with the format, you can teach it to your students. By making data collection and use personal, the data is relevant and relatable to our own contexts. Data we don't know about and things we are unfamiliar with raises two barriers for students; studying data they know closes that gap.

In thinking about how to wade into action research, it's first important to understand what it is and how it can be leveraged to our advantage. This chapter's goal is to show that action research is truly practitioner-friendly and not at all that sort of "swallowing sawdust" experience that most of us think about when we hear terms like data or research.

What is action research and evidence-based practice?

Action research is a systematic, intentional, problem-focused, and solution-oriented investigation. It is context-specific and therefore meaningful and relevant to the researcher (us!). It is also future-oriented: when we engage in action research, we are testing whether or not some action or cycle of actions or interventions will result in improvements in professional practice (Hart and Bond 1995). We may also research to find out, with greater confidence, whether what we are doing is having the desired effect. Action research helps the practitioner bridge the gap between theory and practice, and for educators and school librarians, it is not only an ideal way to better understand and improve our work, it is also a tool for evidence-based practice (Gordon 2006).

Evidence-based practice has its roots in health care, where it is defined as "the conscientious, explicit and judicious use of current best evidence in making decisions about the care of individual patients" (Sackett, Rosenberg, Gray, Haynes, & Richardson 1996, p. 71). In considering its usefulness in education, researcher Ross Todd was an early proponent of evidence-based school librarianship, which he defined as "an approach that systematically engages research-derived evidence, school librarian-observed evidence, and user-reported evidence in the ongoing processes of decision making, development, and continuous improvement to achieve the school's mission and goals. These goals typically center on student achievement and quality teaching and learning." (Todd 2008). As the recent passage of the federal Every Student Succeeds Act (ESSA) reminds us, being able to use evidence as a rationale for decision-making is gaining prominence in how K-12 schools move forward. Teachers and school librarians can gather evidence via action research to help improve instruction, or, in the instance of the examination of program and services, to address the ongoing needs of students and the learning community.

Educators are already using a variety of data and evidence to get a snapshot or sense of instructional and program needs, utilization, and effectiveness. The data sources may include traditional quantitative measures such as test scores, demographics (student, community, and school profiles), comparative costs, availability of resources and user records, and more. However, the most powerful use of these data is in combination with the kind of data that may be culled from student interviews, examination of student work, questionnaires, focus groups, pre/post-tests, observation and field notes, case studies, and several other standard qualitative research methods. Although some numerical data may be collected and analyzed in qualitative studies, they remain distinct from the quantitative style of research. Yes, you read that right. Not all data is quantitative – a point we often tend to forget!

We also neglect to realize that while quantitative studies are the norm for the pure sciences, the social sciences do not lend themselves to the same sort of methodology. Qualitative research probes *why* something happens, rather than documenting the frequency of occurrence. Qualitative work may focus on smaller samples or fewer participants, exchanging scale for depth of insight and understanding. Rather than reporting results statistically, qualitative research is somewhat anecdotal, and therefore well-suited to studying the relationships among student achievement and teaching practice. Action research is an ideal tool for looking at many of those elusive elements of need in education.

In the complex environment of the school, action research provides a structure for teaching in order to:

>> **identify problematic areas in the design, implementation, and evaluation of the instruction;**

>> **develop teaching strategies that generate data about student performance;**

>> **collect evidence using qualitative and quantitative methods in naturalistic settings;**

>> **analyze evidence at the point of need and apply it to the revision of instruction; and**

>> **apply evidence to determine how to improve instruction in the future.**

Action research is flexible, individualized, and usable at any developmental level. It assumes that teachers and school librarians are knowledgeable about their areas of endeavor and gives them power to make decisions (Gordon 2006). It can be carried out by a single educator or by a collaborative group.

One of the more significant qualities of action research is that it puts the teacher and school librarian in the position of accepting more responsibility for her (his) own professional growth (Wood 1988) and, by doing so, to empower the practitioner with the ability to advocate – with evidence – for the practices she (he) values most. Most significantly, action research is a self-reflective process that helps to elevate the academic climate of a school as students see their educators join them in doing research. Students see us as learners who are willing to model the research process.

The bottom line is that YOU can be a researcher with action research, and once you can do it, you can help students become action researchers, too.

The advantage of action research is its immediate impact. Action researchers don't have to wait for a test company to score and return results. The results stay in-house and are immediately put to use to support, communicate, and facilitate change. Consider the use of action research as a platform from which we can take a deep dive into finding out answers or possible strategies to address some fundamental questions about how effective our instruction or delivery of service is in relation to what we are aiming to provide at the local level.

In the action research model, teachers and school librarians pose questions that address the problems related to curriculum or program development and implementation. Consider these potential questions:

- » **Are we teaching the appropriate skills for each level?**
- » **Where are the gaps in instruction?**
- » **Do all students have equal access to resources?**
- » **Is this instructional strategy leading to the results we want?**
- » **What is the impact of our work?**

These types of questions are rooted in a primary question for the teacher and school librarian: *How can I do it better next time?*

Action research follows a series of phases and is an iterative process (Gordon 2006). While presented here in a linear format, good researchers know that all research is iterative. We may reach a point in the process where we realize we need to backtrack. Perhaps we realize our question needs refining or editing because the data we collected is insufficient. Perhaps we realize, when synthesizing, that having more or different data would give us more insight. So as you read through the following stages, keep this iterative – or "go back a few stages" – approach in mind. Especially with novice researchers who are less skilled at predicting how the research might unfold, going back and revisiting stages is to be expected, not a sign of poor planning.

The action research proposal

Whether you are a teacher, administrator, school librarian or a student, the first step in getting started with action research is to develop a proposal (Figure 1). The proposal is a template that provides novice and expert researchers alike with a flexible structure and sequence that prompts the researcher to:

>> **identify the purpose and scope of the research;**

>> **develop and pose researchable questions;**

>> **select appropriate data collection tools;**

>> **develop a plan for data collection and analysis;**

>> **anticipate how and to whom you will present your findings;**

>> **reflect on the process and outcome of the project.**

Planning the overall framework of your action research up front can help you visualize the entire process before you begin. This can help you (and student researchers) anticipate stumbling blocks, plan for possible challenges, and mentally "rehearse" the research activities before beginning them.

Asking a researchable question

The process begins by gathering basic information about the individual or team submitting the proposal. The first significant

Proposal for action research

Submitted by
Date
Research Question or Hypothesis
Project
Data Collection. Please include at least two methods (e.g., interviews, questionnaires, grades, observation journal entries, photographs, student products/projects, formative assessments, focus groups, case studies, content analysis)

Figure 1: The action research proposal guides the researcher into envisioning the action research as a whole.

section is focused on the *Research Question* (or *Hypothesis*). This is often framed as a problem in the form of a researchable question and is derived from an area of your practice where you would like to see improvement. Choose a problem and question that is important to you. Later, if you implement action research for students, try to find opportunities to link their classroom curriculum with research questions for which they have genuine interest or that are meaningful and resonant for them. In both instances, take care as well to create a question which can be effectively measured and evaluated (Table 1).

Strong research questions	Weak research questions
How might setting up a self-checkout station impact our library's circulation? (This question can be measured by comparing previous circulation to future circulation.)	Does self-checkout work? (Weak because we aren't clearly defining what "works" looks like – is it mechanical functioning? successful use by students? increasing circulation?, etc.
How might ten minutes of sustained silent reading impact reading scores? (Strong because we can measure the scores from before tand after the intervention and compare them.)	Do school library hours impact learning? (Hard to measure because there could be many factors impacting learning – how would we know that changing the library hours was the necessary factor?)

Table 1: Strong vs. weak research questions

For instructional problems, it can be helpful to ground the problem in educational theory. This not only aligns your area of concern with an established body of knowledge, but allows educators to engage in meaningful discussions and exchanges about how students learn and what interventions are most appropriate (and when) in order to ensure their success (Ballard, March, & Sand 2009). In general, the work of the constructivists offer us a place to begin to tie action research to theory. Bloom's Taxonomy, Dewey's notion of learning by doing, Gardner's work on multiple intelligence, Piaget's idea of knowledge construction by assimilation and accommodation, Vygotsky's metacognition and the Zone of Proximal Development and Kuhlthau's Information Seeking Process are access points to anchor questions to theory. As an example, a proposal that considers the question, "Are third grade students able to gather information and then demonstrate higher levels of thinking beyond the competency of knowledge"? aligns well with Bloom's Taxonomy because it allows the researcher to gather evidence to assess if students are progressing from the lowest end of Bloom's cognitive domain which includes knowledge toward comprehension, application and ultimately the "higher order" areas of analysis, synthesis, and evaluation. It also lends itself to the development of a secondary question that addresses a performance task, "Will the task of creating a diary and comparison charts promote higher level of thinking?"

Project

The *Project* section of the proposal (you can rename this "area of research" for students) helps to deal with the pragmatic aspects by helping to identify the "Who, What, When" of the process. Some questions to consider at this stage:

> » **What will be studied?**

> » **Who will lead the research?**

> » **Will this be an individually-led investigation or a collaboration with another teacher or groups of teachers (or students/groups of students), or even a school-wide investigation?** The size of the group of researchers does not change the researchable question: each follows the same process and considers the use of similar data collection resources – the difference is that individual action research focuses on a single educator's particular teaching assignment, role or interest, whereas collaborative action research involves at least two participants seeking to address a mutual concern and school-wide action research involves a group: perhaps a discipline-specific team, grade level, or the entire learning community. Support from outside agencies or organizations may be

used or needed in all three approaches – such as working with a college or university, other schools or district personnel or community and state agencies. Support may also involve the need for financial resources to fund staff release time for planning and/or training purposes.

» **When will the research be conducted?** When will data be synthesized? When will results be available? This helps to establish a timeline to fuel progress and build in ac-countability. In your proposal you will have identified a start and end date for this purpose. It can be as short as one instructional period, or extend to a year-long or multi-year investigation. As you get started, it's wise to keep it manageable. In choosing and administering your data collection tools, you have to consider schedules, personnel availability, etc. since action research is designed for you to learn from your results and apply what you have learned as soon as possible.

» **Who will receive the results of the research (and, if ap-propriate, recommendations based on that research)?** This may inform the types of questions that are investi-gated, the types of research instruments used, and the format, or style of the report of findings (Calhoun 1993).

This section of the proposal also includes an opportunity to give a **brief description, or abstract,** of the overall project to ensure it is helpful to those to whom you are making the proposal and/or to someone who may have a similar problem to investigate so that they have an idea of how they might replicate it. By taking the time to consider the abstract in advance, you gain a valuable tool for communicating with stakeholders throughout the pro-cess, a kind of elevator pitch – a short overview of your project that you can share with interested stakeholders. Depending on the scope of your project, the abstract may also have value when shared in a school newsletter, distributed at a parent-teacher or-ganizational meeting, or placed in your annual teaching portfolio.

The *data collection* component of the proposal provides the description of the measurement tools and collection methods you will use to gather data. At least two types of evidence should be collected because having multiple measures allows the researcher to compare and contrast using a wider variety of lenses and increases the reliability and validity of the research.

You might consider some of the following data collection tools:

» **Interviews** – While time-intensive, interviews can give you in-depth insight into how a particular student approaches, thinks about, or processes work responding to specific pre-determined, questions. While in general they are conducted one-to-one and face-to-face, they can also occur via email or via video conferencing.

» **Focus groups** – These allow the researcher to meet with a small sample group of participants (about six to eight people) and record their individual responses to questions as well as how they respond to and interact with other focus group participants. Focus groups help to explore participant needs and how they feel about ways to address those needs. It's important to provide structure and ground rules in conducting focus groups so the session will flow smoothly.

» **Grades and test scores** – Evidence of students' performance using grades, tests, quizzes, homework, and standardized assessment continue to be valuable as these are the traditional data sources that most stakeholders understand and value and their use can help us to communicate results. Nonetheless, they should never be used as the sole source of data. For example, students with test-taking anxiety may underperform on tests but have higher performance levels in small-group projects. By limiting oneself to just test scores, an educator might see an amplified set of weaknesses and miss some strengths.

» **Observation/field notes** – These are the written observations of what the researcher "sees" occurring in the field (the classroom or other learning environment). They reflect only what is going on and are not subject to interpretation as they occur. Over time the researcher will see patterns emerging from this data. As with interviews and focus groups, analyzing the notes takes significant time, though the revealed insights may also be significant.

» **Questionnaires/surveys** – A questionnaire is comprised of questions that respondents answer in a given format – either as open-ended (respondents articulate their own response) or closed-ended (respondents pick an answer from a options provide to them). It is part of an overall survey process which also includes identifying the population to administer the survey to, deciding on the delivery method, striving to ensure questions are valid by considering responder variabilities and then analyzing results. Questionnaires/surveys are useful because data can be gathered from larger populations, and they are relatively easy to tabulate. However, care must be taken to construct questions carefully so that they are understood by respondents, and it helps to develop a script for whomever will administer the survey so that participants hear the same message at the same time and to eliminate any potential bias in the way the survey is presented

» **Checklists/charts** – These can take various forms but are generally pre-designed by the instructor for a student to fill in before, during, and after projects. Examples include a K-W-L chart (what a student knows [K], wants to know [W], and has learned [L] about a topic); teacher checklists which address what content was covered or when new skills or concepts were introduced; and rating/reflection checklists used with students or teachers to assess how they see themselves at a given point in time. Not only are checklists helpful in documenting completion of tasks or attainment of skills but also in tracking time spent on an activity/task.

» **Photographs** – Photo elicitation is a data collection tool defined as showing photographic images during research interviews for participants or subjects to comment on (Lorenz & Kolb 2009). Collier (1957) wrote that more information was elicited from interviews with study subjects when photographs were used to elicit responses during interviews. In addition, the subjects were less easily fatigued by the interview process when the act of looking at photographs was included in the interview process.

» **Journal entries** – Journals are helpful to document the research process from beginning to end. They are usually most helpful when maintained on a daily or at least weekly basis for a longer project period.

» **Rubrics** – While rubrics are also time-intensive to construct and use, they are excellent sources of data since they describe specific indicators and attributes of what student work should include and provide a consistent and accurate scoring mechanism for the work.

» **Students products/projects** – Samples of student performance (assignments, quizzes, tests, as well as projects and presentations) provide rich sources of data by providing evidence of patterns or gaps and are expressions of the level of student learning and the effectiveness and impact of instructional intervention.

» **Portfolios** – These are excellent examples of data collection and evidence over time. Decide in advance what you are measuring. For example, are you looking at each portfolio and giving it a global aggregate score of quality? Selecting the same essay from each portfolio for comparison? Measuring each student's growth and comparing it?

See Appendix A for a complete comparison of the above data instruments.

After you have identified your data collection tools, try to complete your proposal in enough time to ensure that you can set it aside for a few days and review it with fresh eyes so that it is reflective of your best thinking and is achievable. Consider any challenges or barriers to implementation and refine the proposal to address them. If you are doing research that extends beyond your classroom, involves other educators, or collects data that is out of the norm for your school or district culture, now is a good time to run your plan past designated administration.

With the proposal completed, you are now ready to move from planning and into action — collecting data. But before we go there, don't hesitate to consider your proposal as a living document. If, in the course of conducting research, you discover that what you are researching yields little result, is unanswerable with the data collection instruments you have chosen, or runs into other barriers, don't hesitate to return to the proposal to update and retool it. Next stop, data collection!

Sorting and analyzing data

After you have your information in hand, **data analysis** is in order. Again, refer to Appendix A for strategies. The key here is to discover patterns regarding students or their work. What themes and ideas came up repeatedly? Are they consistent? Do they change over time? Sometimes, sorting the information you find into various configurations can yield different insights with each sort. Consider such patterns as:

> » **Chronological order/stages** – categorizing the data chronologically, by importance and by frequency (e.g.,

how often an occurrence repeats) can yield interesting results.

» **Procedures/steps** – Note anything of significance that stands out as you review the procedures used or the steps taken in the study.

» **Causes/effects** – Does the research question still fit the data that is emerging?

» **Problems/solutions** – Does the data collected to address the problems identified in the research questions lead to actionable solutions?

» **Similarities/differences** – Look for what matches your assumptions/educational theory as well as what doesn't fit your expectations or theories of other researchers.

» **Relationships (human/spatial)** – Does the physical environment have any impact on participants or the data collection process and therefore findings?

» **Main ideas and themes** – Watch for ways that the data develops into categories that surface through supporting evidence.

» **Perspectives and attitudes** – Preconceived notions and bias may be variables that emerge and should be noted – context matters.

» **Best-worst/Most-least connections** – These patterns emerge when using questionnaire/survey data collection tools that ask for participants to "scale" or "rank" their preferences or responses and can provide valuable insight.

» **Defining characteristics of the population** – Information related to age (or grade), gender and learning variabilities are important factors.

» **Other variables** – Are there other factors that have been identified as influencing results – especially in an unexpected way?

Apply the action or intervention

After spending so much time engaged in researcher mode, it's easy to think that your work is done, but remember that you engaged in action research in order to figure out how effectively something is working (or not working) and where interventions or changes may be needed. The action research cycle doesn't end with a report! Take what you have learned and implement your recommendations. Notice how much more confident you are with data on your side – data that matters to you!

Presenting the findings

Finally it's important to determine what will be the best methods of reporting your findings and why. First, return to your proposal and confirm the audience that will receive your findings. It may just be data that informs your instructional practice, but it may be that this data has value beyond your classroom or school. Should the superintendent or school board see this? What about a professional organization at a conference? Would sharing it with the parent-teacher organization be a consideration? Hopefully, you can see that it's important to share the results of local action research in numerous ways and with numerous audiences to help build awareness and create understanding of the important work that educators do on a daily basis and/or highlight the achievement of students who undertake the process. For educators there are a number of communities to connect with and places/venues to do so such as:

- » **School teams, departments**
- » **Faculty meetings**
- » **School board**
- » **Professional development meetings**

- » **Social networks**
- » **Regional conferences**
- » **Professional journals**
- » **Digital portfolio**

For students the list might include opportunities to share results with or via:

- » **Other students**
- » **Faculty**
- » **School board**
- » **Parents**
- » **Community groups**
- » **Social networks**
- » **College or job applications**
- » **Digital portfolio**

Be sure to consider the limited time of your audience. Whether your audience is the curriculum director or parents via a newsletter, think about how to take your findings and present them in ways that are visually impactful. Elsewhere in this book, you will find a wide range of strategies for displaying and presenting data in charts, graphs, infographics, and other visualizations. Remember your goal is to communicate your findings in such a way as to spur others to action: to embrace your pedagogical techniques, fund interventions to close instructional gaps, volunteer in your classroom or library, and more. Think impact!

Consider these possibilities:

- » **Classify or categorize findings,** combining several smaller themes into larger patterns.

- » **Similarly, make generalizations about student work,** supporting the assertions with quotes, photos, or other evidence from student work.

- » **Alternatively,** point out notable exceptions to the pattern and why the exception merits attention.

- » **Share annotated student work or artifacts** to help your audience notice the same details, strengths, or weaknesses that you do. For example, you could share three anonymized student paragraphs, noting what makes one weak, one average, and one strong. By adding annotations, you guide your audience to see the work as you see it and to use the same vocabulary and criteria you do to describe it.

- » **Address variables or unexpected issues encountered** – Share what you learned related to unexpected results or surprises and how you handled them.

- » **Discuss supports needed such as funding, release time, or PD** – Make sure you are clear as to what is needed to take action and make progress in addressing the research problem.

- » **Predict what is next** – Often times results of one action research project leads to the identification of additional areas for investigation.

- » **Imagine what if...?**

If this is a high-profile project, you may also wish to create a single graphic that can be posted in Facebook feeds, Instagram accounts, or Twitter accounts. Easy graphic design templates from sites like Canva.com or Creative Commons-licensed icons from TheNounProject.com can give your findings a polished, professional look, even if you're not a professional artist.

As you work on sharing findings, stop occasionally to reflect. Consider these strategies to focus you and keep you energized in the final lap of your research:

» **Return to your proposal and check that you are still on track.** Does your message convey what was learned relative to the original hypothesis?

» **Have you incorporated any unexpected "aha" moments or surprises?**

» **Do you need to not only share findings but also make recommendations based on those findings?**

» **Have your findings pointed you to areas for future research or investigation?** As an iterative and reflective process, action research often leads to yet another question or problem to investigate.

While it's easy for me to make suggestions and provide pointers, the best way I can convey the action research process in action is to share a personal experience in its use and effectiveness.

Action research in action

When I worked as a Director of Library, Media and Instructional Technology in a New England school district, an Assistant Principal colleague and I, functioning as Lead Researchers, were able to use the action research model to deal with questions regarding the use of interactive whiteboards (IWBs). There were varying opinions among decision-makers in our district as to their overall effectiveness – before investing districtwide in a capital expense, we needed to gather data so our decisions were not based solely on hunches and individual perceptions.

Our district decided to solicit proposals from interested teachers in order to test-drive the technology. Proposals were vetted and grant funds used to place IWBs in selected settings across the district. The use of action research took the personal opinions, preferences, and biases of decision-makers out of the equation when we were able to boil down the Primary Research question/hypothesis to:

> "Does the use of Interactive Whiteboard Technology improve the delivery of instruction (efficiency and efficacy) and result in better student performance?"

Using what we knew about our community and its needs, we also designed our study to consider some underlying questions such as:

- » **Will the technology provide increased opportunities** for differentiation related to modalities and the learning needs of Special Education students?

- » **Is there a difference** in the level of engagement in learning exhibited by students during similar lessons with and without the Interactive White Board?

- » **What is the total cost of ownership** for Interactive Whiteboard Technology (including deltas for support, energy, software, hardware, and training)?

- » **What is the impact** (to a greater or lesser degree) on the utilization of other classroom technologies?

Next, we undertook our action research Study Design. First, teachers received training in the use of the technology. This consisted of contracting with a certified IWB trainer and providing a full-day of release time in which the teachers not only gained technical skills but determined in which of the core content areas to concentrate (and) collectively created a protocol to use the technology to deliver instruction and address selected items found in the unit assessment. Monthly after-school follow up sessions were scheduled to provide support and an opportunity for teachers to share their experiences and talk about the merits and weaknesses of the technology. These discussions were recorded and the Lead Researchers noted trends and patterns.

Additional data was collected using pre- and post-intervention student questionnaires and a teacher self-assessment survey was developed and administered. We also asked teachers to keep weekly journals, in which they entered important observations made throughout the duration of the study.

Administrators and Lead Researchers engaged in regular three-minute walk-throughs to log the number of instances in which they observed IWB use and *how* it was being used. The Lead Researchers convened a series of focus groups and conducted individual interviews with both students and teachers in the Fall of the school year in which they were asked questions regarding their experiences with the IWBs. This exercise was repeated in the Spring in order to be able to compare/contrast data and determine if the IWB intervention had impact.

Finally, The research team analyzed Automated Help Desk Records to determine if there were any trends in servicing the whiteboard technology.

The Plan of Action included the following sequence:

1. **Information Technology and Library Media and Instructional Technology Directors** issued request for quotes/request for bids, for identified products and ordered equipment.
2. **Trainer Integrationist** (our job title for the person who designs and delivers professional development for instructional technology integration) developed a training plan/timeline.
3. **Information Technology Director** facilitated installation.

4. **Lead Teachers** met for a training presentation and designed a plan for using/sharing whiteboards. The group discussed elements of research important to the district in different subject areas.

5. **Lead Teachers** trained other partners/team members in small group training facilitated by District Trainer/Integrationist. Each team presented content area plans to the Assistant Superintendent/Director of Library Media and Technology.

6. **Student** samples were collected.

7. **Pre-Questionnaires/Self-Assessment Surveys/Observation** activities conducted.

8. **Teacher Journal Protocol** developed and administered.

9. **Teachers** implemented the project and conducted unit assessments.

10. **Administrators and Lead Researchers** conducted three-minute walk-throughs.

11. **Post-Questionnaires/Self-Assessment Surveys/Observation Journal Protocol** developed and administered.

12. **Student** samples for compare/contrast collected and analyzed.

13. **Data analyzed.**

14. **Recommendations made.**

The findings were reported to the local school board and shared in a publication of the district's web site. Included were a summary as well as charts, graphs, and a review of trends and excerpts from teachers' journals. Our major findings were that although teacher preparation time was significantly increased, the teacher participants all felt the time invested was worthwhile because of the results and because the ability to save and archive their lessons would pay dividends in the future and ultimately ensure more time to focus on direct instruction. Additionally it was noted that the technology paid the best learning dividends in the areas of math and science.

In addition, surprises and lessons learned were noted such as the use of the technology for classroom managements tasks (attendance, lunch counts, etc.) and the fact that this provided additional opportunities for students to hone their skills and make use of the technology transparent. Another surprise encountered was the shift from teacher-directed learning to student-directed learning and the creation of a collaborative culture for learning. The students worked better not only as individuals, but as a group in solving problems and using higher order thinking skills to do so.

We were also careful to note variables that came into play that might have impacted the study, such as the fact that the teacher participants were highly motivated and had high-end technology skills to begin with. These educators were also willing to put in a great deal of time and received considerable training and support throughout the process. Finally, we were gratified to learn that as we were conducting our research a similar, though large-scale study was being conducted by well-known education researcher Robert Marzano, who wrote:

> ...results indicated that, in general, using interactive whiteboards was associated with a 16 percentile point gain in student achievement ..." and" Interactive whiteboards have great potential as a tool to enhance pedagogical practices in the classroom and ultimately improve student achievement. However, simply assuming that using this or any other technological tool can automatically enhance student achievement would be a mistake. As in the case with all powerful tools, teachers must use interactive whiteboards thoughtfully, in accordance with what we know about good classroom practice (Marzano 2009, 81).

Marzano's findings aligned with our own local study and mapped well to our additional conclusion that an important variable in the effective utilization of the technology is the willingness of the teacher to implement and use it to transform practice and that appropriate professional development and other support must be provided throughout in order to sustain the effort and produce positive and sustainable results.

Engaging in action research throughout the pilot project yielded several benefits to our school district. Teachers benefited through renewed understanding of the importance of development of new skills for new pedagogies and instructional design in order to successfully implement the project. Student learning was improved and their time used more effectively because they were engaged and on task as the focus was more on student-directed learning. School board members were able to see how the technology could be used, but were also cognizant of the fact that funding and support for teacher training to ramp up technology skills and especially shifting practice from teacher-driven to student-driven in the implementation would be crucial in any wide-spread adoption.

Action research and the connection to data literacy

It's easy to see how relevant action research was for our district. Imagine how powerful it could be to ask students to consider problems and questions that are relevant for them or the community. Experienced teachers and school librarians understand how action research affords a unique opportunity to provide an authentic learning experience in which students can also learn to engage personally with data and to sort, interpret, and analyze information from data. Additionally action research allows them the chance to develop and evaluate implications as well as to use data themselves to solve problems and communicate solutions. Action research can be harnessed to gather data and construct meaning, giving important context to why and how data matters to students. This starts with discussion among teachers and school librarians to identify collaborative curriculum access points or to address problems that impact student learning in the respective content areas.

Teachers and school librarians can design instructional units in which they serve as coaches, guides, and mentors to students who undertake action research projects. This begins with assisting them to identify problems or areas of interest, pose researchable questions, and write proposals. It extends to encouraging them to anchor questions in a theoretical base whenever possible, and involves working with them to identify the best data collection tools and ways in which to approach data analysis and reporting. Finally, teachers and school librarians work to empower students to share their findings with appropriate audiences and move toward taking action that address the area of investigation.

Conclusion: Time to get your feet wet

Action research presents a unique opportunity for us to renew and refresh our professional practice as well as model and demonstrate to our students that we are engaged in using data and evidence to inform and improve that practice. As you try action research for yourself, I hope you will keep in mind that it is a process, and it is in the data analysis component that the "aha" moment occurs. Findings lead us to the development and application of interventions (the *action* in action research) and often leads to further research.

On a professional level, action research helps us to improve through continual learning and progressive problem solving. It also leads to a deeper understanding of practice and how we can relate it to the greater body of educational theory as well as provides us with an opportunity to contribute to the community in which our work is embedded. We can share the results of local action research in numerous ways and with numerous audiences to help build awareness and create understanding of the important work we do on a daily basis.

Through the use of action research we have the opportunity to influence decision-makers and the community by validating how students learn and achieve in an information environment and because it is grounded in local actions, local processes, it can lead to local, immediate outcomes.

Resources

Ballard, Susan D., Gail March, and Jean K. Sand. 2009. "Creation of a Research Community in a K-12 School System Using Action Research and Evidence Based Practice." *Evidence Based Library and Information Practice* 4 (2): 8-36. Accessed April 20, 2016. http://ejournals.library.ualberta.ca/index.php/EBLIP/article/view/5020 .

Calhoun, Emily. 1993. "Action Research: Three Approaches." *Educational Leadership* 51 (2): 62-65. Accessed April 23. http://www.ascd.org/publications/educational-leadership/oct93/vol51/num02/Action-Research@-Three-Approaches.aspx .

Collier, John. (1957). Photography in anthropology: A report on two experiments. *American Anthropologist* 59: 843-859. Accessed November 27, 2016. http://onlinelibrary.wiley.com/doi/10.1525/aa.1957.59.5.02a00100/epdf .

Coffey, Heather. nd. *Learn NC: K12 Teaching and Learning from the UNC School of Education*. Accessed April 20, 2016. http://www.learnnc.org/lp/pages/4697 .

Gordon, Carol. 2006. "A Study of a Three-dimensional Action Research Model for School Library Programs." *School Library Media Research Online* 9. Accessed April 23, 2016. http://www.ala.org/aasl/slr/vol9 .

Hart, Emily, and Meg Bond. 1995. *Action Research for Health and Social Care: A Guide to Practice*. Buckingham: Open University Press.

Kuhlthau, Carol Collier. 1993. *Seeking Meaning: A Process Approach to Library and Information Services*. Norwood, NJ: Ablex Press.

Little, J.W. (1993, June). Teachers' professional development in a climate of educational reform. *Educational Evaluation and Policy Analysis*. 15(2), 129-152.

LeCompte, M.D. and Schensul, J.J., 1999. *Analyzing and interpreting ethnographic data* (Vol. 5). Rowman Altamira.

Lorenz, Laura S., and Bettina Kolb. 2009. "Involving the public through participatory visual research methods." Health Expectations 12: 262-274. Accessed November 27, 2016. http://onlinelibrary.wiley.com/doi/10.1111/j.1369-7625.2009.00560.x/full .

Marzano, Robert. 2009. "The Art and Science of Teaching: Teaching with Interactive Whiteboards." *Educational Leadership* 67 (3): 80-82. Accessed May 2, 2016. http://www.ascd.org/publications/educational-leadership/nov09/vol67/num03/Teaching-with-Interactive-Whiteboards.aspx .

Sackett, David. L., Rosenberg, William. M.C, Gray, J. A. Muir, Haynes, R. Brian., & Richardson, W. Scott. (1996). "Evidence based medicine: What it is and what it isn't." *British Medical Journal*, 31(7023): 71–72. Accessed November 26,2016. http://www.bmj.com/content/312/7023/71?variant=extract&eaf= .

Sanjek, Roger. 1990. "A vocabulary for fieldnotes." *Fieldnotes: The makings of anthropology.* Chapter 5: 92-121. Cornell University.

Todd, Ross. J. 2008. "The evidence-based manifesto for school librarians: If school librarians can't prove they make a difference, they may cease to exist." *School Library Journal,* 54(4): 38-43. Accessed November 26, 2016. http://www.slj.com/2008/04/sljarchives/the-evidence-based-manifesto-for-school-librarians/ .

Wood, Patricia. 1988. "Action Research: A Field Perspective ." *Annual Meeting of the American Educational Research Association.* New Orleans: American Educational Research Association. 16-17.

Interview	
Good for	In-depth exploration of an individual's thinking, work flow, work processes, problem-solving strategies, beliefs, or other ideas or feelings that may be difficult to capture in student work or artifacts; Interviewer can provide clarification if needed.
Less effective for	Quickly determining patterns across a group. Data does not provide opportunity for quantification.
How time intensive is it to collect data?	Extremely – depending on the age of the student or interviewee, interviews can last as little as five minutes for preschoolers or up to an hour for adults.
How might you record the data you find?	Use an audio recorder to capture all audio (most smartphones come with a preloaded app for this). Make notes throughout the process, noting the time stamp so you can easily go back to the recording and recapture anything you miss.
How time intensive is it to analyze this data?	Extremely. Consider working with a partner to retell the interview based on your notes.
What strategies could you use to analyze it?	Transcribe each idea on to a separate sticky note, then sort all the sticky notes into categories to identify themes, patterns or conflicts. (For more information, search online for "affinity wall" or "affinity diagram").
Other notes	Requires intense analysis.
Focus group	
Good for	Allows for "focus" type interview with a representative sample of respondents.
Less effective for	Proving structure for respondents.
How time intensive is it to collect data?	Requires determining subject availability and scheduling which can be challenging in a school setting.
How might you record the data you find?	Use an audio recorder to capture all audio (most smartphones come with a preloaded app for this). Make notes throughout the process, noting the time stamp so you can easily go back to the recording and recapture anything you miss.
How time intensive is it to analyze this data?	Extremely. Consider working with a partner to retell the interview based on your notes.
What strategies could you use to analyze it?	Transcribe each idea on to a separate sticky note, then sort all the sticky notes into categories to identify themes, patterns or conflicts. (For more information, search online for "affinity wall" or "affinity diagram").
Other notes	Requires intense analysis.

Photographs

Good for	Used in interview and focus group situations to elicit more detailed response from participants than other tools; are especially useful with visual learners.
Less effective for	Proving structure for respondents.
How time intensive is it to collect data?	Requires determining subject availability and scheduling which can be challenging in a school setting.
How might you record the data you find?	Use an audio recorder to capture all audio (most smartphones come with a preloaded app for this). Make notes throughout the process, noting the time stamp so you can easily go back to the recording and recapture anything you miss.
How time intensive is it to analyze this data?	Extremely. Consider working with a partner to retell the interview based on your notes.
What strategies could you use to analyze it?	Transcribe each idea on to a separate sticky note, then sort all the sticky notes into categories to identify themes, patterns or conflicts. (For more information, search online for "affinity wall" or "affinity diagram").
Other notes	Consider the need for photo permissions if you plan to use any photographs of students in reports or publications.

Grades/test scores

Good for	Use as evidence of student performance and instructional effectiveness and in determination of patterns/gaps.
Less effective for	Tendency to over rely on scores as the sole indicator of student understanding or teacher effectiveness.
How time intensive is it to collect data?	Depending on the instrument, can be quick/efficient or can be quick/efficient if retrieving a single data point. Evaluation over time can be time-intensive.
How might you record the data you find?	Electronic grade book and/or database.
How time intensive is it to analyze this data?	Relatively efficient.
What strategies could you use to analyze it?	Sort course or individual assignment grades from highest to lowest; compare individual scores over time; compare scores from this year to those of past years.
Other notes	Single scores do not reflect the nuances of student strengths and weaknesses the way artifacts of student work do.

Observation/field notes

Good for	Gathering first-hand comprehensive (oral and visual) data in authentic context.
Less effective for	Use when there is a need to be unobtrusive so as not to influence the subjects.

How time intensive is it to collect data?	Depending on circumstances, observation can be short and a one-time occurrence, or it can be of greater length and take place over time.
How might you record the data you find?	Audio and/or video recorder.
How time intensive is it to analyze this data?	Transcription is often required and can be time consuming.
What strategies could you use to analyze it?	Pulling out keywords and themes using qualitative data software or index cards.
Other notes	Consider using audio or video recorders (with permission) alongside notes. Record the elapsed time on the recorder next to your notes so you can quickly navigate the recording.

Checklists/charts

Good for	Quick/efficient if retrieving a single data point. Evaluation over time can be time-intensive.
Less effective for	Use when there is a need to be unobtrusive so as not to influence the subjects.
How time intensive is it to collect data?	Depending on circumstances, observation can be short and a one-time occurrence, or it can be of greater length and take place over time.
How might you record the data you find?	Tally methods to record frequencies and percentages.
How time intensive is it to analyze this data?	Easily quantifiable and can be displayed in chart format.
What strategies could you use to analyze it?	Observation of patterns; counting of items; identification of missing items.
Other notes	If checklist is paper-based, consider using a clipboard held at an angle so those being observed cannot see the questions.

Questionnaires/surveys

Good for	Rapid gathering of information to find broad patterns and source of user information (demographics). Provide means for pre/post data collection.
Less effective for	Surfacing nuance or ideas you did not think of when designing multiple choice.
How time intensive is it to collect data?	Closed-end responses can be quickly "counted" through the use of numeric value systems like Likert or rating scales; open-ended responses requiring narrative responses will take more time to sort .
How might you record the data you find?	Data collection instruments serve as the record and rating scales yield data that can be displayed in tables and charts.

How time intensive is it to analyze this data?	The formats of different questions will yield different types of data and questions may be open to interpretations; open-ended questions require more time for analysis.
What strategies could you use to analyze it?	Survey software like Google Forms, SurveyMonkey, or Qualtrics can help visualize closed responses; use coding techniques similar to those for observation/field notes for open-ended responses.
Other notes	Check with school district about where student data can be stored online so you are consistent with district policies.
Journal entries	
Good for	Identifying daily habits and patterns; reflections on what is really happening; can be maintained by teacher or students.
Less effective for	More difficult to collect in a timely manner.
How time intensive is it to collect data?	Must be vigilant and intentional in recording dates and times.
How might you record the data you find?	Head notes or scratch notes LeCompte and Schensul (1999, p.31) describe head notes as, "...memories or mental notes kept ... until such time as it is possible to actually write things down." Scratch notes are jottings written right after an event when it is inappropriate to write during the event itself.
How time intensive is it to analyze this data?	Daily and/or weekly transcription into digital form to assist with trend analysis.
What strategies could you use to analyze it?	Qualitative analysis, such as assigning each concept in thee entry a separate sticky note, which are then arranged to find patterns in data.
Other notes	Prompts may be helpful for student journals.
Rubrics	
Good for	Identifies criteria to measure impact; Provides authentic assessment of student learning and data regarding how students view their own progress;
Less effective for	When data must be collected in a timely manner.
How time intensive is it to collect data?	Need to be well-designed and communicated to and depending on what is being assessed can take significant time.
How might you record the data you find?	Lend themselves to numeric format and can be displayed/represented in a variety of ways.
How time intensive is it to analyze this data?	Somewhat.
What strategies could you use to analyze it?	Consider plugging the points students receive in each category into a spreadsheet so it can calculate various statistical information and reveal patterns.

Other notes	Be careful in how various categories are weighted. Check for balance in your rubric by asking yourself, "How many points are going to demonstration of understanding? How much to following directions? How many to aesthetics?"

Student products/projects

Good for	Samples of student work provide authentic evidence.
Less effective for	Occasions in which data must be pulled together rapidly.
How time intensive is it to collect data?	Need to develop a plan or schedule to collect/harvest data in an intentional manner.
How might you record the data you find?	Collect representative samples at different periods of time to provide evidence of performances and changes over time.
How time intensive is it to analyze this data?	Very.
What strategies could you use to analyze it?	See earlier sections on interviews and focus groups.
Other notes	Some families may be uncomfortable if minimal student work comes home with the student. Consider photocopies or photographs so you have a duplicate from which to work.

Portfolios

Good for	Showing growth and changes over time — artifacts maintained for continuous review.
Less effective for	When data must be collected in a timely manner.
How time intensive is it to collect data?	Need to establish criteria for determining what work will be included.
How might you record the data you find?	Collect representative samples at different periods of time to provide evidence of performances and changes over time.
How time intensive is it to analyze this data?	Very.
What strategies could you use to analyze it?	Similar to Projects.
Other notes	See notes in Projects section above.

If you have five minutes,

Share these rules of thumb in the action research cycle with students:

- Action research is problem-focused and solution-oriented.
- You must frame a problem into a researchable question.
- The question needs to be one which can be measured and evaluated.
- Data collection tools need to be carefully selected.
- Data must be sorted and analyzed in order to discover patterns and outliers.
- Analysis leads to identifying the action/s to address the problem.
- Findings should be shared and reflected upon by an authentic audience.

If you have 30 minutes,

What would action research look like in a high school classroom? Walk through these examples and ask students to begin to think about what data collection tools would be appropriate.

- **Math:** Would the introduction of a peer tutoring program be of benefit to those struggling with advanced math concepts?
- **Social Studies**: Does the difference in levels of Internet access in the home environment impact equal access to the curriculum by students?
- **Science:** Does water quality vary according to zip code?
- **English:** Do cultural and language differences impact the viewpoint of a student related to engagement with books on the required reading list.

If you have one class period,

Extend upon the examples above and engage students in conversations that lead them to how they would follow the rules of thumb as cited.

If you have multiple class periods,

Have students develop an action research proposal for each of the examples as well as extend learning to the creation of either a collaborative or school-wide action research proposal.

Data literacy related standards

The URL below provides data literacy related standards compiled from the Common Core State Standards; Next Generation Science Standards; C3 Voluntary Social Studies Standards; and the American Association of School Libraries. This list should not necessarily be considered exhaustive, but may provide direction to link established Standards to data literacy instruction.

https://tinyurl.com/DataLiteracyRelatedStandards

Visit the following web sites for additional information

Common Core State Standards Initiative
www.corestandards.org

Next Generation Science Standards
www.nextgenscience.org

C3 Voluntary Social Studies Standards
www.socialstudies.org

American Association of School Libraries
www.ala.org/aasl/standards/learning

Data Literacy in the Real World: Conversations & Case Studies

DATA LITERACY IN THE REAL WORLD

Conversations & Case Studies

EDITED BY

Kristin Fontichiaro   Amy Lennex   Jo Angela Oehrli
Tyler Hoff   Kelly Hovinga

This second book has also been created. *Data Literacy in the Real World: Conversations & Case Studies* is designed as a professional learning reference with some components that can also be used directly with high school students. In Part I, we bring the experts to you, providing plug-and-play professional development (PD) via high-quality archived webinars from the 2016 and 2017 4T Virtual Conference on Data along with discussion questions and hands-on activities. In Part II, we share over 40 case studies about data literacy in the real world. With issues drawn from the headlines, these case studies can serve either as PD with colleagues or as classroom conversations.

This title will be available in Fall 2017 in multiple formats including, PDF, machine-readable, Amazon CreateSpace, and Kindle. Find more information at http://dataliteracy.si.umich.edu .

Glossary

Action Research Model – a model of teaching that focuses on collecting and analyzing data in a real life context. Practitioners conduct research on the effectiveness of various activities and lesson plans and then use that research to make informed decisions about their next course of action.

Average – a term for the median, mean, or mode of a data set. Used to describe the most common value. Synonym for *central tendency*.

Bar chart/bar graph – a visualization that displays values through the use of narrow rectangles (bars).

Benchmark statistics – a reliable statistic used to determine the validity or importance of another statistic in a related field.

Bins – consecutive numeric ranges or intervals used in histograms, such as 20-30, 0-100, or 0-1.

Box plot – a visual icon placed on a graph that displays a wide range of numerical values, including the mean, median, first and third quartiles, and maximum and minimum values.

Bubble charts – visualizations that represent the relationship between three separate, numeric variables, one on the y-axis, another on the x-axis, and a third mapped via the the size and/or color of the bubble around the data point itself.

Causation – a relationship of cause and effect in which change in one variable always provokes a change in the other.

Categorical information – information that is sorted into groups according to the presence of named characteristics, such as age or gender.

Central tendency – synonym for *average*.

Chart – a way of organizing information in tabular form, much like a table. Also, a synonym for *graph*.

Cherry-picking – the practice of selecting information that confirms your argument while ignoring information that contradicts your argument.

Choropleth map – a map that conveys information through color shading, where a range of hues demonstrates the density of a variable. Population density is the most common variable mapped on a choropleth map.

Close reading – the process of reading material actively for information while considering the context in which the information is presented and the language which is used.

Computational data – data which results from a simulation or computer model, usually displayed in numeric format.

Confirmation bias – the inherent tendency to favor information that agrees with our pre-existing hypothesis or ideas.

Correlation – term used when one observes a relationship or connection between two or more elements. A correlation does not indicate that one variable causes another to happen. Positive correlation means that variables increase or decrease together, while negative correlation means that one variable decreases as the other variable increases. Much more common than causation.

Data – facts and statistics collected together for reference or analysis. Note that while data is technically a plural term, it is often used either as a singular or plural term in practice.

Datasets – a collection of data points.

Data collection – the process of gathering qualitative or quantitative information through experiments, interviews, focus groups, test scores, surveys, field notes, observations, etc.

Data literacy – the ability to comprehend, evaluate, and synthesize data and numeric information in all of its different forms.

Data point – a single piece of data or information.

Data projection – the act of predicting data trends through statistical analysis.

Data visualization – a display of information in visual form, which may take the form of a table, chart, graphic, infographic, etc., for the purpose of discovering trends, patterns, or anomalies that we would otherwise miss.

Density – the compactness or volume of information associated with a geographic location, variable, or element.

Distribution – the range of values or intervals in a dataset.

Dot plot – a graph that represents data as dots on an x- and y-axis. May be used as an alternative to bar graphs to avoid visual clutter.

Evidence-based practice – decision-making based on research.

Filter function – a function in Excel that allows the user to limit the data they are looking at.

GAP – an acronym used by Reading Apprenticeship program that stands for genre, audience, and purpose.

Graphic visualization – See *Data visualization*.

Frequency – the number of times a variable, instance, or number appears in a dataset.

Goldilocks principle – term for a right-sized dataset. Also, a rule of thumb that says that while some data points will be extremes, most will fall somewhere in the middle.

Graph – a visual diagram showing the relationship between two or more variables.

Histogram – a visualization that shows the distribution of a numeric set of variables, like height or income, in a bar graph-like format, with each bar representing a *bin*, or range of values.

Infographic – a collection of visual, numerical, and text-based bits that together create a compelling argument or synthesis.

Key – See *Legend*.

Labels – words or phrases assigned to the axes or headings of graphs to provide information on what each value represents.

Legend – a text box usually located in the lower right corner of a graph that provides contextual information needed to interpret the graph, such as what specific colors, lines, or shapes represent. Also known as a *key*.

Line chart/line graph – a visualization that uses lines to connect plotted data points.

Logarithmic graphs – visualizations that may use non-standardized distances between intervals to consolidate a wide range of information so it fits into a smaller graph.

Margin of error – the statistical allowance for differences between a sample and the actual population from which the sample is derived.

Maximum – the largest numeric value in a dataset.

Mean – the result after one adds a series of numbers and divides that sum by the total quantity of numbers. Also known as the *arithmetic mean*.

Median – a number that is the midpoint in a range of numbers, so that there is equal probability that a number will fall above or below this number's value.

Metadata – information about a dataset, such as labels, headers, scale, and other information that is required to understand a dataset.

Metrics – a mathematical function that takes a set of numbers and compares the difference in values. Specifically, metrics create standards by which figures and statistics can be judged.

Minimum – the smallest numeric value in a data set.

Mode – the value that occurs most often in a data set.

Online portal – a website that brings together information or links to information from a diverse number of sources.

Outliers – a value that falls outside the expected range of a dataset and is numerically exceptional in comparison to the other values.

Parameters – a measurable factor or number that helps define an operation or sets the conditions by which a study is conducted.

Percentile – the percentage of scores that were lower than that of a given person or instance. On a standardized test, a student scoring in the 93rd percentile means 93% of the scores were lower than the student's.

Pie chart – showcases the parts of a whole or percentages of a total through the use of "slices" within a circle.

Pivot table – function in Excel allowing users to create a temporary table of a specific column (or category) and check for duplicates in the data.

P-value – a statistical term that refers to evaluating the significance of a hypothesis. While widely used in scholarly work, the importance of calculating p-value has been debated of late.

Quartiles – the three values that divide a numeric dataset into four equal parts.

Qualitative data – information that is best captured in words or "qualities." For example, answers in an interview are qualitative data.

Quantitative data – data that is measured by counting and/or in numbers.

Range – the difference in values from the maximum to the minimum.

Research question – the question or hypothesis that is used as the grounds for experimentation or research.

Regression analysis – a statistical process for determining the relationships among variables, specifically one independent variable and a number of dependent variables (causation instead of correlation).

Sample – a part or fraction that represents a larger group. Using a sample in lieu of studying a larger group is cost-effective and efficient, but to be accurate, samples should be representative of that whole group and large enough to discern patterns.

Scatterplot/Scatter graph – a graph in which each data point is represented by a dot. Lines do not connect the dots.

Segment – a portion of a whole, such as a slice in a pie chart.

Self-reported – an adjective that describes data donated by and about participants. When people report data about themselves, there is a tendency to provide answers skewed toward one's "best self."

Skew – A distribution is considered skewed if, when graphed, one of its "tails" is longer than the other.

Sort function – an Excel feature that that allows the user to sort and sequence the information in a spreadsheet's column.

Statistics – a branch of mathematics focused on the collection, analysis, interpretation, presentation, and organization of quantitative or numerical data.

Storyframing – a process tool designed and named by Connie Williams in which students use sticky notes to experiment with the content and format of an infographic.

Table – a set of data arranged in rows and columns.

Terms of art – specialized terminology, or jargon, associated with a particular field of study.

Variables – A characteristic or object that can be counted.

Vetted – describes information which has been checked by a professional for accuracy.

Waffle chart – a square graph used to compare percentages between different categories.

Web polling – a survey conducted over the Internet.

Web portal – see *Online portal*.

Wireframing – a rapid model showing the placement of images, graphic design and content of a web page or document.

Contributors

Debbie Abilock co-founded and leads the education vision at NoodleTools, Inc., a teaching platform of integrated research tools for note-taking, outlining, citation, document archiving and annotation, collaborative research and writing. A *Library Journal* Mover and Shaker, she has worked on numerous local, state, and national boards and currently is on Granite State's (NH) National Advisory Board to create a new M.S. in School Leadership for future school principals, library media specialists, and experienced teachers that will blend online learning with extended supervised clinical experiences. Known for her innovative curriculum design and instructional strategies, she lectures and consults internationally. She co-authored a book on the varied professional development roles of school librarians (*Growing Schools*, Libraries Unlimited 2012) and served as founding editor of the AASL journal, *Knowledge Quest*. She writes "Adding Friction," a column about thoughtful teaching and learning, for *School Library Connection*.

Susan D. Ballard is a Senior Lecturer and Program Director for the Master of Science in School Leadership Program (with School Library certification) at Granite State College of the University System of NH. She is a Past-President of AASL (2012-13) and the retired Director of Library, Media, and Technology Services for the Londonderry (NH) School District, a recipient of the National School Library Media Program of the Year (2000). She currently serves as a member of AASL's Standards and Guidelines Editorial Board and is a member of Julie Todaro's ALA Presidential Initiative Steering Committee. She is also a member of the Advisory Board for Teacher Librarian, the Board of Directors for the Q.E.D. Foundation and the Leadership Council of the National Collaborative for Digital Equity. Susan has published numerous articles in a variety of professional and scholarly journals including one selected by the Library Instruction Round Table of ALA as one of the Top Twenty Library Instruction Articles of 2009. Among various awards, she was the first-ever recipient of the NH Excellence in Education Award (EDie) for Library Media Services.

Tasha Bergson-Michelson is the Instructional and Programming Librarian for Castilleja School in Palo Alto, CA, where she builds curricula based on the notion that strong research skills lower the bar to curiosity. Since 1995, Tasha has been exploring what makes for successful information literacy instruction in corporate, non-profit, subscription, and school libraries, and through after school programs and summer camps. Most recently, Tasha was the Search Educator at Google, where she wrote an extensive series of Search Education lesson plans, the Power Searching MOOCs, and – most importantly – collaborated with other librarians around the world to explore the most effective ways of teaching research skills. In 2014 Tasha was designated a Mover and Shaker – Tech Leader by *Library Journal*.

Jennifer Colby is a High School Teacher Librarian at Huron High School in Ann Arbor, MI. She coordinates SAT training for students at her school and provides resources to help teachers integrate SAT skills into all content areas. She also works with students and teachers in her district to practice the skills necessary to take the Michigan Student Test of Educational Progress (M-STEP). In her spare time she writes informational texts for elementary students.

Kristin Fontichiaro is a Clinical Associate Professor at the University of Michigan and principal investigator on the Supporting Librarians in Adding Data Literacy Skills to Information Literacy Instruction project (IMLS RE-00-15-0113-15). A *Library Journal* Mover and Shaker and member of the American Library Association's inaugural class of Emerging Leaders, she has written several books for educators, librarians, and K-12 readers.

Lynette Hoelter is an assistant research scientist and Director of Instructional Resources at ICPSR and a research affiliate of the Population Studies Center at the University of Michigan. At ICPSR, she is involved in projects focusing on assisting social science faculty with using data in the classroom, including the Online Learning Center and TeachingWithData.org, and generally oversees efforts focused on undergraduate education. Lynette is also a Co-Principal Investigator of the Integrated Fertility Survey Series, an effort to create a dataset of harmonized variables drawn from national surveys of fertility spanning 1955-2002. Her research interests include the relationship between social change and marital quality, gender in families, and the study of family and relationship processes and dynamics more broadly. She has also taught for the department of sociology and the survey methodology program at the University of Michigan.

Justin Joque is the Visualization Librarian at the University of Michigan. There he assists users in finding, manipulating, analyzing, and visualizing diverse types of data. Before becoming the Visualization Librarian, Justin was a Spatial and Numeric Data Librarian, also at the University of Michigan. He completed a Master's of Science of Information at the University of Michigan — School of Information with a focus on Information Analysis and Retrieval and his Ph.D. in Communications at the European Graduate School.

Jo Angela Oehrli is a former high school and middle school teacher who helps students find information on a wide range of topics as a Learning Librarian at the University of Michigan Libraries -- Ann Arbor. In addition, she supports the students in the Women in Science and Engineering Residential Program and the students in the Michigan Research Community Residential Program as well as undergraduates across campus. She has published articles on library instruction, served as Chair of ALA LIRT's Top Twenty Committee, serves on the ACRL Instruction Section Executive Board & the LOEX Advisory Board, and has worked as an adjunct lecturer for UM's School of Information & the College of Literature, Science and the Arts. She also supports the research and instructional needs for those throughout the university community who are studying children's literature at any level.

Jole Seroff is Director of Library and Information Services at Castilleja School in Palo Alto, CA. She began her career in urban public schools in Memphis, TN. She collaborates with faculty to infuse curriculum with research skills and a focus on intellectual freedom. She also implements humanities-based, hands-on learning through letterpress printing. She is lover of poetry, and works closely with student writers. In her free time she enjoys birding, museums, and factory tours.

Susan Smith is Library Director at The Harker School in San Jose, California, where she has worked for 12 years. She holds an MLIS from San Jose State University, and a BA from Duke University. Smith oversees a team of seven professional librarians on four campuses, preschool through high school, where information literacy is embedded across the disciplines as librarians collaborate with teachers on hundreds of lessons each year. Teaching research skills in a rigorous college prep environment, Smith is committed to teaching data literacy to K-12 students and providing teachers with the professional development necessary to support such instruction. She frequently speaks at SF Bay Area and national conferences on professional development, information literacy, and news literacy. Publications include co-authoring "An Argument for Disciplinary Information Literacy" in *Knowledge Quest* May/June 2016, and "Growing Information Literacy School –Wide," published in *Growing Schools: Librarians as Professional Developers*, edited by Debbie Abilock, Kristin Fontichiaro, and Violet Harada, Libraries Unlimited 2012.

Tierney Steelberg received her Master of Science in Information in 2016 from the University of Michigan School of Information, where she specialized in library and information science. She is currently the Instructional Technology Librarian at Guilford College.

Wendy Stephens is an Assistant Professor and School Library Program Chair at Jacksonville State University. A high school librarian for fifteen years, she earned National Board Certification in Library Media in 2008. A past president of the Alabama Library Association, she has served as ALA Councilor-at-Large, on the EMIERT Executive Board, and on the United States Board on Books for Young People Board of Directors, and was chosen as an ALSC Bechtel fellow in 2016. She has a Ph.D. from University of North Texas, and dissertation research focused on the interaction of reading practice and student attitudes surrounding literacy and libraries.

Martha Stuit is the 2015-2016 project assistant on the Supporting Librarians in Adding Data Literacy Skills to Information Literacy Instruction project. She is a 2016 graduate of the University of Michigan School of Information with a Master of Science in Information with a specialization in library and information science. Prior to returning to school, she was a reporter.

Connie Williams is a National Board Certified Teacher Librarian and taught in junior high and high school libraries in Petaluma, CA. She is a past president of the California School Library Association, a governor appointee to the California State Library Services Board, and a member of the ALA Government Documents Round Table Government Information for Children Committee. She has authored articles and chapters on school library advocacy, infographics, primary sources, and the Question Formulation Technique. Connie is an Adjunct Librarian and Instructor at the Santa Rosa Junior College and works at the Sonoma County Public Library. She blogs for Knowledge Quest at: http://knowledgequest.aasl.org/author/cwilliams/ .

Index

CPSIA information can be obtained
at www.ICGtesting.com
Printed in the USA
LVHW071757141121
703306LV00008B/201